LEADERSHIP IN DIETETICS

Achieving a Vision for the Future

Anne M. Barker, EdD, RN
Mary Beth Foltz Arensberg, PhD, RD
M. Rosita Schiller, RSM, PhD, RD

THE AMERICAN DIETETIC ASSOCIATION

Library of Congress Cataloging-in-Publication Data

Baker, Anne M.

Leadership in dietetics: achieving a vision for the future/Anne M. Barker, Mary Beth Foltz Arensberg, M. Rosita Schiller.

p. cm.

Includes bibliographical references and index.

ISBN 0-88091-137-9

1. Dietetics—Practice. 2. Leadership. 3. Organizational behavior. I. Barker, Anne M., II. Arensberg, Mary Beth Foltz. III. Schiller, M. Rosita.

[DNLM: 1. Dietetics. 2. Leadership. WB 400 B2541 1994]

RM218.5.B35 1994

658.4'092'024613—dc20

DNLM/DLC

for Library of Congress 94-31016

CIP

Foreword

We are living in an era of intense change. There may well be no other period in history that can match the sweeping changes of the last 20 years. Recently we've witnessed historical, political, and scientific events that were unimaginable just a few years ago. We feel the impact of these events in virtually every aspect of our lives, but perhaps nowhere more directly and dramatically than in healthcare.

The majority of dietetics professionals work in healthcare settings and experience firsthand the effects of economic trends, technological advances, and societal shifts. A number of these trends are greatly affecting the healthcare environment, including revolutionary developments in technology and treatment, the "graying" of America, new delivery systems, managed care, and shifts in payment systems.

If dietetics professionals are to be in the vanguard of the new healthcare, they must be knowledgeable about what is happening in the world at large—they must anticipate trends and understand how those trends affect the profession. They must analyze where they are now and where they are going, then develop strategies to get where they want to be.

This requires a willingness to embrace change, to venture into uncharted territory. Dietetics professionals must have courage and trust their own judgment. They must understand and anticipate the forces of change. They must capitalize on opportunities and challenges. They must be willing to seek counsel and build partnerships outside their profession. They must be bold enough to challenge the status quo and dare to take risks. And they need to strike that delicate balance between what is tried and true and what needs to be changed.

How is this accomplished? How can dietetics professionals deal with constant change and prepare for uncertain future? How can the profession be positioned to ensure that members assume their rightful place in the vanguard of healthcare?

To do this, dietetics professionals must use a full range of business skills, particularly the ability to market and sell their services and profession. However, excellence in dietetics and in business is not enough in these complex times. To master the kind of change that is sweeping throughout society and our profession, to function in the forefront of a changing healthcare environment, rather than as part of "the pack," dietetics professionals must learn and apply the principles of good leadership.

The American Dietetic Association (ADA) has a long tradition of fostering leadership development among its members. Several years ago, when strategic initiatives were developed to give members a competitive advantage, the concept of a leadership initiative was born. Through this initiative, Association leaders committed themselves to offering members opportunities to reshape the world in which they practice dietetics.

The ADA Leadership Initiative supported the development of *Leadership in Dietetics*. A brief look at the table of contents conveys its scope and importance. Written primarily for students and practicing dietetics leader-managers in all areas of practice, *Leadership in Dietetics* will benefit anyone in the profession or anyone who has an interest in what dietetics professionals do and how they do it.

The authors' central theme of change provides a critical perspective on the profession of dietetics today. The material on leadership theories and societal trends presents a compelling case for the need for change and for dynamic leadership. Traditional views of "who is a leader" are challenged. As they map out a route to success, the authors see all dietetics professionals as leaders. They view leadership as an exciting practice and discipline—an integral part of practicing dietetics in these volatile times.

The book's premise is that the healthcare environment is changing the way dietetics professionals work and use their resources. People—not technology, dollars, or regulations—are identified as the main determinant of organizational success. It is people who will determine whether high-quality/cost-effective healthcare can and will be delivered and how it will be done.

For a professional group that has traditionally emphasized getting the task done, the shift to the significance of the individual as the key factor for success requires a dramatic mind shift. While Total Quality Management (TQM) and Continuous Quality Improvement (CQI) initiatives in many organizations showcase this concept, the authors of *Leadership in Dietetics* provide readers with a new perspective on developing people's potential and working in collaboration with others.

The blend of theory, discussion, and case studies in *Leadership in Dietetics* challenges all dietetics professionals to refocus their perceptions of the world and to reshape their role in the context of what is happening in society.

Dietetics professionals have the education, the skill, and the knowledge to provide a new generation of leadership. No one in healthcare is more knowledgeable, has better professional expertise, or is better trained in nutrition than we are. Now we have to prepare ourselves further, to position ourselves for leadership roles. *Leadership in Dietetics* can be a key to developing the strategies needed to shape the way healthcare is delivered in this decade and in the next century.

Susan Calvert Finn, PhD, RD
President, 1992–93
The American Dietetic Association

Preface

Although the struggles to implement a personal dream of dietetics are real, challenging, complex, and at times seemingly futile, there is help. The authors of this book are optimistic about dietetics and the role it can play in the future. This optimism stems from the abundance of workable, contemporary leadership theories and strategies that are available to guide dietetics leaders. By thinking about and adapting these theories and strategies, dietetics leaders can begin to design work environments that satisfy the needs of dietetics professionals and enhance the quality of their care and services.

Being a dietetics professional in a leadership position is not easy. The cry for dietetics leadership has been heard for decades. It is an echo of the cry for leadership in our society. But this leadership crisis need not be lamented. It can be looked on as a time to reassess values about people, leadership, leaders, dietetics, and dietetics practice. In this reassessment, threads of hope can be found. Dietetics professionals are more assertive and more educated than in the past. In one way, this means that work environments should undergo major renovations—an awesome task. From another perspective, it means dietetics professionals are increasingly capable of contributing to the care of the individual patient and to the healthcare of the society as a whole. Employees and dietetics professionals have new values, including a paradoxical need to belong while at the same time achieving as individuals. In dietetics, it is relatively easy to create a climate that appeals to those needs because dietetics involves helping others. This is not necessarily true for people employed in other types of work. By focusing on our heritage of caring and by designing dietetics organizations that both facilitate teamwork and recognize and allow individuals to achieve, dietetics leaders can address current dissatisfactions in the profession.

Traditional management skills, such as finance, budgeting, marketing, and staffing, are important ingredients for successful dietetics leadership in today's healthcare environment, but they are not enough. Dietetics needs leaders with new skills to transform dietetics organizations into spirited, exciting, successful workplaces where dietetics professionals can excel. This book attempts to weave together current and classic leadership theories and strategies and apply them to contemporary dietetic practice. The seminal work of James MacGregor Burns, *Leadership*, provides the theoretical framework for the book. His inspirational work focuses on political leaders. Warren Bennis and Burt Nanus, the authors of *Leaders: Strategies for Taking Charge*, and other contemporary authors apply Burns' theory to business organizations. Specifically, the chapters on vision, social architecture, trust, and deployment of self (self-regard) are the four transformational leadership strategies proposed by them, and each is the subject of a chapter.

An earlier version of this book was written by Anne Barker for nurses. It was first published in 1988 by Williams & Wilkins as *Transformational Leadership in Nursing: A Vision for the Future*. Shortly thereafter, the publisher withdrew from the nursing text business and turned over publication rights to the National League for Nursing, which published a reprint in 1992. While conducting her doctoral dissertation research on transformational leadership in dietetics, Mary Beth Foltz Arensberg came across the book. Barker's message seemed as applicable to dietetics professionals as it was to the nurse leader-managers for whom it was originally intended. We are grateful to the National League for Nursing for granting permission to update and revise the text to include current concepts from the field of dietetics.

Leadership in Dietetics was written for two audiences: dietetics students and practicing dietetics leader-managers. Because it was derived from a nursing book, it clearly deals with healthcare. Although the principles of leadership apply across the board, the terminology and examples will not have the same relevance to all practitioners. Dietetics professionals in hospitals and long-term-care facilities may find the book more useful than those working in school foodservice, communications, government, and private practice. To help readers apply the theories to actual practice, we have included a case study and discussion questions at the end of each chapter. Explanations of discussion questions are in the appendix. These can be used to stimulate further discussion. In the real world of dietetics management, there is seldom only one correct approach. Similarly, there are many ways to interpret the case study questions. The case studies can be used in the classroom for group discussions, or the reader can study them independently to gain insight from applying theory to practice.

In this book we struggled with semantics. One struggle involved the need to avoid sexist language. The second was more difficult—avoiding the use of terms such as "subordinate", "superior", and "boss". These terms in many ways conflict with the philosophy of the book. Some authors and organizations are beginning to use the term "associates" to refer to employees. We opted not to use this or any other unfamiliar term, but limited our use of traditional hierarchical language to those instances when their use clarified the discussion. Lastly, this book evolved out of a conviction that all dietetics professionals, and especially those in management positions, must be leaders; therefore, the term "leader-manager" is used throughout the book to convey this ideal.

Acknowledgments

This work is a compilation of many years of experience for each of us authors. We wish to acknowledge the many individuals in both nursing and dietetics who served as leadership models and mentors. To all those who have touched our lives, we are truly grateful.

Anne Barker,
Mary Beth Foltz Arensberg,
and M. Rosita Schiller

There are many people who have contributed to my thinking, values, and convictions. In my work as a nurse executive, I was most influenced by Jennie Umbal McKoy, the first transformational nurse leader with whom I had the privilege of working. She was, without doubt, my best mentor. I am further appreciative of many nurses and students who throughout my career have challenged me and helped me to develop my leadership beliefs. These individuals taught me that if one provides an exciting, participatory work environment in which people are recognized, people will respond and achieve excellence for nursing and patients. Because of them, I am convinced that the ideas in this book work.—**A B**

In my doctoral work, I am grateful to Virginia M. Vivian, my advisor, for her personal guidance and tireless support to help me complete my study of leadership in dietetics. M. Rosita Schiller has served as a mentor and teacher to me and to many dietetics professionals, and I appreciate having had the opportunity to work with her in developing this text. Susan Calvert Finn, one of the profession's outstanding leaders and a colleague of high regard, forged the path for transformational leaders in dietetics, and I applaud her for expanding the horizons of the profession. I thank my husband, parents, and friends for encouraging me to pursue my goals.—**M B F A**

Throughout the years I have been inspired by the leadership of many individuals with whom I associated in my religious community, The American Dietetic Association (ADA), and various institutions. The sisters to whom I am particularly grateful are Sisters Helen Marie Burns, Mary Gretchen Elliot, Agnes Mary Mansour, Maurita Sengelaub, and Mary Sharon Wedig. The leadership of ADA presidents Anita Owen, Susan Calvert Finn, and Sara Parks has influenced me and many others within the profession, and we all owe much of ADA's progress to their tireless service. I wish also to thank my doctoral advisor, Virginia M. Vivian, for her continued encouragement; Mary Beth Foltz Arensberg, my colleague, for her creative thinking and undying enthusiasm; Juanita Williams, my secretary, for her expert assistance; and my family and friends for their loving and faithful support of my work.—**M R S**

About the Authors

Anne Barker, EdD, RN—Dr Barker is Associate Professor and Director, Nursing Programs, for Sacred Heart University in Fairfield, Connecticut. She received her education doctorate in nursing administration, executive role, from the Teacher's College of Columbia University, and her master's degree in nursing from Catholic University of America in Washington, DC. Prior to accepting her position at Sacred Heart University, Dr Barker was Associate Director of Nursing for Bridgeport Hospital and has also served as Chief of Nursing Service for the Veterans Administration Medical Center in West Haven, Connecticut. Dr Barker has many publications on leadership in nursing, including her book *Transformational Nursing Leadership: A Vision for the Future.* She has given numerous presentations and workshops on transformational leadership and empowerment to multidisciplinary groups of heathcare professionals.

Mary Beth Foltz Arensberg, PhD, RD—Dr Arensberg is manager of Nutrition Services for the Ross Products Division, Abbott Laboratories, in Columbus, Ohio. She earned a doctorate in nutrition from The Ohio State University. She received her master's in nutrition from the Boston University Sargent College of Allied Health Professions after completing a clinical dietetic internship at the New England Deaconess Hospital. Among her professional activities, she has given presentations on nutrition support, nutrition screening, service marketing, strategic planning, and leadership at a number of local, state, and national health professional meetings. Her publications include articles on marketing specialized nutrition services, the image and role of the dietitian, nutrition screening, and leadership.

M. Rosita Schiller, RSM, PhD, RD—Dr Schiller is Professor and Director of the Medical Dietetics Division, School of Allied Medical Professions, The Ohio State University, in Columbus, Ohio. She earned her doctorate in foods and nutrition at Ohio State. She is the author of numerous articles and book chapters on topics related to dietetics practice, marketing dietetics services, quality assurance, role delineation, leadership, and dietetics education and research. Dr Schiller coauthored *Handbook on Managing Clinical Nutrition Services* and *Total Quality Management for Hospital Nutrition Services.* She has lectured to physicians, nurses, dietitians, other healthcare professionals, and the public on such topics as diet and cancer, obesity, health promotion, curriculum development, research methodology, and motivation.

Contents

1

Leadership in Crisis: The Need for New Theory

Chapter Objectives

1. Discuss and cite examples of the leadership crisis in dietetics and society.
2. Recognize the need for new leadership theory and strategies in dietetics.
3. Describe the historical development of leadership theory over the past century.
4. List five major leadership theories and describe their basic premises.
5. List the strengths and weaknesses of five leadership theories.
6. List three components of an effective leadership theory.
7. List five characteristics of a successful dietetics leader.

Introduction

Today in all of society there is a seemingly unending, universal search for leadership. This exploration is occurring during an era when a combination of societal forces portends a radically different future. With the rapid development of technology, society is being transformed from an industrial to an information society. Compounding the complexity of this major transformation is a general shortage of people entering the work force in Western society. In some areas, such as dietetics, these shortages may be regional rather than nationwide. Moreover, the values of this work force are changing. In the industrial era, from which present society is emerging, the importance of human resources was secondary to energy and mass production. In an information society, the maximization of human potential is the single greatest challenge for managerial leadership today.

These forces are increasing the demands on managerial leadership in organizations. At the same time there is a decrease in the authority of managers, a questioning of the infallibility of management decisions, and uncertainty regarding management tasks. Moreover, the potential of the rest of the work force to contribute to the organization in meaningful ways has increased. The relationships between managers and their staff are undergoing significant change. This change requires new leadership theory and new strategies that will appeal to the values of the contemporary work force. Organizational employees will no longer be satisfied with hierarchical organizational structures and depersonalized, bureaucratic policies and procedures.

As society searches for leadership during this time of rapid and fundamental change, the dietetics profession searches as well. For dietetics, there are additional forces and issues to consider, both in the healthcare industry and within the profession. The cost-constrained healthcare environment of the 1980s and 1990s has resulted in the beginning of major transformations and government reform in the healthcare industry, including changes in the organizational structure of healthcare facilities, new modes of healthcare delivery, alterations in the locations at which patients receive their care, increasing regulations, and competition in the marketplace. Within the dietetics profession, there is pervasive concern about the profession's future role and dissatisfaction with salaries and opportunities for advancement.

These complex interrelated forces demand new leadership in society and in dietetics. The conceptual framework for this book, transformational leadership (see chapter 3), can provide a new leadership paradigm. Transformational leadership can offer guidance to leaders in dietetics to make the profession thrive.

The Leadership Crisis

Leadership in society as a whole is plagued by three problems: increased complexity, lack of commitment, and decreased faith in leaders (Bennis and Nanus 1985, p 7–12). First, society and organizations are becoming more and more complex:

> This is an era marked with rapid and spastic change. The problems of organizations are increasingly complex. There are too many ironies, polarities, dichotomies, dualities, ambivalences, paradoxes, confusions, contradictions, contraries, and messes for organizations to understand and deal with (Bennis and Nanus 1985, p 8).

The changes in our society profoundly affect how leaders lead organizations. Thus many traditional management techniques have become obsolete. Yet now, more than ever, we need good leaders, because leadership is directly linked to organizational success. Bass (1990) noted that leadership was often regarded as the single most critical factor to the success or failure of institutions. Thus managerial leaders must begin seeking new ways to communicate, make decisions, think, and act quickly.

Furthermore, there is evidence of a second crisis in leadership. This crisis involves a decrease in employees' commitment to their work, which results in decreased productivity in many of our nation's organizations. Yanklevich and Associates (1983, p 6–7) surveyed the nonmanagerial work force and found that fewer than 25 percent of the people surveyed said they were currently working at their full potential; 50 percent said they did not put effort into their job more than is necessary to keep it; 75 percent said they were not as effective as they could be; and 60 percent said they did not work as hard as they used to work. Leaders and supervisors may be part of the problem. In the workplace it has been documented that when immediate supervisors are considered, 60 percent of workers said their supervisors are the major cause of job-related stress (Clark et al 1992).

The third leadership problem is a lack of leader credibility, which affects the relationship between managers and employees. Due to the mass media, which publicizes the unethical behaviors of public leaders and more assertive behaviors on the part of followers, leaders are being scrutinized and criticized by followers as never before. People are questioning and challenging authority. This questioning and challenging is not limited to political leaders, but extends to leaders in business, industry, and healthcare as well. The roots of this problem can be found in our nation's emphasis on the bottom line and on personal material success.

Dietetics faces many of the same leadership challenges faced by society in general. A leadership crisis exists in dietetics, where job satisfaction and salaries have been continuing concerns. In quoting statistics from the 1990 American Dietetic Association membership survey, Owen (1994) noted that:

- 67 percent of dietitians had no budget under their control;
- more than 50 percent of those in dietetics positions earned $20,000 to $35,000 annually; and
- 39 percent of those in primary dietetics positions supervised no employees.

Paralleling the growing recognition of the leadership crisis in society and dietetics is the increasing understanding of the necessity of leadership for effective organizational change. In fact, it is this concept that most clearly distinguishes "leaders" from "managers." Specifically, when managers implement change in an organization it is often "planned change." Managers function within the existing organizational structure. They make small changes in the process perhaps, but they do not alter fundamental constructs or worker motivation. This provides for incremental but not necessarily significant organizational gains.

Leaders, on the other hand, are not typically confined by structure. They make changes more readily in organizational cultures and ultimately in the workers themselves. Thus leaders provide an opportunity for more effective change and significant organizational gains. Kotter (1990) distinguished the functions of management and leadership in this way: management helps keep an organization on time and on budget, whereas leadership produces movement through constructive or adaptive change.

Another consideration is the level at which leadership is exhibited within an organization today. Often the leadership of an effective and popular chief executive officer or president is singled out as the reason for organizational success. Day and Lord (1988) note that differences in executive leadership might explain up to 45 percent of an organization's performance. More important, researchers have documented that effective organizations have leaders not just in the executive ranks but also at lower levels of management (Wilson et al 1990, Yammarino and Bass 1990, Sashkin and Burke 1990). Current research in leadership is being redirected on how to identify and foster leadership skills at many organizational levels.

Likewise, in dietetics there is a strong need for leadership at all levels of responsibility. Pacesetters in the profession have been sounding the leadership alarm for the past fifteen years (Huenemann 1981, Hoover 1983, Wylie-Rosett et al 1990, Rinke and Finn 1990, Finn 1991, Dodd 1992a, Dodd 1992b, Schiller et al 1993). Few, however, have responded, and a specific approach to dietetics leadership has never been defined. The distinction between managerial and leadership skills is often blurred by the profession, further adding to the confusion. To answer the leadership call there is clearly a need to design and implement an approach for effective leadership development in dietetics that builds on both past and present theories.

Historical Development of Leadership Theory

As early as the times of Plato and Confucius and the writing of the Old and New Testaments, scholars and philosophers have attempted to understand and describe leadership. The real impetus to study leadership in a systematic, scientific manner occurred during and after World War I. The leadership theories of the last century have their base in industrial organizations and society (Fig 1-1). They have provided significant knowledge that has facilitated current and future theory development. No schools of leadership, however, have emerged out of the immense reservoir of leadership data and analysis. This is true partly because scholars have worked in separate disciplines and subdisciplines in pursuit of different questions and problems.

Figure 1-1. Leadership and motivational theories.

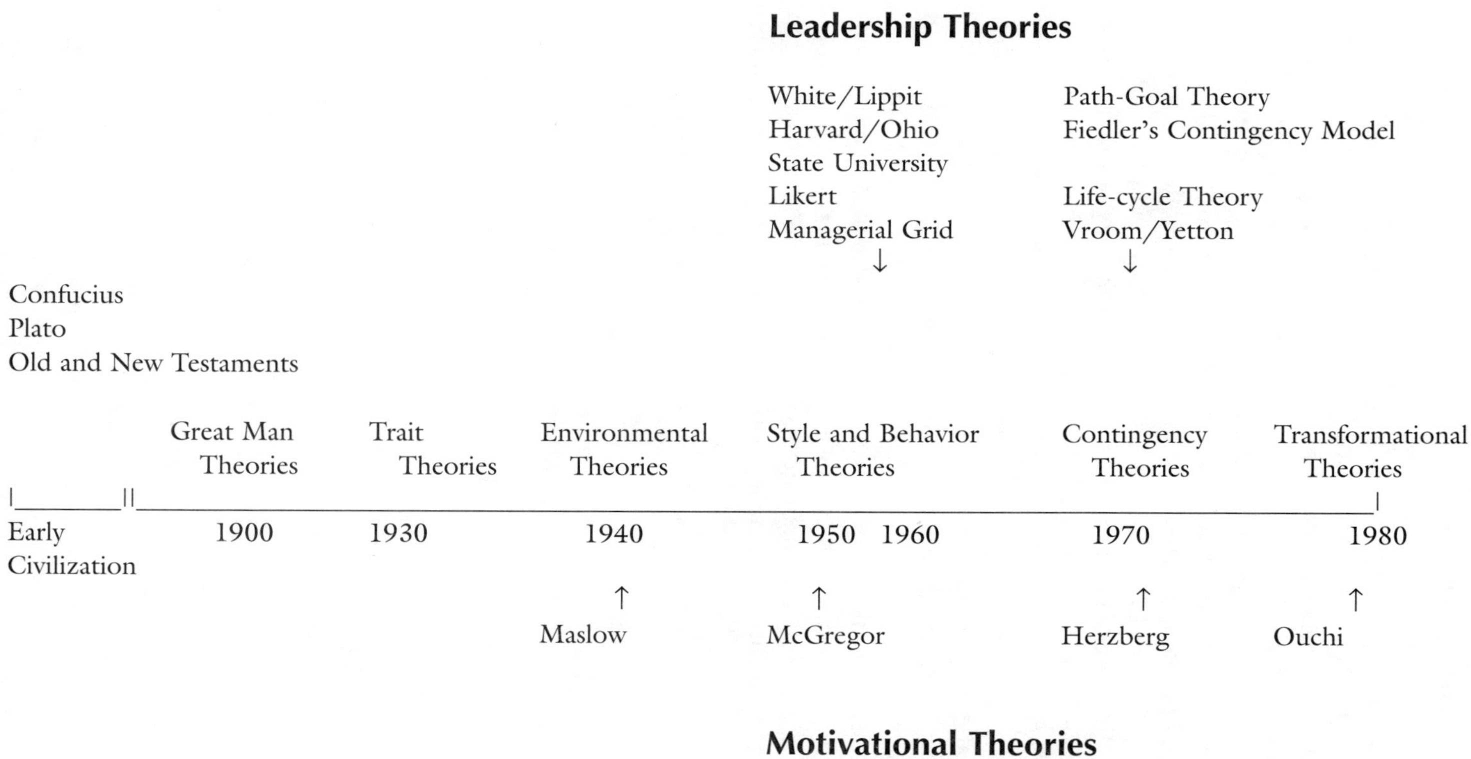

Society is now on the brink of an intellectual breakthrough in leadership theory (Burns 1978, p 3). In fact, Clark et al (1992) observed that in the past fifteen years, the number of articles on leadership increased at twice the rate of articles in general.

The following review of leadership theories is important to the understanding of transformational leadership. However, the theories reviewed are incomplete, because they are basically limited to two dimensions: the tasks of managers and their relationships with others. The theories do not consider the values of people, nor do they help explain why some organizations achieve success and excellence and why others do not. In chapter 3, a theory will be presented that is relevant to an information society and responds to the future. Books on leadership and management (and management books in general) abound with similar summaries of the historical development of leadership theories. The extensive additional readings in appendix B provide for further study of leadership theories. To offer the reader a greater appreciation of transformational leadership, the following summary identifies important themes in the seminal works on leadership.

One of the predominant themes of the works that follow is that a democratic, participatory style is generally most effective. The situational theorists suggested the use of different leadership styles in different situations. This is a concept with much common sense and some research to support it. The participatory style of management, however, has the most overall support. This style includes having a positive, supportive relationship with followers. Additionally, the theories also suggest that managerial leaders need to attend to the tasks and goals of the organization as well as to interpersonal relationships with followers. Another important concept that can be gleaned from this review is that the behaviors and attitudes of leaders directly affect followers' satisfaction and productivity. All three of these themes provide a foundation for transformational leadership theory.

Great Man Theories and Trait Theories

The earliest leadership theories centered on the study of the traits and characteristics of the leader, such as personality, social traits, and physical characteristics. By studying "great men" such as Caesar, Alexander the Great, and Jefferson, theorists searched for and listed attributes that differentiated the leader from the led. Because these studies described the characteristics of important historical figures, they were called "great man" theories. These attempts later evolved into trait theories, which were developed by observing leaders in groups or by asking people to describe characteristics of preferred leaders.

Both of these early efforts to study leadership, although helpful, failed to identify any sufficiently universal traits in leaders. Characteristics that distinguished the leader from the follower or attributes that could help predict who would or would not be a successful leader were lacking (Stogdill 1974, p 35–65). Nonetheless, the failure to find these traits is important to the understanding and practical application of leadership theory. A person does not have to possess a certain rigidly defined set of attributes to be a leader. Dietetics leaders who are responsible for choosing lower-level managers are cautioned against making a list of desirable traits and searching for a leader by measuring people against the list. A better approach is to look at candidates' past behaviors and accomplishments and to gain an understanding of the person's values and beliefs about leadership and dietetics. Traits such as initiative and intelligence, which are generally accepted to be characteristics of leaders, can be nurtured and developed in others.

Environmental Theories

Several early theorists advanced the view that leaders arise as a result of certain circumstances and events. Thus they proposed that the situation itself plays a large part in determining both the qualities of the leader and who the leader will be. For example, George Washington was a successful leader because the events of the American revolution brought out his skills and abilities. Like trait theories, however, these environmental theories were inadequate. They provided no assistance in predicting a leader's abilities or in helping to develop future leaders (Stogdill 1974, p 17).

An underlying belief of both environmental and trait theories is that leaders are born, not made. This concept is not in tune with the basic values in today's society, nor is it accurate. Leaders are and can be developed. Leadership can be learned. It is not an easy task, but it happens every day.

General Approaches to Leadership Theory

In this category, the major focus is on the behaviors, activities, and styles of leaders. It is important to note that little attention is paid to followers and situations in these theories.

Styles of Leadership. One of the earliest and most famous studies looked at specific leader behaviors, primarily that of decision making and control. The researchers described three styles of leadership behavior: *autocratic*, *democratic*, and *laissez-faire*. These styles were placed on a continuum. At one end is the autocratic leader, described as directive, exerting a high degree of control, and allowing no participation in decision making. On the other end of the continuum is the laissez-faire leader, who gives complete freedom to the followers group and provides no direction, resulting in a passive approach. In the middle is the democratic leader, who exerts a low degree of control but is active in stimulating the group. The democratic leader allows participation in decision making while providing guidance and direction (White and Lippit 1960).

The most important finding arising from this work is that leadership behavior directly influences the climate and productivity of the group. Further research and transformational leadership theory strongly embrace this belief. A second, important theme is that, overall, the democratic leadership style is the most successful. This style allows participation in decision making while simultaneously supporting, guiding, and counseling the followers. Although later situational theories suggested that a leader's style should change to fit the situation and the characteristics of the followers group, a participatory, supportive style remains a common premise in many theories and is a basic premise in this book as well.

Leader Behaviors. Leader behavior was the emphasis of two parallel research programs at Harvard University and The Ohio State University. At Harvard, Bales (1958) identified two important behavioral dimensions of leadership: behavior centered on task accomplishment and behavior centered on interpersonal relations. He found that leaders typically exhibited high levels of both types of behavior.

Over the course of many years, studies of leadership behavior were also conducted at The Ohio State University. From these studies, two similar leader behaviors, called consideration and initiating structure, consistently surfaced. Consideration refers to a wide range of activities that describe leader-follower interactions. Consideration behaviors cause leaders to display regard for the followers, satisfy their needs, and provide a supportive work environment. Initiating structure refers to the role of the leader to provide structure to accomplish the tasks of the organization and to direct the work group toward attainment of organizational goals. It includes activities such as assigning and organizing work, providing feedback for work performance, clarifying roles, and defining policies and procedures. These activities are similar to the classic management principles of planning, organizing, directing, and controlling (Rue and Byars 1986, p 385).

Much of the research conducted to verify this theory of leader behaviors has resulted in conflicting findings about the relationship between initiating structure and employee satisfaction. However, leaders that scored high on both initiating structure and consideration questionnaires appear to have more cohesive, harmonious, and productive groups of followers (House 1971, p 321). This research further supports and expands the belief that a democratic, participatory, supportive style is effective if combined with attention to tasks and goal accomplishment.

Likert's Four Systems of Leadership. Likert's (1967) four systems of leadership evolved out of studies conducted at the University of Michigan, which revealed that supervisors of highly productive work groups gave general supervision, delegated authority and responsibility, and were employee-rather than production-oriented (Rue and Byars 1986, p 387). Likert's four systems of leadership are described below:

1. The *exploitative authoritative* style of leadership is one in which the leader exploits subordinates.
2. The *benevolent authoritative* style is paternalistic in nature, yet the decision making and control are authoritarian, using direct hierarchical pressure for results.
3. The *consultative* style is one in which the leader maintains the decision-making prerogative but seeks input from and consults with employees.
4. In the *participative* leadership style, decisions are reached by group consensus with the leader serving to give direction.

In agreement with previous theories, Likert claimed that the participative leadership style, called the system 4 manager, is the most effective. Effectiveness was measured by the productivity of the work group, the level of cost containment, positive employee attitudes, and good labor-management relationships.

The Managerial Grid. Closely related to the initiating structure and consideration perspective is the *task* vs *relationship* orientation of Blake and Mouton (1985). Rather than seeing these orientations on a single continuum, however, Blake and Mouton developed a managerial grid that placed the two elements together bipolarly. They described four combinations and styles of leadership. A leader with a high task orientation and a low relationship orientation has the *authority/obedience* style of management. In this style, the leader's efforts are directed at efficiency of task completion with minimal consideration for people. A manager using the opposite style, *country club* management, emphasizes a concern for people (a high relationship orientation), resulting in a relaxed atmosphere and workplace. The i*mpoverished* manager, who scores low on both the relationship and task orientations, exerts little effort to accomplish the tasks or to relate with people. The *team* manager combines a high degree of concern for people with a high degree of concern for the task.

The purpose of the grid and of the work of these two researchers is to help managers identify their style by use of a questionnaire. Blake and Mouton claim that the team management style of leadership is the most desirable. From this work, empirical research has demonstrated that both the people- and task-related behaviors of leaders are important. The transformational dietetics leader cannot ignore either the people in the organization or the tasks of the organization. Both tasks and people will be explored in this book; however, they will be discussed as integrated rather than as separate entities.

Situational Leadership Theories

The basic premise of situational leadership theories is that different leadership styles are needed in different situations. For example, some research showed that a democratic, participatory, permissive style is not necessarily most effective in every situation (Morse and Reimer 1956). Vroom (1960) found that the most effective style was, in part, determined by the characteristics of employees. Thus he suggested that leaders need to adapt their style to the situation at hand. The situational theories contributed two new elements to the development of leadership theory: the situation and the follower. These theories are prescriptive, attempting to tell leaders how to act in a given situation.

Path-Goal Theory. The central underlying concept of the path-goal theory is consideration of what motivates individuals. In this theory, motivation to behave in a particular manner is seen as the result of two related functions. First is the expectation that a particular behavior will result in a particular goal. Second, how strongly a person desires the goal will influence the behavior. The role of a leader is to clearly define desirable goals and to remove obstacles that could stand in the way of goal accomplishment (House 1971).

The path-goal theory also suggests that there are four leadership styles that the leader can choose to employ in a particular situation:

- *Directive*—The authoritarian style previously discussed.
- *Supportive*—The leader is friendly, approachable, and shows concern for others.
- *Participative*—The leader asks for and uses suggestions to make decisions.
- *Achievement-oriented*—The leader sets goals for subordinates that cause subordinates to strive for higher standards and the leader shows confidence that they can attain the goals.

Depending on the situation, House suggested, the same leader could use varying styles. There are two situational factors: the personal characteristics of subordinates and the environmental demands with which the subordinates must cope to accomplish goals and satisfy their needs. Thus far, research has shown that for ambiguous tasks the leader should use a directive style. For stressful, frustrating, dissatisfying work, a supportive style is appropriate. Finally, for nonrepetitive, unclear tasks, an achievement style is warranted. A participatory leadership style was prescribed when subordinates were highly ego-involved in a decision or task and when the decision or task was ambiguous (Rue and Byars 1986, p 388).

An example of applying varying management styles would be the same dietetics manager using each of the four styles in different situations. In an emergency situation in which the tasks are ambiguous and seldom encountered, a directive style should be used. For handling the daily stressful (and sometimes frustrating) work, the dietetics manager should choose a supportive style. In a situation in which the work group is facing a major change, such as the implementation of a new system of care delivery, the leader should use an achievement style by setting high standards and showing confidence in the group. Last, to accomplish goals in which people have expressed a variety of opinions and beliefs, a participatory style would be most appropriate.

Fiedler's Contingency Theory. The contingency model of leadership effectiveness sought to integrate person, process, and situation (Fiedler 1967, Fiedler and Chemers 1974). It was also the only theory at the time based on specific leadership traits and behaviors. The main premise of the theory is that the effectiveness of the leader is contingent upon two factors: the motivational system of the leader and the degree to which the leader has control and influence in a particular situation. This theory consisted of two parts: ranking the leader's style and analyzing the situation.

To rank the leader's style, Fiedler and Chemers developed and administered a questionnaire called the "Least Preferred Co-Worker." The questionnaire ranked the leader as either *task-motivated* or *relationship-motivated*. These two elements are similar to the initiating structure and consideration perspective of previous theories. Next, Fiedler and Chemers analyzed the situation based on three elements and characterized the situation as either favorable or unfavorable. The first element, the *leader-follower* relationship, is the degree of friendliness of the leader and the extent to which others trust and respect him or her. *Task structure,* the second element, is the degree of structure entailed in a particular job. The third element is the *position power* of the leader. This refers to the formal power and influence of the leader, particularly his or her authority to reward and punish. Using these dimensions, the researchers developed eight classification schemes, which are prescriptive suggestions for matching a leadership style with a situation.

Fiedler and Chemers viewed leadership situations on a continuum. In the most favorable situation for the leader, the relationship between the leader and followers is good—characterized by mutual trust, respect, and friendliness. The task is structured—that is, the goals of the task are known, the elements are defined, and goal completion is probable. The leader is powerful, having formal influence over others. In this situation, a task-oriented leadership style is recommended. Likewise, in unfavorable situations in which the relationship is poor, the task is unstructured, and the power of the leader is weak, a task-oriented style is prescribed. A relationship leadership style is recommended, however, when the elements in the situation are moderate.

Life-cycle Theory. Hershey and Blanchard's (1977) life-cycle theory grew out of The Ohio State University study of leader behaviors. This theory placed an emphasis on the behavior of the leader as it relates to the characteristics of the follower. First, researchers looked at follower maturity as it related to a specific task. The elements of follower maturity are as follows:

- The capacity to set high but realistic goals for self
- The willingness and ability of the follower
- The education, experience, job maturity, and psychological maturity of the follower

The researchers proposed that as the maturity level of the follower increases in relation to a specific task, the leader should reduce task behaviors and increase relationship behaviors. Hershey and Blanchard had a slightly different definition of task and relationship behaviors than that of previous theories. They considered task behaviors to be the extent to which a leader engages in one-way communication by explaining how to accomplish tasks. They defined relationship behaviors as the extent to which a leader engages in two-way communication by providing socioemotional support and facilitating behaviors. They viewed these behaviors as bipolar (Table 1-1).

Vroom and Yetton's Contingency Model. Vroom and Yetton (1973) composed a contingency model that attempted to specify situations that would affect the effectiveness of decision making. They proposed that the decision-making process was affected by three factors:

1. Quality/rationality of decision
2. Acceptance/commitment by subordinates to execute decision effectively
3. Amount of time required to make decisions

Based on these factors, a decision tree was developed to guide leaders in a choice of appropriate levels of subordinate participation. Research using the model documented that a leader's willingness to use participative decision making was affected more by the decision-making situation than an autocracy-democracy "style." For example, leaders were more willing to use

Table 1-1. Hershey and Blanchard's Leader Behaviors and Resultant Leadership Styles

Leader Behaviors		Leadership Style
Task	**Relationship**	
High	Low	**Telling**—defines the task; explains responsibilities; gives time frames for task completion; one-way communication
High	High	**Selling**—balances concern for goal accomplishment with values, needs, and attitudes of followers; is in control but seeks input
Low	High	**Participating**—concern is for how to get the group to work together to accomplish the task
Low	Low	**Delegating**—takes a low profile; is available for consultation

participation in situations requiring a high-quality, technically adequate solution than in situations that were trivial or had no technical component. Thus Vroom and Yetton expanded the earlier work of White and Lippit (1960) and Likert (1967), who had considered only leadership style as a factor in evaluating leadership.

Motivational Theories

These theories focus on the needs and motivation of followers and examine factors that satisfy followers or decrease their dissatisfaction. According to these theories, a satisfied employee is more productive than a dissatisfied one. Furthermore, these theories claim that the performance of the organization as a whole is a function of individual employee satisfaction and morale. There is conflicting evidence in the research regarding these basic premises; some scholars believe that the issues are more complex than this simple cause-and-effect relationship. Few managers would deny, however, that employee satisfaction is a desired end—if not for its ability to enhance productivity, at least for its ability to provide a positive work environment.

Theory X and Theory Y. At the hub of McGregor's work (1960) is the belief that leaders' attitudes about human nature influence their leadership behavior. Consequently, he proposed that there are two types of leaders, *theory X* and *theory Y*. Theory X leaders consider people as lazy, unmotivated, irresponsible, and unintelligent, and believe that workers will work only as much as is necessary to keep their jobs. These leaders feel they must direct and control people, supervising them closely and motivating them through a system of rewards and punishments. In contrast, theory Y leaders believe that work itself can be motivating and rewarding and that workers can be trusted to work hard without constant supervision. The major function of theory Y leaders, therefore, is to provide support for workers. This support includes providing a satisfying work environment by removing obstacles, providing guidance, and encouraging growth.

Herzberg's Dual Factor Theory. The concept that job satisfaction and job dissatisfaction are not direct opposites but are, in fact, separate but related entities is important to understanding Herzberg's theory. Herzberg (1966, p 72–74; 1968) labeled factors that affect worker satisfaction and worker dissatisfaction as *hygiene* and *motivation* factors, respectively. Hygiene factors are those elements of the job environment that, when present, avoid unpleasantness in the work environment. They include company policy, administration, salary, supervision, interpersonal relationships, and working conditions. If any of these factors does not meet worker expectations, the worker will be dissatisfied. Motivation factors are concerned with job content rather than job environment. If present, they result in employee satisfaction. Motivation factors include those elements that people need to grow and develop psychologically, such as achievement, recognition for achievement, the work itself, advancement, and responsibility.

In applying this theory, the dietetics manager should consider that those factors that cause dissatisfaction, such as salary, do not reversely cause job satisfaction. In other words, if an employee considers his or her salary appropriate, this does not mean he or she is necessarily satisfied with his or her job. Similarly, factors that result in satisfaction, such as achievement, do not cause dissatisfaction when not present; rather, they cause a lack of satisfaction.

In his research, Herzberg found that three motivation factors—the work itself, opportunity for advancement, and responsibility—were the most important for long-lasting, positive attitudes about work. He believed that the only way to motivate people is to give them challenging work in which people assume responsibility and achieve success. Although his work is three decades old and there are valid criticisms of his theory, his premises point leaders in an appropriate direction. His theory suggests to leaders how they may determine what may or may not enhance employee motivation and satisfaction.

Theory Z. Intentionally alluding to McGregor's theory X and theory Y, Ouchi (1981, p 71–94) described an alternative leadership approach, theory Z. His basic premise is similar to other motivational theories: an increase in job satisfaction, brought about by attention to humanistic management, results in improved employee satisfaction and productivity. Ouchi's work is rooted in a comparison of Japanese and American management. He began by listing the characteristics of "type Z" companies. These include long-term employment, slow evaluation and promotion, nonspecialized career paths, collective decision making and responsibility, and a holistic concern for people. Ouchi purported that the theoretical basis for why type Z companies are successful is that they have achieved a high state of consistency in their organizational cultures. He likens Z companies to clans in which the associations among people are intimate. In a clan, people's individuality is less important than teamwork and agreement on working toward a common goal. Yet people in a clan are socialized so that their personal needs and values are naturally consistent with the common good. Thus people in Z organizations report a higher degree of autonomy and freedom than employees of other organizations.

Expectancy Theory. One of the most recent motivation theories, expectancy theory, was developed by Beer et al (1984), who suggested that rewards will serve as motivators only under certain circumstances. Specifically, employees must:

- Believe that effective performance or behavior leads to certain rewards
- Feel that the rewards offered are attractive
- Believe that a certain level of individual effort will lead to achieving the organization's standards of performance (Beer et al 1984, p 121–122)

Schiller and Wolf (1994) note that the expectancy model of motivation helps explain why salaries alone serve as poor motivators in dietetics. With low salaries, any increase adds only a few pennies more to each paycheck. Rarely is there a perceived association between goal achievement and salary increases.

Implications for Dietetics

Almost every article or book written in the last decade that discusses leadership begins by arguing the need for new leadership theory and strategies. Peters and Waterman (1982), Bennis and Nanus (1985), Bass (1985), Berlew (1986), Manz and Sims (1989), Anderson (1992), Nanus (1992), and Reynolds (1994) are just a few examples. The theories presented in this chapter are not wrong; they are simply unfinished. They do not consider the new values of people who are no longer fulfilled solely by their work and by being treated with respect. These theories do not explain why some organizations are enthusiastic and successful while others are not. The answers to these questions can, at least in part, be found in the theory of transformational leadership.

As the reader proceeds throughout the book, the behaviors of an "ideal" leader will be discussed. Such leaders exhibit the transformational leadership behaviors needed in today's healthcare organizations. These behaviors include some of those already discussed in this chapter, but also include many new ones. The effective leader needs to be able to balance the tasks of the organization (organizational goals) with his or her skills in dealing with people. To best work with others, the leader must understand the values, motives, and aspirations of others. The motivational theories reviewed in this chapter direct the dietetics leader toward providing an environment in which people can achieve and be successful, have a sense of belonging to the team while maintaining a sense of self, and seek self-actualization in their professional work.

Application to Dietetics Practice: Case Study

The Setting

A director of food and nutrition services in a seven-hundred-bed hospital recently submitted her resignation in order to pursue a new career goal. During her four-year tenure, the director successfully implemented a clinical ladder, set up a continuous quality improvement program, and decreased employee turnover.

Current Situation

Upon her departure, the director receives the following letter from the vice president to whom she reported:

> Dear Maria:
>
> My reaction to your official announcement that you are leaving the Medical Center is that it is an unmitigated disaster for the institution. Very few departures in recent years will have had a comparable adverse impact on the functioning of this hospital.
>
> You are a rare commodity: a savvy, highly intelligent, highly skilled, professionally adept, wise, insightful visionary. You are an understanding, flexible, firm thinker as well as a doer who works extremely well with colleagues, superiors, and those reporting to you. You can compromise without capitulating, say no without being negative, take chances without being reckless, be innovative without being destructive, and have warmth and charm without being weak. When you lead, others want to follow. When you collaborate, your colleagues are enriched. Your very presence in a meeting is assurance of at least one source of reason, considered judgment, and an attempt to accommodate. You will be sorely missed. You have made a difference; let there be no doubt about it. I wish you the best in your new endeavors.
>
> Sincerely,
> A. M. Bellows

Case Study Discussion

1. What traits does this dietetics leader possess? Do these traits ensure leadership success?

2. Does this letter indicate the leader's ability to attend to both the tasks of the food and nutrition services department and the people with whom she works (ie, consideration and initiating structure)?

3. How would you classify her leadership style using Blake and Mouton's managerial grid? Using theory X and theory Y?

4. What characteristics does this dietetics leader exemplify that are not included in the theories discussed thus far?

5. How do you think this dietetics leader might motivate staff?

6. Does the letter reflect the dietetics leader's skills in dealing with dietetics professionals' dissatisfactions with their practice? Why or why not?

7. Does this letter reflect the leader's ability to use different leadership styles in different situations?

8. Which of Maria's specific traits would you like to develop further in yourself?

References

Anderson T. *Transforming Leadership: New Skills for an Extraordinary Future.* Amherst, Mass: Human Resource Development Press Inc; 1992.

Bales RF. Task roles and social roles in problem-solving groups. In: Maccoby EE, Newcomb TM, Harley EL, eds. *Readings in Social Psychology.* 3rd ed. New York, NY: Holt, Rinehart & Winston; 1958.

Bass BM. *Leadership and Performance Beyond Expectation.* New York, NY: Free Press; 1985.

Bass BM. *Bass & Stogdill's Handbook of Leadership: Theory, Research, and Managerial Applications.* 3rd ed. New York, NY: The Free Press; 1990.

Beer M, Spector B, Lawrence PR, Mills DQ, Walton RE. *Managing Human Assets.* New York, NY: The Free Press; 1984.

Bennis W, Nanus B. *Leaders: Strategies for Taking Charge.* New York, NY: John Wiley & Sons; 1985.

Berlew DE. Leadership and organizational excitement. In: Williamson JN, ed. *The Leader-Manager.* New York, NY: John Wiley & Sons; 1986:99–104.

Blake RR, Mouton JS. *The Managerial Grid III*. Houston, Tex: Gulf Publishing; 1985.

Burns JM. *Leadership*. New York, NY: Harper & Row; 1978.

Clark KE, Clark MB, Campbell DP, eds. *Impact of Leadership*. Greensboro, NC: Center for Creative Leadership; 1992.

Day DV, Lord RG. Executive leadership and organizational performance: suggestions for a new theory and methodology. *Journal of Management*. 1988;14:453–464.

Dodd J. The leadership challenge. *J Am Diet Assoc*. 1992a;92:225–226.

Dodd J. The words of leadership. *J Am Diet Assoc*. 1992b;92:1006.

Fiedler FE. *A Theory of Leadership Effectiveness*. New York, NY: McGraw-Hill; 1967.

Fiedler FE, Chemers MM. *Leadership and Effective Management*. Glenview, Ill: Scott Foresman; 1974.

Finn SC. The decade of the dietitian: leadership can make it happen. *Topics in Clinical Nutrition*. 1991;6:1–7.

Hershey P, Blanchard KH. *Management of Organizational Behavior: Utilizing Human Resources*. 3rd ed. Englewood Cliffs, NJ: Prentice-Hall Inc; 1977.

Herzberg FH. One more time: how do you motivate employees? *Harvard Business Review*. 1968;46:53–62.

Herzberg FH. *Work and the Nature of Man*. Cleveland, Ohio: World Publishing Co; 1966.

Hoover LW. Enhancing managerial effectiveness in dietetics. *J Am Diet Assoc*. 1983;82:58–61.

House RJ. A path-goal theory of leadership effectiveness. *Administrative Science Quarterly*. 1971;16:321–338.

Huenemann RL. Leadership and quality in nutritional care: our role in today's world. *J Am Diet Assoc*. 1981;78:124–128.

Kotter JP. *A Force for Change: How Leadership Differs From Management*. New York, NY: The Free Press; 1990.

Likert R. *The Human Organization: Its Management and Values*. New York, NY: McGraw-Hill; 1967.

Manz CC, Sims HP Jr. *Superleadership: Leading Others to Lead Themselves*. Englewood Cliffs, NJ: Prentice-Hall, Inc; 1989.

McGregor D. *The Human Side of Enterprise*. New York, NY: McGraw-Hill; 1960.

Morse NC, Reimer E. The experimental change of a major organizational variable. *J Abnorm Psychol*. 1956;52:120–129.

Nanus B. *Visionary Leadership: Creating a Compelling Sense of Direction for Your Organization*. San Francisco, Calif: Jossey-Bass Publishers; 1992.

Ouchi W. *Theory Z: How American Business Can Meet the Japanese Challenge*. Reading, Mass: Addison-Wesley Publishing Co; 1981.

Owen AL. Women as managers. *Topics in Clinical Nutrition*. 1994;9:1–7.

Peters TJ, Waterman RH. *In Search of Excellence: Lessons From America's Best-Run Companies*. New York, NY: Warner Communications; 1982.

Reynolds J. *Out-Front Leadership: Discovering, Developing, and Delivering Your Potential*. Austin, Tex: Mott & Carlisle; 1994.

Rinke WJ, Finn SC. Winning strategies to excel in dietetics. *J Am Diet Assoc.* 1990;90:935–938.

Rue LW, Byars LL. *Management: Theory and Application.* Homewood, Ill: Richard D Irwin Inc; 1986.

Sashkin M, Burke WW. Understanding and assessing organizational leadership. In: Clark KE, Clark MB, eds. *Measures of Leadership.* West Orange, NJ: Leadership Library of America Inc; 1990:297–326.

Schiller MR, Foltz MB, Campbell S. Dietitians' self-perceptions: implications for leadership. *J Am Diet Assoc.* 1993;93:868–876.

Schiller MR, Wolf KN. Motivating clinical staff: new variations on an old theme. *Clinical Nutrition Management Newsletter.* 1994;13:1–6.

Stogdill RM. *Handbook of Leadership: A Survey of Theory and Research.* New York, NY: The Free Press; 1974.

Vroom VH. *Some Personality Determinants of the Effects of Participation.* Englewood Cliffs, NJ: Prentice-Hall Inc; 1960.

Vroom VH, Yetton PW. *Leadership and Decision Making.* Pittsburgh, Pa: University of Pittsburgh Press; 1973.

White RK, Lippit R. *Autocracy and Democracy: An Experimental Inquiry.* New York, NY: Harper & Brothers; 1960.

Wilson CL, O'Hare D, Shipper F. Task cycle theory: the processes of influence. In: Clark KE, Clark MB, eds. *Measures of Leadership.* West Orange, NJ: Leadership Library of America Inc; 1990.

Wylie-Rosett J, Wheeler M, Krueger K, Halford B. Opportunities for research-oriented dietitians. *J Am Diet Assoc.* 1990;90:1531–1534.

Yammarino F, Bass BM. Transformational leadership and multiple levels of analysis. *Human Relations.* 1990;43:975–995.

Yanklevich D. *Work and Human Values.* New York, NY: Public Agenda Foundation; 1983.

2

Societal and Healthcare Transformations

Chapter Objectives

1. Explain how projected future possibilities will affect dietetics and healthcare.
2. Compare and contrast industrial and information societies.
3. Define structural change.
4. Discuss how changes in information processing and communications will affect healthcare and dietetics.
5. List three major social trends.
6. Discuss how concerns for cost and quality will change healthcare.
7. Define semiautonomous work units.
8. Describe the required characteristics of future leaders.

Introduction

This chapter is about the predicted future of society, organizations, and healthcare and the implications for dietetics and leadership. There is nothing incontrovertible about the information presented here. No one can predict with absolute certainty what the future holds. By analyzing current trends and examining them through computerized models, however, futurists such as Naisbitt (1982, 1994), Tapscott and Caston (1993), Martel (1986), and Toffler (1970), have theorized about possible future scenarios.

It may seem difficult, as dietetics leaders struggle everyday for the survival of the profession, to think about the future. However, the nutrition leader's understanding of projected possibilities for society and healthcare will help him or her prepare for and gain a better foothold in the uncertain future of dietetics.

Few periods in history can be labeled as transforming. Today we are living in one of those periods. The transformation is unusual as compared with others (the most recent being the Industrial Revolution). Unlike those of the past, today's society is aware that the transformation is occurring: the transformation is being studied and hypotheses about the future are abundant. Kuhn (1962) labeled transforming periods in history as paradigm shifts when the working values and assumptions upon which people structure their daily lives become inappropriate. These assumptions then break apart to be replaced by more appropriate ones.

Furthermore, the healthcare system in this country faces two major, conflicting challenges in the next decade: the control of healthcare costs and the provision of high-quality care to all clients. These two factors, in combination with societal trends and changes in the role of healthcare providers, are fundamentally altering the healthcare delivery system in this nation.

Structural and Cyclical Change

There are two types of societal change: structural and cyclical. Structural changes are fundamental transformations of an activity or institution that are irreversible and require permanent adjustment on the part of society. Cyclical changes, however, do not involve a change in the structure of society; they are temporary and do not require permanent adjustment. Examples of cyclical changes are business, economic, and demand-supply cycles (Martel 1986, p 19–34).

The structural changes of society and healthcare are the subjects of this chapter. There are a variety of ways to classify the structural changes facing society. Simplistically, they can be categorized as either technological or social trends. As with most attempts to categorize complex ideas, however, the classification is not exact. The two categories overlap; technological changes bring about social ones and vice versa. In the following discussion, the impact of structural technological and societal trends on healthcare will be discussed.

Technological Trends

The technological changes facing society and healthcare are occurring because of electronic breakthroughs during the past half century. Recently, the miniaturization of electronics with the concomitant decrease in their cost has laid the foundation for fundamental structural changes in society and healthcare.

The Emerging Information Society

The most pervasive, pivotal, and profound structural trend is the transformation from an industrial to an information economy. This transformation is occurring because of society's increased and growing capability to handle information using the electronic technology of computers. In the last four decades, the development of equipment to store, process, and distribute information has resulted in information replacing energy as the new transforming societal resource. In contrast to fossil fuel, the primary resource of the industrial age, information is a growing resource that cannot be depleted. This fact, combined with advances in electronic, genetic, and other technologies, means that information will be society's most important resource and the demand for it will continue to increase.

Industrial Society. To fully appreciate the changes that are occurring and will most likely continue to occur, it is helpful to first discern the elements of an industrial society. For most of history, human labor was society's principal resource until energy was harnessed in the 1800s, creating the large-scale production of goods and the means to transport and distribute them rapidly.

The primary resources of industrialization are fossil fuel, steam energy, and electricity. The industrial society maximized and "massified" the world through the mass production and distribution of goods, mass communication, and mass education. The values of education were punctuality, obedience, and rote and repetitious work. This resulted in the standardization of goods, services, currencies, and even time. The Industrial Revolution was characterized by big cities, centralized governments with concentrated political power, and big corporations. Socially, the family structure changed from large, extended families of the agricultural era to the nuclear family. These smaller family units were more mobile and thus could move to the big cities (Toffler 1986).

The attributes and working assumptions of the industrial society are breaking apart and are no longer working. This is a reflection of the current paradigm shift. Today society faces major problems:

- The economic strength of our nation is faltering.
- Corporations are breaking up or downsizing.
- Workers are dissatisfied with their work environment.
- Productivity is down.
- The welfare system does not produce recipients who contribute to the productivity of the nation.
- The healthcare system is too expensive, provides limited access for some people, and is dehumanizing.

- Families are in crisis.
- The environment is polluted.
- Traditional energy sources are becoming depleted.

Centralized big governments, which, in the past, were able to respond to crises, are not able to deal with the current problems facing society.

Information Society. Today some call the new era the *postmodern* or *postindustrial age;* others call it the *information society.* The distinction between the two terms is not clear. In this book, the latter term will be used. An economy is called an information economy when the percentages of products and employment involved in the service industries exceed those involved in manufacturing and other industrial activities. In an information economy, the major business is information—or a major part of the business is processing and distributing information.

The information society began in 1956–1957. Ironically, this was during the height of the industrial economy in this country. In 1956 white-collar workers outnumbered blue-collar ones for the first time in this nation's history. In 1957, with the space exploration of the Soviet Union's *Sputnik*, global communications became a reality (Naisbitt 1982, p 12). In the 1990s the information age is already going through its first paradigm shift, evolving into a second era. This modern era is driven by the demands of the new, competitive business environment on the one hand and profound changes in the nature of computers on the other (Tapscott and Caston 1993, p xi).

Society's increased and growing capability to handle information means changes in all activities in society, including work. Owen (1984) notes that the level of change involved is fundamental, yet subtle; therefore, people tend to dismiss it as overly simplistic and ignore it. Such behavior can be a great risk to the dietetics profession, individual careers, institutions, companies, and the economy as a whole. Leaders must appreciate the larger shifts that are restructuring society or fall into the trap of acting on assumptions that are already outdated (Owen 1984).

In an information society the service sector, including services provided to producers, services provided directly to consumers, and services provided to society as a whole, is and will continue to be the fastest-growing component. The high-tech industries, including computers, software, and related businesses, will continue to grow. Their growth, however, will not be as rapid as the "low-tech/no-tech service jobs," such as foodservice and healthcare workers (Martel 1986, p 91–107). Furthermore, legislation such as the American Disabilities Act opens up a whole new segment of society for employment in service industries and in other jobs.

Toffler (1986, p 15) claimed that the major difference in today's and tomorrow's societies is diversity. Naisbitt (1982, p 231) calls this a move from either/or to multiple options. One significant factor contributing to diversity is the new era of competition. Tapscott and Caston (1993, p 4–5) explain that competition comes not only from traditional adversaries in traditional markets or from new entrants to a specific industry or economic sector but also from the disintegration of barriers to previously insulated and protected markets. Evidence of the trend of diversity is ubiquitous. Scientists are looking at a variety of energy sources besides fossil fuel, such as sun, water, and wind. There is no longer a "typical" family structure. The selection of foods now available in the grocery store, including the wide range of salad dressings, ice cream, and ethnic foods, clearly demonstrates the diversity trend.

Healthcare has experienced this diversity as well, primarily because of recent cost-cutting and healthcare reform efforts. Hospitals are diversifying into related ventures, such as ambulatory care centers, satellite clinics, physician group practices, and home healthcare. Some have begun to sell medical/surgical products. Others have entered into ventures not connected with healthcare, such as catering. Still others are forming strategic networks and alliances with different healthcare providers, including those once outside their service area (eg, as rural/urban hospital alliances) or even with onetime competitors, such as the hospital down the street. Alternatives to the traditional system of healthcare delivery have burgeoned, particularly health maintenance organizations (HMOs), preferred provider organizations, and independent practice associations. As other healthcare providers (such as dietitians, nurses, and social workers) successfully challenge the physicians' monopoly on healthcare, consumers and payers of healthcare will have more choices about who will provide care, where that care will be provided, and at what cost.

Robotics. Although this form of technology is in its infancy, it deserves special attention because the use of robots in healthcare and dietetics is not unforeseeable. It has the potential to drastically alter foodservice. In the 1950s there were dreams that robots could perform those chores that humans found to be laborious, such as housekeeping and cooking. This dream has not been realized. The sophisticated circuitry and programming to manufacture such robots has thus far proven to be too expensive. Robots are currently used for tasks such as assembling delicate electronic parts, handling nuclear waste, and exploring space.

For healthcare, the development of robots is also in its infancy. In some healthcare fields, however, they are being tried for routine tasks. Although their use in healthcare will grow slowly because of their costliness, their proposed use is important to dietetics. The psychomotor skills of foodservice staff are slowly diminishing in importance while the need for decision making, creativity, and innovation is expanding.

Technology and Healthcare

The two most important technological advances for healthcare are the miniaturization of electronics and the new biology. In healthcare there will be more computer-assisted diagnostic techniques, the development of supple prosthetics, improved therapeutics, and improved management information systems. The biological revolution is likely to be even more pervasive and more important to the future of healthcare than electronics. Genetic engineering offers great potential, such as the elimination of some diseases and new and effective drug therapies (including artificial red blood cells, improved chemotherapies, and antirejection drugs). Along with improved drug therapy will come the ability to administer drugs through implantable devices that reduce the side effects of many medications. In the area of nutrition, technology has provided breakthroughs such as fat substitutes and has led to the development of effective disease-specific medical nutrition therapies.

The rapid development of sophisticated medical technology over the past thirty years has caused a dilemma for society. In one way, it has contributed to noninvasive diagnoses, improved drugs, improved life expectancy, and fewer complicated invasive procedures—all of which benefit society. Technology, however, has also contributed to increased healthcare costs. In addition, the use of technology to prolong death unnecessarily does not significantly contribute to the quality of life of some individuals and becomes an ethical issue. Thus it has become necessary to protect the public from ineffective, unnecessary technology while ensuring that the life-enhancing possibilities of biomedical technology can flourish.

Communications

The most important asset of business and healthcare in an information society (besides people) is the rapid communication of dependable information. In order for businesses to compete successfully, decisions have to be based on accurate and timely information. Parallel to the growth of information, structural changes are altering communications. The two major structural changes that are occurring in communications involve the print media and the electronic media. These new technologies enable communications to be directed to distinct, small segments of the population; at the same time, information can be sent to an entire nation, several nations, or even the world. This contributes to the functioning of the world as a global village in which values and attitudes can be widely shared and adopted.

Print Media. The print media are growing, but slowly. In the future they may decline. Newspapers have been the most affected thus far. Where once there were two or more major newspapers in most big cities, now there is usually only one. The next print media to be affected are periodicals. The large general-purpose magazines have already experienced a decline in readership. Many magazines and journals have had their formats revised to appeal to smaller audiences. This change is reflected on the newsstands, where one can find numerous periodicals and journals (more than twenty thousand of them exist) written only for diverse, segmented audiences. Other periodicals are altering their distribution channels. For example, a number of professional journals are reaching readers electronically via CD-ROM disks and integrated computer networks.

In dietetics the technology is already available to replace traditional print sources of information. Administrative and other reference documents, such as policy and procedure manuals, can be stored electronically. Detailed nutrient composition tables and menus are now developed, stored, and accessed with the aid of computer software. Communications are faster, easier to keep updated, less bulky to store, and more accessible to a greater number of users.

Electronic Communications. The second structural change will be in the continued boom of electronic communications and in interactive electronics. The information superhighway is fast becoming a reality, in part because of new and emerging technologies and electronic communications, which have become progressively less expensive and of better quality. For example, wired cable television provides the hardware technology for interactive communications. Patients may use this technology to communicate directly with healthcare providers and receive treatment at home.

Radio, like the print media, is also switching from broadcasting to "narrow casting" by marketing to smaller segments of the audience. Radio signals can also be used to communicate with people for such purposes as paging, reminding people to take a medication, and warning families or healthcare providers of an emergency. Thus both interactive electronics and radio signals will alter where people receive healthcare and the frequency of interactions between patients and healthcare providers.

Three fundamental shifts occurring in the application of computers have further expanded opportunities. Personal computers are giving way to work-group computing, improving communication and leading to productivity and responsiveness gains. Separate information systems within an organization are being restructured into integrated systems. Integrated systems allow workers to move beyond organizational hierarchy, because layers of management are not necessary when information is instantly available electronically. Third, computer systems are now extending the reach of organizations outward to link enterprises with their suppliers, distribution channels, and ultimately with consumers (Tapscott and Caston 1993, p 14–18).

Structural changes in communications are creating new ways of doing business and rearranging relationships between senders and receivers of information. People no longer have to meet face-to-face to exchange ideas, make decisions, receive training, or buy or sell a product. Telephones, fax machines, and Voice Mail have already altered communications. With the broader use of computers, physical contact can be entirely eliminated and the nature of human interactions transformed.

Preliminary studies of people communicating solely through computers show that this interaction is not necessarily positive. In these studies, people frequently resorted to emotional language, took a longer time to reach agreement, and made more extreme final decisions than when they communicated face-to-face (Martel 1986). These findings have implications for dietetics leaders, who are already finding themselves increasingly using computers to communicate with others.

Social Trends

Along with these technological changes, social transformations are occurring that have implications for dietetics and healthcare. In some instances technological advances beget social changes. For instance, improved technology has increased life expectancy. At other times, the relationship is not quite as clear. Yet the technological and social changes discussed here are best viewed as interrelated and interconnected.

Demographics

The population growth of the world is slowing. In some countries the growth may begin to decline in the next decade. At the same time, life expectancy is increasing. These two structural changes in the population have led to new altered family relationships and changes in the composition of the work force. Furthermore, dependency ratios will change with more older adults dependent on a smaller, younger work force to contribute to Social Security and Medicare. The single most important change in the composition of the work force is the entrance of women. This lowers the overall fertility rate and is partly responsible for the predicted lowering of population growth. In addition, women's participation in the work force alters social needs such as child care and health needs (Martel 1986, p 107–127). Finally, as women have entered management, they have begun to alter leadership styles from the traditional autocratic approach toward more participatory leadership.

Demographic changes in the next thirty years will have a dramatic effect on healthcare. In a nationwide survey of sixteen hundred healthcare experts, the aging of America was identified as the most critical issue facing the future of the healthcare delivery system. This issue was considered more important than even costs and quality of care (Wesbury 1988, p 59). Furthermore, the shrinking American family, a disproportionate increase of elderly women who are poorer than elderly men, and an increase in minorities means fewer personal resources for healthcare and an increased need for long-term-care programs.

With an increasing elderly population comes a greater need for attention to nutrition. The elderly are at higher risk for poor nutrition than are other segments of the population. This is because of factors such as poverty, social isolation, dependency, disability, and chronic disease (Posner et al 1993). Coalitions such as the Nutrition Screening Initiative have formed to focus greater attention on the nutrition needs of the elderly and to implement routine nutrition screening and intervention. Dietetics professionals must continue to take a leadership role in efforts like these to ensure high-quality care and a high quality of life for the elderly.

Education

The educational advancement of the entire world population is another of the structural changes occurring today. In 1980 school enrollment of people aged six through twenty-three exceeded 50 percent for the first time in the history of the world. In the United States in the last twenty years, the overall increase in college-prepared individuals has increased from 11 percent to 21 percent.

Education changes how people act and think and what they need and want. With education, people attain the knowledge and skills to work in higher-paying jobs. This improves their purchasing power and standard of living, which adds wealth to society. Furthermore, education increases people's awareness and facilitates their participation in decision making, making them less apathetic and submissive.

The improved educational level of society affects healthcare as well. As people become more educated, they are able to better understand their own health and take responsibility for it. Since dietetics has traditionally assumed responsibility for teaching nutrition and for valuing a preventive health approach, this societal trend can provide exciting opportunities for dietetics professionals as healthcare educators. In the future, the demand for dietetics professionals in acute care may decline while the demand for their teaching and preventive care skills in outpatient and home care may increase.

Work and Values

The values of people in society are changing. With reduced work hours, wages above subsistence level, and higher levels of educational achievement, work is no longer the central feature of people's lives. Workers have acquired property, new skills, and other interests. Like other aspects of society, workers are diverse. They come from a variety of ethnic backgrounds, life-styles, family structures, and value systems. Furthermore, workers have a decreased respect for and no longer are in awe of authority.

These changed attitudes and values indicate that people have new expectations of organizations and managerial leaders. For themselves, people want respect, recognition, dignity, and an opportunity to be successful and advance. They want work that will increase their self-esteem and self-actualization. From the job itself, people want work that is challenging, rewarding, meaningful, and not boring. Employees want a work environment that is conducive to health, safety, and comfort. From the organization, especially managers, employees want organizational structures that allow participation in decision making. In addition, contemporary workers need to have their opinions, attitudes, and beliefs listened to and respected.

Specific Healthcare Trends

As has been discussed, trends in healthcare reflect societal trends. Some other healthcare trends, however, are specific to the industry. These include cost containment, quality assurance, access to care, ethical issues, the changing roles of physicians, healthcare reform, and managed care. Each of these trends has implications for dietetics.

Costs

The concern over rising healthcare costs became evident in the late 1970s. In 1983 the crisis in the Medicare fund and its projected failure, combined with a concern for the overall national deficit, resulted in new legislation. The law implemented prospective reimbursement in the form of diagnosis-related groups. Hospitals became motivated by the bottom line, which forced them to function as cost-effective businesses rather than as altruistic organizations. These federal efforts to control healthcare, though, have not proven effective. Medical care continues to consume an increasingly larger percentage of the gross national product. In fact, if the growth rate of medical care continues to parallel that of the last decade, healthcare expenditures could consume the entire economy by 2020 (Dwyer et al 1994, p 8).

Another structural change is also evident in the locations at which people receive their care. For example, the decreased length of stays in hospitals has greatly affected other sectors of the healthcare industry. Ambulatory care, long-term care, and home healthcare have burgeoned. The acuity of patients being cared for in their homes has increased, causing opportunities as well as problems for this sector of the healthcare delivery system. Likewise, the acuity of patients in long-term-care facilities has also increased. Current technology has facilitated this structural change by eliminating the need for hospitalization for some diagnostic tests (eg, laser technology) and surgeries (eg, cataract extraction).

All these events have increased competition among the many sectors of the healthcare industry, because every sector is scrambling for the diminishing healthcare dollar. To secure more dollars under a managed care or capitated system, each healthcare facility has to compete with other service providers as well as with other sectors of the healthcare market. Theoretically, the winners of the competition will be those who can provide the highest quality of care at the lowest cost.

What does the future hold? The changes already witnessed in the healthcare system are expected to continue. Experts predict that there will be more consolidations, downsizing, mergers, acquisitions, competition and marketing, managed care, HMOs, and bankruptcies in the years ahead. Many hospitals are already joining networks. In the very near future, most, if not all, hospitals will be part of a corporate structure. Several scenarios have been predicted:

1. Hospitals will consist of only emergency rooms, operating rooms, and intensive care units.
2. Hospitals will specialize (eg, some will be surgical centers, others maternal-child centers).
3. Short stays of one to two days will occur in areas remote from the major hospital, perhaps by expanding an already existing satellite ambulatory care center.

Quality

With fewer dollars to finance healthcare, many people are concerned that the quality of care will decrease. At the same time, the consumer movement, which is affecting the provision of goods and services throughout the nation, is demanding the assurance of quality from the healthcare industry.

Quality of care is a nebulous term that must be more clearly defined in the future. More objective, quantitative data that are agreed-upon indicators of quality will need to be available to consumers. The release of data by the Health Care Financing Administration (HCFA) comparing the mortality rates among hospitals was one of the early attempts to provide these data. More recently, report-card measures, such as the Health Plan Employer Data and Information Set (HEDIS), which was developed to rate managed care organizations, reflect an ongoing focus on quality.

Quality of care is receiving increased attention from the Joint Commission on the Accreditation of Healthcare Organizations (JCAHO) and HCFA. In particular, JCAHO has moved away from quality measures that evaluate process toward quality measures that judge outcomes. This means that healthcare facilities will need to measure quality outcomes and make the necessary improvements. Dietetics professionals must contribute to institutional quality initiatives; Schiller et al (1994) have made available tools and techniques to manage the quality of nutrition care services.

To process and have this type of data readily available, hospitals are already purchasing and designing integrated computerized management information systems. In addition, healthcare professionals are now being asked to demonstrate clinical effectiveness. For example, dietetics professionals must be able to document the impact of medical nutrition therapy on patient outcomes. All these data will assist hospitals in their efforts to ensure quality to consumers and other interested parties. The information will also help hospitals to demonstrate their competitive edge when marketing their services to the community or to a managed care organization.

Access to Care

Not only have the costs of healthcare not been controlled, but there is less equity in the provision of health services than there was three decades ago. The current system functions in a piecemeal fashion—funding from both public and private sources is increasingly incapable of meeting the healthcare needs of society. Furthermore, the number of uninsured Americans has reached a crisis proportion. Healthcare reform is one possible solution for this problem, but only if the tough question is addressed: how do we increase access while holding the line on rising healthcare costs?

Ethical Concerns

The forces challenging the healthcare delivery system have created major ethical dilemmas for the nation and for healthcare providers. Cost containment and quality assurance, combined with new technology and the increasing aging population, warrant and stir debate on many issues. Should there be limitations on who receives what kind of care? For instance, should a total hip replacement be limited to people under seventy years of age if it will be paid for with Medicare funds? Can those people older than seventy who can pay for it with out-of-pocket funds be allowed to have this procedure? Will the seventy-two-year-old denied a total hip replacement become wheelchair bound and drain even more resources from the system than the procedure? Similarly, should some patients (such as patients with Alzheimer's disease) who do not have a physiological condition limiting swallowing be given tube feeding? Or should they be denied this treatment and suffer progressive malnutrition and its complications?

Physicians

The multiple forces altering the role, status, and finances of physicians portend new opportunities for all healthcare providers. Physicians have dominated the healthcare system, and this dominance has had a significant impact on the overall system and its functioning. There is evidence, however, that this is changing. The dominance of the physician is giving way to a more pluralistic system. Physician relationships with healthcare facilities, consumers, other providers, and the government are undergoing fundamental, irreversible change.

For instance, in this era of competition and cost containment, hospitals are purchasing physician practices and entering joint ventures or mergers with physicians. Fewer physicians are in private practice and, in fact, the solo practitioner may be virtually extinct by the end of the decade. These trends alter the nature of the relationship between physicians and healthcare administrators to one of either employee/employer or business partners.

In some cases, physicians are buying healthcare facilities and so changing their role to employer. There is also a trend to hire salaried medical directors in hospitals and managed care organizations to oversee both the cost and quality issues of physician practices. More physicians are becoming the employees of healthcare facilities rather than the users of healthcare facilities—a trend that is expected to continue well into the next century. Physicians are now beginning to feel professional and bureaucratic conflicts that they did not feel in the past as they shift toward more integrated, collaborative relationships with hospitals and other healthcare providers.

Physician-consumer relations are also changing. With more information about healthcare available to the public, consumers are more aware and more assertive about their own healthcare. Physicians are no longer revered and given as high a status in this society as they once were. In fact, often the opposite is true. People are questioning physician salaries, particularly those of specialists, as excessive and not warranted given the quality of medical care provided and the limited time the patient actually spends with the physician.

Physicians are being challenged by other healthcare providers, such as dietitians, nurse practitioners, physician assistants, and social workers, who believe they can deliver high-quality healthcare in a more cost-effective manner than physicians. Many nonphysician providers, including nurses, social workers, and physical therapists, have successfully challenged the once legally sanctioned monopoly given to physicians through licensure. This trend is certain to continue, with much resistance from physicians, as other providers demonstrate to payers that they can provide similar services at a lower cost.

Physicians are facing major changes in how they are reimbursed for their services. With Medicare moving toward relative value payment scales, physicians are being paid more for counseling and education and less for medical procedures. This trend, coupled with the move toward managed care, portends an explosion in the need for family practitioners and a glut of specialists.

Healthcare Reform and Managed Care

Healthcare reform is driven by the trends of cost (the need to control escalating expenditures) and access (the need to provide healthcare coverage for the uninsured). Issues at the center of the debate include what basic benefits should be provided, at what cost, and who pays. There are no easy answers. Although the final outcome of federal legislation has yet to take shape, many states have already enacted reforms. One common approach in a number of these reform measures is managed care. The managed care model is not new; however, healthcare reform is accelerating managed care's evolution and speed of implementation.

By definition, managed care includes the full range of healthcare structures and strategies for focusing on decreases in fragmentation of care and increases in quality and cost efficiency (Dwyer et al 1994, p 11). Managed care can encompass everything from the typical fee-for-service or indemnity plan, in which consumers have a broad range of choices in healthcare service providers and their care may be "managed" by a simple utilization review, to the most tightly controlled managed care model, the HMO, in which consumers have limited choices in service providers and the treatment protocols are very specifically defined (Tootell 1993).

Dwyer et al (1994, p 15–16) explain that managed care is already shaping how and where care is delivered. Specifically, there is a movement toward vertical integration by hospital systems to offer services across a continuum of care. Managed care is also affecting who delivers care, with primary care viewed as the main gatekeeper for managed care. Finally, a shift is occurring in who accepts responsibility for care. Organizations that were self-insured are moving away from this practice because of the risk associated with managing the total healthcare of their employees. It is certain that many healthcare professionals and providers will have an unprecedented opportunity to carve out a niche in the new managed care healthcare arena.

The Future Organization

Two major changes are occurring in organizations. The first is the development of small, semiautonomous work units. The second is the cry for a new type of leader to guide these work groups.

Semiautonomous Work Units

The current and emerging electronic technology of communications and the importance of information as the primary resource will continue to profoundly affect the workplace. The new organization will be composed of small work units that are interconnected with other small work groups and integrated with larger corporations via electronic networks. Different authors have used various names for these work groups: *electronic cottage* (Naisbitt 1982, p 35; Toffler 1986, p 18), *atomized organizations* (Deal and Kennedy 1982, p 177), and *semiautonomous federal units* (Kinsman 1986, p 20). Kinsman described this change as a move from hierarchy to heterarchies, with each unit supported by a central matrix, the corporation. He likened this central organization to a sponge. Each unit is supported by the central matrix and can absorb the needed support from it. At the same time the semiautonomous work groups nourish the central organization by their profitable activity in the marketplace.

More recently, Naisbitt (1994, p 12–13) put a new spin on the trend of semiautonomous work units, defining them in terms of today's changing world. He explains this as the global paradox, where the bigger the world economy, the more powerful its smallest players. Thus the entrepreneur becomes the most important player. Already today, big companies are decentralizing and reconstituting themselves as networks of entrepreneurs.

Parker (1994, p 4–5) further explains that teams have become an important strategy in today's competitive environment. These new-styled teams are composed of people from a variety of functions who may be friends, enemies, or strangers, but by working as a unit can generate the potential for powerful organizational change. They can weave together a cross-functional design that is an amalgam of many cultures. Similarly, in the hospital, there is a move away from departmental and unit bureaucratic structure toward patient-focused care and other decentralized models that are more attuned to quality and patient needs.

The locations in which people work will also change. More people will work in their homes or at small local sites rather than in big cities. Toffler (1986, p 19), in an informal interview with factory managers, found that 25 percent to 35 percent of people currently employed could work at home and could communicate with the factory by computer. Although it seems impossible to envision dietetics professionals working exclusively in their homes to care for patients, some patient counseling, such as weight or diabetes management, can and increasingly more could be done through electronic communications and monitoring. This would probably reduce the number of face-to-face interactions between private practice and outpatient dietitians and their clients.

Why are so many business scholars predicting this change from big corporations to semiautonomous work groups? One reason is that small work groups are better able to respond locally, quickly, and creatively than larger systems. This is a vital ability in a complex, rapidly changing, highly competitive environment. Furthermore, smaller work units are integral parts of the overall trend from centralization to decentralization.

Appealing to the new workers' need for a sense of belonging, small work units will help foster in workers a sense of the organization belonging to them, rather than they belonging to the organization. At the same time, the individual's innovative abilities and creativity will be highly prized. This appeals to another value of the new worker: meaningful, challenging work. Since the computer will perform "left brain" activities, the role of intuition and creativity in workers will be the most needed and valued asset. Thus each person will be expected to be an in-house entrepreneur. The relatively intimate, simple work environment will best support this individual entrepreneurship. Kanter (1983, p 354–355) explained the importance of what she called "corporate entrepreneurs." She believed that top managers can set priorities, demand quality, and look for ways to cut costs, but it is the middle managers and below who put form to these strategies.

Decisions in semiautonomous work units will be reached democratically. The use of consensus decision making allows everyone's opinions, ideas, and beliefs to be sincerely listened to and considered by the group. Since it is highly unlikely that everyone will always support the same strategy, there will be an understanding that once a strategy is undertaken, everyone will give it time and support to be tried.

The units will use ad hoc groups to make decisions, to plan, and to forecast trends. Ad hoc groups, committees, or task forces are ones that form, take action, dissolve, and reform again when necessary. They have been used extensively in organizations for some years. The major difference in the new ad hoc groups is that the leadership of the groups will be more flexible than today. The best person for the task at hand will be the best person to lead the group. The leader does not have to be a manager. To an increasing degree, staff dietitians will lead those task forces that affect their work.

Each work group will be responsible for its own success. However, there will be some financial arrangements with the larger corporation. The best current example of this is seen in franchises, which are tied to the larger corporation and pay a fee for group advertising, purchase of supplies, and so forth.

These small, autonomous units and the parent corporations will need to respond to a number of stakeholders. Bottom-line financial success will not be the only measure of performance. The new work units will need to show concern for the environment, customers, employees, communities, society, and shareholders.

Handy (1984) described a slightly different scenario for the organization of the future. He believes there will be three types of employees:

- A small, professional/managerial support core
- A fringe of self-employed "outworkers" who function individually or in cooperation with others on a jobbing basis
- An outer ring of part-time, temporary employees that will be a flexible work force

Whether this design will become a widespread reality is not known. Elements of the design, however, are already evident. For instance, in dietetics, the use of staffing agencies to provide "outworkers" to food and nutrition services is becoming more common. Senge (1990b) explains the new work force in this way: "In an increasingly dynamic, interdependent and unpredictable world, it is simply no longer possible for anyone to 'figure it all out at the top.' The old model, 'the top thinks and the local acts,' must now give way to integrating thinking and acting at all levels."

The Future Leader

The leader-employee relationship will change in the future. The now-sharp distinction between managers and workers will blur. The leader will work alongside followers. He or she may best be viewed as the first among equals rather than as a person having autocratic or paternalistic power (Kinsman 1986, p 20). The new leader will need to exhibit a fundamental belief in human beings by acknowledging their expertise, trusting them, and sharing power with them.

The role of the new leader will be vastly different than it is today. The primary roles will be to empower others to be their own leader and to foster a learning organization. People will transform themselves and their organizations through personal commitment based on the deeply felt understanding that comes from collaborating with others and learning through that experience (Tapscott and Caston 1993, p 283). Senge (1990a, p 340) notes:

> In a learning organization, leaders are designers, stewards, and teachers. They are responsible for building organizations where people continually expand their capacities to understand complexity, clarify vision, and improve shared mental models—that is, they are responsible for learning.

The leader's own creative and intuitive skills will be important, but the new leader will design systems that enhance these learning skills in others. Because decision making will be participatory, the leader will have to develop skills of persuasion, rather than merely ordering people to do tasks.

Deal and Kennedy (1982, p 189) suggested that the role of the future leader of semiautonomous work units will be to structure and negotiate appropriate economic and financial arrangements with the central core organization. In doing this, the leader will need to balance the legitimate concerns and interests of both parties. The leader will also build a culture of pride in being part of the central organization. One phenomenon of striking importance in future organizations is that this leadership can come from anywhere in the organization—from the chief executive officer to the bottom of the hierarchy (Tapscott and Caston 1993, p 283–284).

Implications for Dietetics

In the future, organizations, healthcare, and dietetics will be radically different from today. For dietetics, the predicted changes can be positive ones. Dietetics leaders need to begin to incorporate the ideas and elements of this future into practice today.

All dietetics staff have the potential to become in-house entrepreneurs. There are two major benefits of this possibility. First, if dietetics professionals are empowered to be innovative and creative, they will be more satisfied in their need for achievement. Second, by empowering dietetics staff, the organization will profit. Like many other groups in a hospital or healthcare facility, dietetics staff have an intimate understanding of how the organization works along with its strengths and weaknesses. For the most part, however, dietetics professionals have not been given the resources to contribute meaningfully to the overall organization. In the future this can change by giving staff the necessary time, money, space, information, and knowledge to become in-house entrepreneurs.

Society will continue to become even more dependent on information as a resource. Computers, and even robots, will perform psychomotor tasks and monitoring. Therefore, a dietitian's skills in assessment, planning, evaluation, teaching, and decision making will be more valued and more important to society. Dietetics organizations should be revising the dietetic practice environment so that these skills are nurtured and enhanced. In addition, the task orientation of professional practice needs to be de-emphasized and the intellectual orientation needs to be enhanced. This change in orientation will not be easy. Dietetics professionals, as well as society in general and healthcare providers in particular, often describe the profession by the tasks that dietitians perform. Thus the transition from a task orientation to an intellectual orientation will take time, patience, and significant work with the public. The change, however, is inevitable, and dietetics professionals should prepare for it.

The workplace itself will undergo significant changes as well. A diminishing number of dietetics practitioners will be employed in smaller, more acute hospitals. The role of the dietitian in this setting will also change. The decreased emphasis on tasks and an increase in intellectual activities will be evident in this setting. The need to somehow balance the increased acuity of patients in hospitals with fewer dietitians and more "healthcare extenders" is a challenge that dietetics leaders will be addressing over the next several years. Another anticipated change is increased opportunities for consultants and more dietetics professionals employed in skilled nursing facilities and home care agencies. Dietetics leaders must be prepared to meet these needs while still documenting the effectiveness and outcomes of their services and maintaining high standards of patient care. All these changes and challenges call for new leadership strategies. Dietetics needs creative, innovative leaders as well as followers. These leaders will be faced with a combination of societal, healthcare, and professional issues that are currently transforming today into an uncertain future. Dietetics leaders will need not only a vision of the future but also a definite strategy for realizing this vision. Transformational leadership theory and strategies are the beginnings of such a blueprint for success.

Application to Dietetics Practice

Because of the forward-looking nature of the information presented in this chapter, no case study is given. By discussing the following questions, however, readers can review the chapter's main concepts.

1. Describe one positive and one negative outcome of computerization in dietetics.
2. What are the possible benefits to the dietetics profession from improved global communications?
3. What opportunities do cost containment and the growing elderly population open to dietetics?
4. Are semiautonomous work units in healthcare a credible, future reality?
5. What will be the characteristics of future dietetics leaders?

References

Deal TE, Kennedy AA. *Corporate Cultures: The Rites and Rituals of Corporate Life.* Reading, Mass: Addison-Wesley Publishing Co; 1982.

Dwyer WA, Johnson EQ, Nagy-Nero D, Smith KG, Viall C. *Winning the Managed Care Game.* Columbus, Ohio: Ross Products Division, Abbott Laboratories and The American Dietetic Association; 1994.

Handy C. *The Future of Work.* London, England: Pan Books; 1984.

Kanter RM. *The Change Masters: Innovation for Productivity in the American Corporation.* New York, NY: Simon & Schuster; 1983.

Kinsman F. Leadership from alongside. In: Adams JD, ed. *Transforming Leadership: From Vision to Results.* Alexandria, Va: Miles River Press; 1986:19–28.

Kuhn TS. *The Structure of Scientific Revolutions.* Chicago, Ill: University of Chicago Press; 1962.

Martel L. *Mastering Change.* New York, NY: Simon & Schuster; 1986.

Naisbitt J. *Global Paradox: The Bigger the World Economy, the More Powerful the Smallest Players.* New York, NY: William Morrow & Co; 1994.

Naisbitt J. *Megatrends: Ten New Directions Transforming Our Lives.* New York, NY: Warner Books; 1982.

Owen AL. Challenges for dietitians in a high-tech/high-touch society. *J Am Diet Assoc.* 1984;84:285–289.

Parker GM. *Cross-functional Teams: Working With Allies, Enemies, and Other Strangers.* San Francisco, Calif: Jossey-Bass Publishers; 1994.

Posner BM, Jette AM, Smith KW, Miller DR. Nutrition and health risks in the elderly: the Nutrition Screening Initiative. *Am J Public Health.* 1993;83:972–978.

Schiller MR, Miller-Kovach K, Miller MA. *Total Quality Management for Hospital Nutrition Services.* Gaithersburg, Md: Aspen Publishers Inc; 1994.

Senge PM. *The Fifth Discipline: The Art and Practice of the Learning Organization.* New York, NY: Doubleday & Co; 1990a.

Senge PM. The leader's new work: building the learning organizations. *Sloan Management Review.* Fall 1990b.

Tapscott D, Caston A. *Paradigm Shift: The New Promise of Information Technology.* New York, NY: McGraw-Hill Inc; 1993.

Toffler A. Beyond the breakup of industrial society: political and economic strategies in the context of upheaval. In: Williamson JN, ed. *The Leader-Manager.* New York, NY: John Wiley & Sons; 1986:9–28.

Toffler A. *Future Shock.* New York, NY: Bantam Books; 1970.

Tootell M. Opportunities in managed care. In: Mathieu-Harris M, Foltz MB, eds. *Finding Your Niche in the Managed Care Market.* Columbus, Ohio: The American Dietetic Association and Ross Products Division, Abbott Laboratories; 1993:2–5.

Wesbury SA. The future of health care: changes and choices. *Nursing Economics.* 1988;6:59–62.

3

Toward a Theory of Leadership

Chapter Objectives

1. Develop a personal belief about transformational leadership.
2. Define leadership, transactional leadership, and transformational leadership.
3. Apply Maslow's theory on the hierarchy of needs to dietetics practice.
4. List five possible ways to manage conflict in followers' values.
5. Distinguish between power and leadership.
6. Discuss contemporary personal and organizational values.
7. Discuss the ten roles of managers.

Introduction

Transformational leadership is about change, innovation, the empowerment of others, and power *with* others, not *to* others. In the daily work of dietetics, the need to make changes in dietetics departments is evident. The changes are needed not only to solve current problems and dissatisfactions but also to help dietetics thrive in the future. To help the profession accomplish these goals, dietetics leaders will need to use a variety of strategies:

- Create new visions that give a sense of meaning and purpose to the work of dietetics.
- Develop new, trusting relationships between dietetics managers and staff.
- Design working environments that support a commitment to organizational and professional visions and goals and that empower employees.

- Use one major resource—themselves—to achieve organizational success.

Unfortunately, there are no prescriptions for transformational leadership. Researchers have formulated instruments to rank transformational leadership skills and abilities. They have also developed tools to help people strengthen these skills (Bass 1985, Posner and Kouzes 1991, Sashkin and Burke 1990, Wilson et al 1990). Research performed on a number of these instruments indicates that certain variables appear to be related to transformational leadership, including demographic and experiential variables (such as gender, training, and education), situational variables, effectiveness outcomes, and the beliefs of those rating the leader.

There is also descriptive work on leaders, starting with James McGregor Burns' (1978) Pulitzer Prize–winning book, *Leadership*. His work is limited to extensive descriptions of famous political leaders, such as Mahatma Gandhi, Franklin D. Roosevelt, Woodrow Wilson, and John F. Kennedy. Burns, however, claimed that his concepts did not apply only to this elite group of men. In fact, he argued that transformational leadership can be seen in the daily routines of life. Parents, teachers, preachers, and corporate managers are and can be transformational leaders.

Since Burns' seminal work, other authors have carried the concept of transformational leadership from the purely political arena to that of corporations (Adams 1986, Bennis and Nanus 1985, Paul 1982, Roberts 1985, Tichy and Devanna 1986, Vardaman et al 1986) and organizations (Bass 1990, Kouzes and Posner 1991, Sashkin 1990). These authors used Burns' concepts as a foundation for their observations about transformational or transforming leaders.

A number of management books written in the last ten years describe corporations and corporate leaders that have successfully adapted to a changing environment. The authors describe leadership characteristics and practices that do not explicitly have transformational leadership as their theoretical foundation. These works are not based on the traditional leadership theories reviewed in chapter 1 (Kanter 1983, Naisbitt and Aburdene 1985, Peters and Austin 1985, Peters and Waterman 1982, Manz and Sims 1989, DePree 1989, Bellingham and Cohen 1989, Kotter 1990). Other authors use terms such as *organizational excitement* (Berlew 1986), *charismatic leadership* (House 1976), or *empowerment* (Leatherman 1992) to describe new theories of progressive management. In dietetics there is also a call for a new form of leadership (Wylie-Rossett et al 1990, Huenemann 1981, Hoover 1983, Rinke and Finn 1990, Finn 1991, Dodd 1992a, Dodd 1992b, Schiller et al 1993, Parks 1994).

All these scholars, whether or not they refer to the specific tenets of transformational leadership, have addressed common themes:

- Past leadership theories are not enough to help organizations move toward the uncertain, rapidly changing future.
- People in organizations want to have a sense of purpose and self-worth.
- New leaders and new leadership strategies are imperative.

The most significant finding of all these studies is that all successful organizations have one thing in common: innovative leadership.

A leader's effectiveness can be significantly influenced by his or her insight into personal behaviors, attitudes, and beliefs. In other words, a leader's ability to be introspective enhances his or her ability to lead. In the works of the motivational and the behavioral theorists reviewed in chapter 1, it was seen that a leader's behavior and view of human nature directly affect his or her ability to be effective and successful. Stated another way, what the leader believes about followers, about leadership, and about the relationship between leaders and followers becomes a self-fulfilling prophecy. This chapter presents a new philosophical approach to dietetics leadership that, we hope, will enable dietetics leaders to view the leader-follower relationship in a more contemporary way.

Transactional and Transformational Leadership

Defining leadership and its two types, transactional and transformational, is important to the understanding of Burns' (1978) theory. His theory of transformational leadership and his general definition of leadership make up the conceptual framework for this book. His general definition of leadership is as follows:

> Leadership over human beings is exercised when persons with certain motives and purposes mobilize, in competition or conflict with others, institutional, political, psychological, and other resources so as to arouse, engage, and satisfy the motives of followers (Burns 1978, p 18).

Several important features of this definition will be considered in further sections of this chapter:

- The relationship of leaders and followers
- The values, motives, and needs of the leader and followers
- The dynamics of competition or conflict with others
- Power

Transactional Leadership

Transactional leadership occurs "when one person takes the initiative in making contact with others for the purpose of exchange of valued things," which may be economic, psychological, or political (Burns 1978, p 19). It is thought to be more common than transformational leadership. Transactional leadership is an exchange to satisfy the needs of the leader and the follower. The leader and the follower have separate but related purposes; they are not bound together in pursuit of common goals. For example, a dietetics manager exchanges a salary for the services of employees to provide nutrition care to patients. The dietetics professional and the dietetics manager have separate purposes. The dietitian or dietetic technician receives from this transaction a salary that "buys" a standard of living and, perhaps, fulfillment of some personal and professional need. At the same time, the dietetics manager receives the benefit of staffing the hospital. Since this is one of the responsibilities of dietetics managers, their purpose is also fulfilled. In this example, the "exchange of the valued thing" is money for the service of a dietetics professional for some agreed-upon amount of time.

Transformational Leadership

In contrast, transformational leadership "occurs when one or more persons engage with others in such a way that leaders and followers raise one another to higher levels of motivation and morality" (Burns 1978, p 20). Transformational leadership implies a relationship in which the purposes of the leader and followers become fused, creating unity, wholeness, and a collective purpose. Collective purpose is crucial to the concept of transformational leadership. There is only one measure of success of the transformational leader: the realization of the intended social change (or purpose) that satisfies the needs and motives of the leader and the followers. The change must have a positive impact on the well-being of both the leader and the followers, one that is consistent with their values.

Transformational leadership changes followers. Followers are able to grow and develop because their needs are met and new needs, aspirations, and values emerge. Thus followers may become leaders as they grow and develop.

Transformational leadership in dietetics is not as rare as one might initially think. It is easier to observe such leadership by looking at results than at the process. A dietetics work environment functioning under transformational leadership would have the following characteristics:

- Low turnover of staff
- Readily apparent, high staff morale
- Enthusiastic approach to patient care

- Staff working together with team spirit
- An understanding on the part of each staff member of the department's goals and purpose
- People expressing a sense of achievement and belonging
- Satisfied patients and families

To better understand the elements of transformational leadership, a further look at several key components of Burns' general definition of leadership is necessary. As stated before, these include the leader-follower relationship; values, motives, and needs; conflict and competition; and power.

The Leader-Follower Relationship. Burns' choice of the word *engaged* to describe the leader-follower relationship is significant. It denotes binding, interlocking, meshing, and involvement. It is a fully sharing relationship based on trust. The leader has a sense of belonging to the group while simultaneously having a sense of self.

The engagement of the leader and followers occurs when the leader recognizes, appeals to, and acts on both the leader's and the followers' values and motivations. The result of the relationship is the arousal and satisfaction of the motives, values, and aspirations of all. It brings out the best in followers.

Values, Motives, and Needs. Central to Burns' theory are the values and needs of the leader and the followers. *Values* are enduring beliefs that a specific mode of conduct (*modal* or *instrumental* values) or end states of existence (*end* or *terminal* values) are personally and socially preferable to alternative modes and ends. Modal values may be such things as honesty, courage, and fair play. End values may be such things as equality, salvation, and world peace (Rokeach 1968, p 159–161).

Values are organized into a hierarchical structure and substructures. In other words, values are a learned organization of rules for making choices and resolving conflicts. Situations often occur in which there is a conflict in the values that a person holds. For example, dietetics middle managers are often faced with the choice between two conflicting values. The dietetics manager may wish to satisfy a value to support his or her superior and to follow strategies that advance the overall goals of the facility, but this could conflict with another value to support the dietetics staff and to enhance their practice. This conflict occurs in many arenas, such as policy making and strategic planning.

Values have internalized cognitive and affective components, as well as behavioral components. Specifically, values function to:

- Set standards for behavior by defining specific criteria for action

- Develop and maintain a person's attitude about a particular thing or situation
- Justify one's own actions and attitudes as well as to judge others
- Assist in decision making by defining specific criteria with which to make choices among alternatives
- Motivate people by internalizing the values so deeply that they help define personality and behavior (Burns 1978, p 74–75)

Burns based much of his work on Maslow's (1970, p 35–88) hierarchy of needs. These needs, which are intrinsic rather than extrinsic, include physiological, safety, belongingness and love, esteem, self-actualization, and aesthetic (Fig 3-1). Maslow organized them into a hierarchy of relative prepotency. Once a lower-level need is gratified, a higher-level need emerges and dominates the person. Satisfied needs no longer serve to motivate the individual.

The *physiological* needs (not an inclusive list) include food, water, rest, sleep, elimination, breathing, and activity. The next level of needs, *safety,* includes security, stability, dependency, protection, freedom from fear, anxiety, and chaos, and the need for structure, order, law, and limits. The *belongingness and love* needs include affection, friendship, having a spouse, and enjoying affectionate relationships with people in general. The *esteem* needs encompass self-esteem and the esteem of others. The self-esteem needs include a desire for strength, achievement, adequacy, mastery and competence, confidence in facing the world, independence, and freedom. Human beings desire the esteem of others in the form of prestige, status, fame, recognition, attention, importance, dignity, and appreciation. The

Figure 3-1. Maslow's hierarchy of needs.

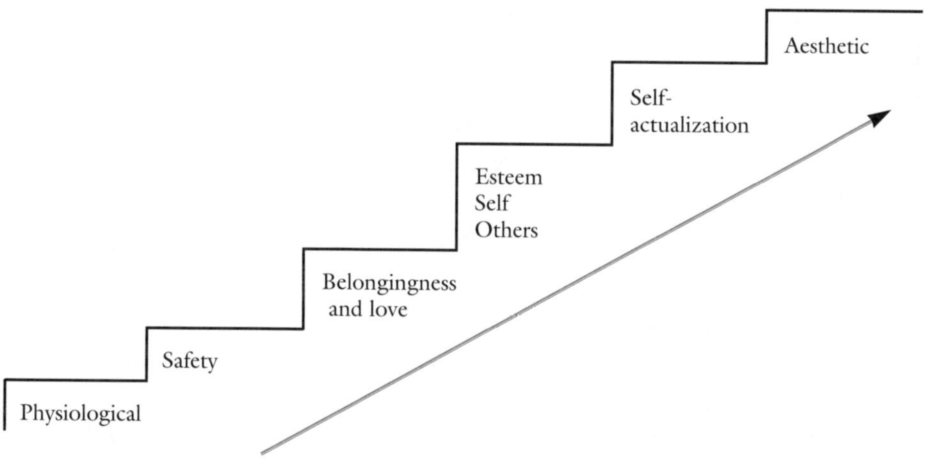

need for *self-actualization* is an idiosyncratic need—to fulfill one's purpose in life. This is the highest of individual aspirations and involves growth, striving for excellence, and a quest for identity and autonomy. According to Maslow, a sixth level of need exists in some people. This is the *aesthetic* need, which Maslow defined as the need to experience and enjoy beauty.

In dietetics organizations today, most attention has been paid to the first three levels of need. There has been an emphasis on salaries and on the safety and security of working conditions. More recently, there has been a move toward participatory management and autonomy in the delivery of dietetics services. These managerial changes are thought to develop a sense of belonging. However, two other needs—esteem (both of self and from others) and self-actualization—often go unmet among people in organizations today.

Maslow postulated a number of beliefs about his hierarchy of needs. He stated:

- The hierarchy is not rigid. In fact, people who are exceptions to this hierarchy exist, albeit rarely.
- The hierarchy is not unidirectional; that is, people can and do regress.
- Satisfaction of needs is relative. In other words, one does not totally achieve satisfaction of one level of need before the next need emerges.
- Needs are not mutually exclusive. There may be multiple motivations for a certain behavior, and some behaviors may not be motivated by any of the basic needs.
- The theory might not be universal for all cultures.

Maslow's theory has come under a great deal of criticism and scrutiny (Brockett 1975, Fox 1982, Wahba and Bridwell 1976). It is certainly beyond the scope of this work to present the arguments supporting Maslow's theory and those not supporting it. However, the theory should be read and used with some hesitancy and with an awareness of its possible shortcomings. For the purpose of this book, Maslow's theory does not have to be accepted literally. It may be imprecise and does lack conclusive, empirical evidence. A hierarchy of needs, as such, does seem to exist. The needs identified by Maslow are valid and are well documented by descriptive and historical works.

According to Burns, leaders operate at a level of need and value higher than that of followers, but not so high as to lose contact with followers. Leaders exploit conflicts in the need and value systems of their followers, see contradictions, and arouse a sense of dissatisfaction to force followers to resolve these conflicts. Leaders help followers gratify lower levels of needs so that higher ones emerge and elevate consciousness. Thus the fundamental act of leadership is to induce people to be aware of and clarify their needs, to be conscious of what they feel, to define values meaningfully, and to induce them to relevant, purposeful action (Burns 1978, p 75–76).

Conflict and Competition. Conflict permeates and characterizes the relationships of human beings. No group of people is totally harmonious, a fact observed daily in our work and personal lives. Conflict is not necessarily bad; if the conflict level is too high or too low, however, it will not promote growth and change. For instance, a totally compatible group would be void of process and structure. Thus conflict can be a source of growth, development, learning, interdependence, and pressure for change—or it can be harmful and only divide people.

Organizational conflict arises because of rapid and unpredictable rates of change, new technological advances, competition for scarce resources, differences in cultures and belief systems, and the variety of human personalities. The organizational conflict with which the leader must be concerned has two forms: conflict within the followership group itself and conflict with others, both inside and outside the organization. For example, the dietetics executive finds organizational conflict within the dietetics department or work group, from other departments within the healthcare facility, and from outside the organization itself.

To deal with conflict within followership groups, leaders first act as catalysts. They arouse followers' consciousness, see and articulate the contradictions in values and needs, arouse dissatisfaction, and ultimately force choices that result in the intended change. Leaders make followers dissatisfied with something so the followers will mobilize and act. Transformational leaders constantly assesses the character and intensity of the followers' willingness and ability to act.

For smaller, homogeneous followership groups, the leader will have to deal primarily with the leaders of other groups that have opposing needs and values. For example, the clinical nutrition manager could be in competition with the foodservice manager for budget, personnel, and recognition of staff members. For larger, more heterogeneous followership groups, the leader will have to face competing interests and goals within that constituency. Dietetics executives, for example, manage the conflicts of the inpatient dietetics staff as well as those of the dietetics professionals who may be in other departments in the medical center (eg, surgery, outpatient services, home care units, and independent weight loss centers). The role of leaders is to express, shape, and curb conflict. They capitalize on and embrace conflict in the followership group and with others instead of avoiding it. Their roles, however, do differ, depending on the source of the conflict. The leader uses a variety of skills to handle or manage organizational conflict. Each situation calls for a different set of skills.

The skills used depend on whether the conflict is inside or outside the followership group and on what resources are available to the leader. Leaders may:

1. Define the grievances and wants of followers
2. Act for followers in their dealings with other clusters of followers and with others inside and outside the organization
3. Influence the intensity of the conflict
4. Deviate and innovate to mediate between the claims of their groups and those of others
5. Modify leadership in recognition of preferences of followers
6. Act directly on behalf of the followers
7. Bargain with others
8. Override certain follower motives
9. Within limits, soften or sharpen the claims and demands of followers (Burns 1978, p 36–41)

In dietetics and healthcare facilities, many forms of conflict exist: for power and prestige, between managers and employees, between line and staff personnel, between members with different professional affiliations or kinds of expertise, among the various departments, each with different goals that contribute to the overall mission of the organization, and other personal and idiosyncratic conflicts. It is the wise dietetics leader who acknowledges the existence of conflict, assesses its sources, and determines how to express and shape conflict for the growth and development of the organization and its people.

Power. In the past decade in dietetics there has been an emphasis on power: what it is, how to get it, how to use it, and how not to lose it. This concern for power is a result of dietetics professionals, as a group, feeling powerless. Power has been defined in terms of the personal attributes of people with power, the positional resources of power holders, the social relationships of power holders and power recipients, control over scarce resources, and the psychodynamics of power relationships (Gabarro 1978, p 298).

Burns (1978, p 9–28) has a different perspective on the topic, one that is helpful in understanding transformational leadership. He views both power and leadership as relationships. Leadership is a form of power. "Raw" power has the capacity to be negative; leadership is positive. Burns defined power as the process by which a person with certain motives and goals has the capacity to secure changes in the behavior of others and in the environment. This is done by using resources in one's power base, which may include economic, political, institutional, or personal skills. This definition implies that power is a relationship among people. It involves the intention or purpose of both the person with power and the recipients of the power. Hence, power is collective. Thus power in transformational leadership is best viewed as a means to get things done rather than as an end in itself.

Power has three elements: the motives and resources of the power holder, the motives and resources of the power recipient, and the relationships among all of these. A simple equation follows:

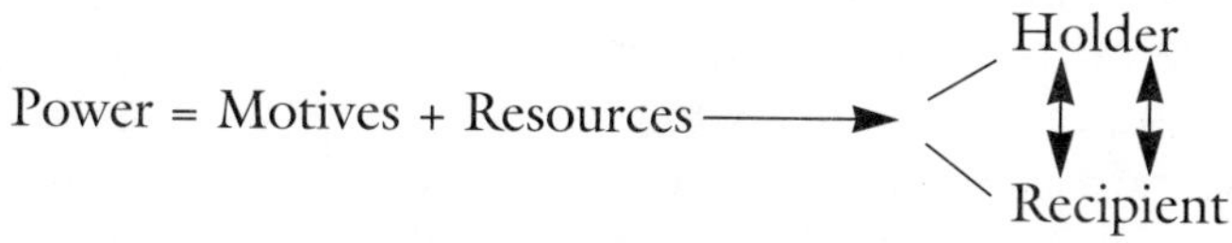

In this equation, the motives of a dietetics manager may be to give all dietetics staff a salary above $75,000. The resources to achieve this goal, however, are not present in the healthcare system today or will not be in the near future. Thus the dietetics manager has no power to achieve this goal. In contrast, all dietetics professionals have the resources to starve patients. Except in rare, pathological instances, there is no motivation to do so. Again, there is no power. When there is no motive to achieve a particular end, resources diminish. Likewise, when there are no resources, motives are inactive. Without motive or resources, there is no power. Because resources are limited and motives may be in short supply, power is seen as elusive and limited.

As stated previously, leadership is a form of power having a collective purpose. With power, the purpose may serve only the power wielder. The motives of the power wielder may or may not coincide with the respondents' wants, but may only meet the goals and aspirations of the power wielder. Power may be coercion or control. Leadership is not. Crucial to the power of a transformational leader is purpose, which is always in the best interests of the leader and followers.

Transformational leadership is about power and empowerment. Empowerment is the creation of an environment that ensures that people in the organization will get the power they need to innovate and be creative. It is power circulation and power access (Kanter 1983, p 156–160). Empowering dietetics professionals is the way to solve the pervasive feeling of powerlessness in the profession. Dietetics managers and employees need appropriate amounts of power to be innovative, creative, and successful.

Sources of Leadership

Burns (1978, p 49–137) departed from previous theories of leadership by considering how people become leaders. He believed there are both social and psychological sources of leadership. The social sources are the family, schools, political system, self-esteem, social role taking, and sense of purpose. The family rewards the child for compliance and punishes for deviance using standards established by the parents. Later, formal schooling sharpens attitudes and behaviors. In adolescence, the need for self-esteem, the perception of esteem by others, and the need for and capacity for social role taking work to bring out the potential for leadership.

No definitive work has been accomplished in the study of the psychological sources of leadership. However, some significant information has been gathered. Studies of animals revealed that they indulge in various forms of leadership, which indicates some evidence of biological sources. Psychoanalysis, a Western invention, has not yielded any helpful results in the study of leadership. Psychobiography, in which the biographies of famous leaders are studied psychoanalytically, has produced a paucity of data. This retrospective approach attempts to look at the formative influences of early life. It has been criticized because it overemphasizes childhood influences and ignores learning from other people and from one's experiences, successes, and failures.

Burns stated that Maslow's hierarchy of needs probably furnishes the best information regarding leadership development. Sources of leadership lie in the transformation of biological wants into needs and social aspirations. The lifelong process of needs fulfillment culminates in leadership skills and the motivation to lead. Although genetic inheritance has a direct impact on the evolving personality, strong cultural, environmental, and political influences work in concert with genetics. The need for affection that Maslow defined may well be the primary source of leadership, combined with social influences and political forces.

Burns' propositions about the origins of leadership in each person have been further researched and defined. Bennis and Nanus (1985) studied successful organizational leaders and documented four strategies of transformational leaders, stressing the idea that transformational leadership is not so much the exercise of power itself but the empowerment of others.

Bass (1985) undertook significant research to define his own theory of transformational leadership. In expanding on the theory of Burns (1978), Bass postulated that transformational leaders did not necessarily need to move followers to higher levels of needs along Maslow's hierarchy (1970); instead, leaders could be transformational by broadening the current needs of the followers at their existing levels. A second significant difference was that Burns saw transformation as a process for furthering good, not evil. Bass argued that even evil leaders were transformational, despite the methods employed, because transformation occurred. A final difference, and perhaps the most important, was that Burns perceived transformational and transactional leadership at opposite ends of a single continuum. Bass proposed that leaders exhibited a variety of leadership patterns but that most leaders employed both transactional and transformational leadership in varying amounts.

Bass (1985) tested his theory by developing and validating an instrument to measure transformational and transactional leadership. Sashkin and Burke (1990) also developed a model and instrument for transformational leadership. They argued that their instrument more adequately incorporated key theoretical elements of transformational leadership—power and its use within organizations—than did Bass' instrument. Posner and Kouzes (1990) also developed a model and instrument for transformational leadership, emphasizing followers and leadership, or the group level of analysis.

What is significant in Burns' thesis and those of other researchers who have expanded on Burns' work is the concept that leaders are not born, they are made. Although many factors may play a role in one's inclination for leadership, leadership can be developed. The major abilities and competencies of leadership can be learned, enhanced, and nurtured. Most of the learning takes place in the experiences of leadership—the successes and failures that the leader has each day.

Contemporary Personal and Organizational Values

It is important to understand the values that people in general and dietetics professionals in particular bring to their work. In addition, new values are emerging within organizations. These values provide the underpinnings of leadership in contemporary organizations.

Personal Values

Complex, interrelated factors are responsible for the fundamental changes in the values of individuals in today's organizations. These factors include higher levels of educational achievement, more leisure time, increased dependence on each other, rapid change, and greater levels of affluence. Work, although important, is no longer the central feature of people's lives. Many people now feel that work should contribute to their self-meaning as well as to the well-being of the organization and society as a whole. Because of this, people are voicing new social values, including these needs:

- A higher quality of work life
- A balance between work and play for a well-rounded life-style
- To be treated with dignity as human beings
- To play a role in organizational decision making by having their opinions, attitudes, and beliefs respected
- To do work that is satisfying, rewarding, and meaningful
- To be empowered to be creative and use their skills and talents (Martel 1986, p 156–174)

Organizational Values

The values of organizations are changing. Tannenbaum and Davis (1969, p 67–86) argued that we are in the midst of value transitions within organizations. Their work, although more than twenty years old, is still pertinent to today's organizations and leaders. Their summary of organizational values (Table 3-1) is used as the framework for this discussion.

Views of Human Nature. The old organizational beliefs about human nature were negative. Organizations thus adopted designs that controlled people's behavior, such as hierarchical structures with fixed job descriptions, evaluation systems that focused on the negative aspects of performance or avoided evaluation altogether, and rigid methods of rewards and punishments.

New organizational values see humans as basically good. Organizations are being redesigned in concert with this belief. Thus, in some progressive organizations, the evaluations of people are focused on their growth and development as human beings. Rather than being confined to fixed job descriptions, people in these organizations are able to use all their talents and skills.

Organizational Behaviors. Old organizational values are reflected in behaviors that are not authentic and carry a negative connotation (Table 3-1). In contrast, the new organizational values create positive behaviors. In today's organization, there is a move away from game playing and the avoidance of risk and conflict and a move toward risk taking, managing conflict constructively, and collaborating with others. Furthermore, the use of one's intuition and the acknowledgment of one's feeling are slowly becoming acceptable behaviors.

Contemporary Organizational Designs

Values and organizational designs change slowly. The new values held by people and by organizations and current organizational designs are asynchronous. Some organizations embrace the new values more fully than do others. The old, hierarchical structures of organizations are still prevalent today despite new, emerging organizational values. Organizations are just beginning to restructure their designs, management systems, and philosophies not only in response to the new attitudes about human nature but also because of the productivity crisis in corporate America. One reason the semiautonomous work unit (see chapter 2) is expected to become prevalent is because it responds to the new societal values.

Dietetics professionals, too, are bringing new values to their practice and they are searching for meaning in their professional lives. These values are evidenced in the many new behaviors seen in the dietetics profession:

- The feminist perspective that is now part of the profession
- Attempts to develop collegial relationships with physicians and nurses
- The drive to raise the competence levels of dietitians and dietetic technicians
- The implementation of participatory management in food, nutrition, and dietetics
- The renewed focus on the centrality of nutrition in optimal health
- Greater initiative and autonomy in the workplace (Isaacs 1991, Finn 1990, Finn 1991, Hill 1991)

Managerial leaders are faced with a paradox: people want to stand out, to fulfill their own purpose, to feel unique and worthy (independent); at the same time, they want to avoid isolation and to belong (interdependent). Transformational dietetics leaders must appeal to all these needs to achieve organizational and professional success.

Table 3-1. Organizational Values and Behaviors

Old	**New**
Man is lazy, incapable of change, and untrustworthy	Man is good, capable of change, and can be trusted
Resisting and fearing differences, rewarding loyalty and uniformity	Acceptance of differences, using them for creativity
Ignoring feelings	Use of feelings
Rational, logical decision making using hard data	Use of intuition as well as rational decision making
Maskmanship and game playing	Authentic behaviors
Power for personal use and prestige	Power for organizational use, and empowerment of all
Avoidance of conflict	Use of conflict
Avoidance of risk taking	Taking risks
Competition	Collaboration

From Tannenbaum and Davis (1969).

Leadership vs Management

Many writers have explored the differences between managers and leaders. Missing from Burns' theory is the integration of leadership and management in organizations in a practical sense. Mintzberg (1973, 1975) has provided a useful definition of managers and a model for the managerial role. A manager is a person in charge of a formal organization or one of its subunits. The manager has two basic goals: to ensure that the organization produces its goods or services efficiently and that it serves the needs of those persons who control it (Mintzberg 1973, p 166).

Mintzberg's work unifies the elements of leadership with the managerial role. He found ten roles common to the work of all managers. (Roles are a set of observable behaviors belonging to an identifiable position.) Everything a manager does can be categorized into one of these ten roles; however, each role is not isolated. Mintzberg studied the content and purposes of managers' work and divided these managerial roles into three groups: interpersonal roles, informational roles, and decisional roles (Table 3-2).

Interpersonal roles are a part of the formal authority of the manager within the organization and involve interpersonal relationships with others. Because of these interpersonal interactions, the manager is a central person in the communications that occur in the organizational unit and so performs *informational roles.* Using the information gathered from these interpersonal and informational roles, the manager plays an important part in making decisions for the organizational unit. This is the *decisional role.*

Model of Organizational Success

Figure 3-2 depicts a model for achieving excellence and success in dietetics organizations. Excellence and success can be defined in dietetics as the result of a balance of organizational, professional, and personal values. The result is the provision of high-quality nutrition care to clients (which fulfills organizational and professional goals) and staff satisfaction with their work environment (which fulfills personal needs and aspirations).

At the base of the organizational model, supporting the whole, is the leader-follower relationship. This relationship is characterized by mutual trust and engagement. All members of the organization bring values, purposes, aspirations, needs, and motives to their work. These values reflect those of people in contemporary society. In addition, the distinct values of the dietetics profession must be incorporated. Leaders use themselves to appeal to the values and aspirations of the followers.

The organization also has a distinct set of values and norms that form its social architecture. In the successful organization, the talents of the people

Table 3-2. Mintzberg's (1975) Ten Managerial Roles

Managerial Role	Behavior
Interpersonal	
Figurehead	Represents the organization on formal ceremonial occasions
Liaison	Interacts with peers in the organization, other colleagues, and people outside the vertical chain of command to gain favors and gather information
Leader	Motivates and guides staff
Informational	
Monitor	Scans the environment for information, asks for information from subordinates and peers, and receives unsolicited information
Disseminator	Transmits information into the organization
Spokesman	Sends information into the external environment
Decisional	
Entrepreneur	Initiates change to improve the unit and to adapt to a changing environment
Disturbance handler	Takes charge when the organization is threatened and when there is conflict and pressure beyond the managers' control
Resource allocator	Decides where the organization will expend its efforts
Negotiator	Deals with situations in which the manager feels compelled to enter negotiations on behalf of the organization

match the organizational tasks and goals. In other words, the needs of the followers and those of the organization must be in balance and harmony. Therefore, for most dietetics leader-managers, there is a need to reorganize food and nutrition service departments by making changes that will empower the dietetics staff.

The essence of leadership is purpose. Practically speaking, the leader must have goals for the organization and for him- or herself. It is the vision and dreams of the leader that provide inspiration and direction to the organization.

Implications for Dietetics

In this chapter a different perspective of leadership theory is presented. The theory, as applied to dietetics, is just a beginning. The dietetics leader-

Figure 3-2. Quest for excellence: a model for organizational success.

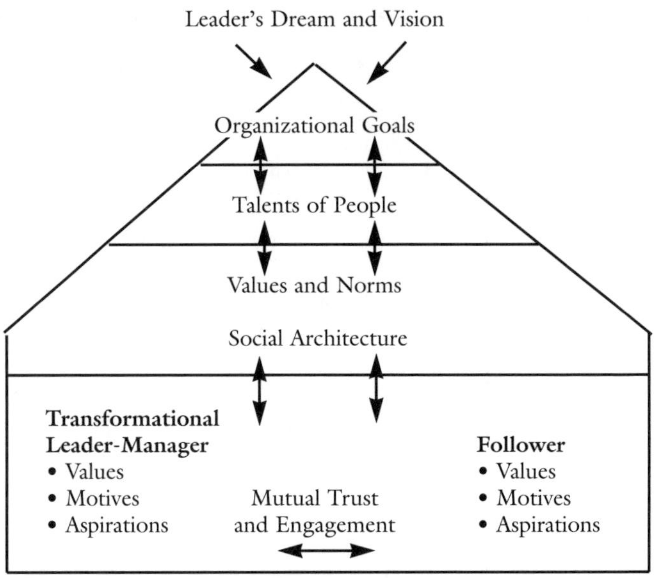

manager now should consider how to apply the concepts to practice. More important, each leader-manager should consider the consistency between the theory and personal behaviors. For example, the dietetics leader can consider the definition of transformational leadership and apply it to personal practice. Questions to consider during this introspection follow:

- How would I describe my relationship with followers?
- Do I trust them?
- What is my view of power? Do I give others the necessary resources to be powerful as well?
- What do I value? What are my goals? What do followers value? What are their goals? Are my values and goals consistent with those of the followers?
- Do I use conflict constructively?
- How does my organizational unit compare with the characteristics of a transformational leadership situation such as the one discussed below?

Although many scholars attempt to distinguish between management and leadership, separating the two concepts may not be practical. It has been helpful to the study of both concepts over the past century to examine them separately. It is not important, however, in the application of theory for organizational success. In every situation a dietetics leader or manager doesn't ask, "Is this my leadership role or is this my managerial role?" The basic underlying element of dietetics managerial success is the integration of both management and leadership into the role; the person who achieves this is called the "leader-manager." The dietetics leader-manager is an individual in food and/or nutrition services who holds a formal line position of authority and engages followers by appealing to their motives, values, and aspirations to achieve the goals of the organization and the dietetics profession.

Application to Dietetics Practice: Case Study

The Setting

The hospital is a midsized community hospital in an urban setting. It employs a department head to oversee foodservices (which are provided by a major contract company), nutrition services (which are headed by a clinical nutrition manager), and an education unit (which offers nutrition education programs for the public and professional experiences for dietetics students from the nearby college).

Current Situation

Based on recent staffing cuts, changes in dietetics practice, the administration's expectation of increased revenue from nutrition services, and staff dietitian complaints of burdensome routine activities (such as screening for nutritional risk and menu checking), the clinical nutrition manager proposes to restructure nutrition services. This restructuring includes an emphasis on the identification and treatment of patients at nutritional risk, the creation of dietetic technician positions, and the expansion of reimbursement opportunities.

The clinical nutrition manager presents her idea to the department head, who is pessimistic that such a restructuring will be effective. The department head prefers to delay any clinical restructuring, focusing instead on increasing revenue by offering brand-name items for purchase by staff and visitors.

Staff dietitians express their desire to have the assistance of dietetic technicians, but they are reluctant to modify their roles, which would shift current practice to an emphasis on the identification and treatment of nutrition problems and nutritional risks. The staff also seems reluctant to generate revenue, stating that they do not have time to develop such a plan or keep up with billing forms.

The clinical nutrition manager is convinced that the mode of clinical nutrition services at the hospital needs to change to maintain quality standards, achieve reimbursement and revenue goals, and improve dietetics staff morale. She is not sure how to proceed.

Case Study Discussion

1. What is the value conflict in this situation?

2. Would you describe this clinical nutrition manager as a transformational leader? Why or why not? Is the department head a transformational leader? Why or why not?

3. What should the clinical nutrition manager do?

References

Adams J, ed. *Transforming Leadership: From Vision to Results.* Alexandria, Va: Miles River Press; 1986.

Bass BM. *Bass & Stogdill's Handbook of Leadership: Theory, Research, and Managerial Applications.* 3rd ed. New York, NY: The Free Press; 1990.

Bass BM. *Leadership and Performance Beyond Expectations.* New York, NY: The Free Press; 1985.

Bellingham R, Cohen B. *Leadership Myths and Realities.* Amherst, Mass: Human Resource Development Press; 1989.

Bennis W, Nanus B. *Leaders: Strategies for Taking Charge.* New York, NY: John Wiley & Sons; 1985.

Berlew DE. Leadership and organizational excitement. In: Williamson JN, ed. *The Leader-Manager.* New York, NY: John Wiley & Sons; 1986:99–104.

Brockett C. Toward a clarification of the need hierarchy theory: some extensions of Maslow's conceptualization. *Interpersonal Development.* 1975:6:77–90.

Burns JM. *Leadership.* New York, NY: Harper & Row; 1978.

DePree M. *Leadership Is an Art.* New York, NY: Dell Publishing; 1989.

Dodd J. The leadership challenge. *J Am Diet Assoc.* 1992a;92:225–226.

Dodd J. The words of leadership. *J Am Diet Assoc.* 1992b;92:1006.

Finn SC. Dietetics: a new decade and a new century. *Topics in Clinical Nutrition.* 1990;5:59–71.

Finn SC. The decade of the dietitian: leadership can make it happen. *Topics in Clinical Nutrition.* 1991;6:1–7.

Fox WM. Why we should abandon Maslow's need hierarchy theory. *Journal of Humanistic Education and Development.* 1982;21:29–32.

Gabarro JS. The development of trust, influence, and expectations. In: Athos AG, Gabarro JS, eds. *Interpersonal Behavior: Communications and Understanding in Relationships.* Englewood Cliffs, NJ: Prentice-Hall Inc; 1978.

Hill L. Women's changing work roles: implications for the progress of the dietetic profession. *J Am Diet Assoc.* 1991;91:25–27.

Hoover LW. Enhancing managerial effectiveness in dietetics. *J Am Diet Assoc.* 1983;82:58–61.

House RJ. A theory of charismatic leadership. In: Hunt JG, Larson LL, eds. *Leadership: The Cutting Edge.* Carbondale, Ill: Southern Illinois University Press; 1976.

Huenemann RL. Leadership and quality in nutritional care: our role in today's world. *J Am Diet Assoc.* 1981;78:124–128.

Isaacs BL. Survival of the clinical dietitian in the 1990s. *Topics in Clinical Nutrition.* 1991;6:15–23.

Kanter RM. *The Change Masters.* New York, NY: Simon & Schuster; 1983.

Kotter JP. *A Force for Change: How Leadership Differs From Management.* New York, NY: The Free Press; 1990.

Kouzes JM, Posner BZ. *The Leadership Challenge: How to Get Extraordinary Things Done in Organizations.* San Francisco, Calif: Jossey-Bass Publishers; 1991.

Leatherman D. *Quality Leadership Through Empowerment: Standards of Leadership Behavior.* Amherst, Mass: Human Resource Development Press; 1992.

Manz CC, Sims HP. *Superleadership: Leading Others to Lead Themselves.* Englewood Cliffs, NJ: Prentice-Hall Inc; 1989.

Martel L. *Mastering Change.* New York, NY: New American Library; 1986.

Maslow AH. *Motivation and Personality.* 2nd ed. New York, NY: Harper & Row; 1970.

Mintzberg H. *The Nature of Managerial Work.* New York, NY: Harper & Row; 1973.

Mintzberg H. The manager's job: folklore and fact. *Harvard Business Review.* 1975;53:49–61.

Naisbitt J, Aburdene P. *Reinventing the Corporation: Transforming Your Job and Your Company for the New Information Society.* New York, NY: Warner Communications; 1985.

Parks SC. Challenging the future: dietetic leadership in the twenty-first century. *Courier.* 1994;33:5.

Paul MF. Power, leadership, and trust: implications for counselors in terms of organizational change. *Personnel and Guidance Journal.* 1982;60:538–541.

Peters TJ, Austin N. *A Passion for Excellence: The Leadership Difference.* New York, NY: Warner Communications; 1985.

Peters TJ, Waterman RH. *In Search of Excellence: Lessons From America's Best-Run Companies.* New York, NY: Warner Communications; 1982.

Posner BS, Kouzes JM. Development and validation of the leadership practices inventory. *Educational and Psychological Measurement.* 1988;48:483–496.

Posner BZ, Kouzes JM. Leadership practices: an alternative to the psychological perspective. In: Clark KE, Clark MB, eds. *Measures of Leadership.* West Orange, NJ: Leadership Library of America; 1990:205–215.

Rinke WJ, Finn SC. Winning strategies to excel in dietetics. *J Am Diet Assoc.* 1990;90:935–938.

Roberts NC. Transforming leadership: a process of collective action. *Human Relations.* 1985;38:1023–1046.

Rokeach M. *Beliefs, Attitudes, and Values.* San Francisco, Calif: Jossey-Bass Publishers; 1968.

Sashkin M. *The Visionary Leader: Trainer Guide.* 3rd ed. King of Prussia, Pa: Organization Design and Development; 1990.

Sashkin M, Burke WW. Understanding and assessing organizational leadership. In: Clark KE, Clark MB, eds. *Measures of Leadership.* West Orange, NJ: Leadership Library of America; 1990:297–326.

Schiller MR, Foltz MB, Campbell S. Dietitians' self-perceptions: implications for leadership. *J Am Diet Assoc.* 1993;93:868–876.

Tannenbaum R, Davis SA. Values, man, and organizations. *Industrial Management Review.* 1969;10:67–86.

Tichy NM, Devannna MA. *The Transformational Leader.* New York, NY: John Wiley & Sons; 1986.

Vardaman B, Wimer J, Dugat S. Transforming leadership. *Baylor Business Review.* 1986;4:5–8.

Wahba MA, Bridwell LG. Maslow reconsidered: a review of research on the need hierarchy theory. *Organizational Behavior and Human Performance.* 1976;15:212–240.

Wilson CL, O'Hare D, Shipper F. 1990. Task cycle theory: the processes of influence. In: Clark KE, Clark MB, eds. *Measures of Leadership.* West Orange, NJ: Leadership Library of America; 1990:185–204.

Wylie-Rossett J, Wheeler M, Krueger K, Halford B. Opportunities for research-oriented dietitians. *J Am Diet Assoc.* 1990;90:1531–1534.

4

Organizational Change

Chapter Objectives

1. Describe three conditions necessary for change.
2. List five characteristics of a transformed future.
3. Discuss four techniques to create a sense of urgent dissatisfaction.
4. List five indications that people are resisting change.
5. Explain why it is difficult to understand the change process.
6. Describe three change tools that the dietetics professional can use on a daily basis.
7. Compare and contrast responding to change with solidity vs doing so with resilience.

Introduction

Change involves the crystallization of new action possibilities (new policies, new behaviors, new patterns, new methodologies, new products, or new market ideas) based on reconceptualized patterns in the organization. The architecture of change involves the design and construction of new patterns (or the reconceptualization of old ones) to make new, more productive, actions possible (Kanter 1983, p 279).

This definition implies that change takes many forms and can occur in a variety of ways. Seldom is change a dramatic, one-time breakthrough. Rather, it is a step-by-step accumulation of accomplishments that have been implemented deliberately and slowly. Thus change is elusive and hard to measure. Rarely can one pinpoint an exact time when a change began or ended. Change may mean a complete overhaul of the mission, goals, and people of the organization. More often, change may be the act of rethinking and repackaging existing organizational elements.

Transformational Change in Organizations

The purpose of transformational leadership, as its name denotes, is change—change that appeals to the values and needs of the leader and the followers. In organizations, change is revitalization through the development of and commitment to a realistic, successful future. Commitment to a vision, however, is not enough. In nutrition and dietetics, organizational transformation also includes the redesigning of organizational structures and departments.

Three conditions are necessary to transform institutional food and nutrition departments or other environments in which dietetics professionals may work:

1. Dissatisfaction with the present
2. A vision of a preferred future
3. A social architecture that commits people to the vision

This chapter and the following three discuss change from the perspective of transforming dietetics services to create departments or other organizational units characterized by success and excellence.

Planned Change

Most books that discuss organizational change propose models of planned change. These proposed models focus on changes within the existing structure. They provide valuable guidance for instituting new programs, such as establishing a reimbursement plan for medical nutrition therapies, or for solving well-defined problems, such as improving patient satisfaction with institutional foodservices. These planned change techniques, while often helpful, do not give guidance for transforming organizations.

Transforming Change

In contrast to changes within the existing structure, transforming changes are those made to the structure itself. Nutrition departments are structurally transformed by leaders who appeal to the values and goals of the people in the organization, manage dissatisfaction, provide vision, and structure the organization for professional dietetics practice. Transforming change, like planned change, is well thought-out and deliberate.

Recognizing the Need for Change

The traditional approach to change is that the leader recognizes and desires a particular change and orchestrates a complex process to bring about the desired outcome. The elements of this process differ among theorists, but generally include the following:

- Assessing the people and the environment
- Determining change strategies
- Implementing the strategies
- Evaluating the effect for intended results

There is one common concept among change theories: others will resist the change. Thus, in order to be successful, the leader persuades and coaxes others. It is generally agreed, however, that change is much too complex and people are much too diverse for any one theoretical prescription to guarantee success. Furthermore, in the confusion and muddle of day-to-day activities, the dietetics professional seldom has the opportunity to apply the concepts of planned change models. Transformational change is not accomplished by manipulating people or by applying some arbitrary change formula, but rather by appealing to people's values and motivation to realize excellence for all (Conner 1993, p 200-215).

At times, the dietetics professional may not see the need for change where it exists. Thus the first thing that must happen before a transformation of nutrition services can occur is for the dietetics professional to become dissatisfied with current reality. If a leader-manager is not sensitive to the need for change or is not willing to change, others in the department are less likely to be innovative and creative. In other words, the leader will not be able to empower others to enact change.

Ironically, healthcare organizations and the people who run them are not always sensitive to the need for change. This phenomenon happens because organizational thresholds of awareness for change are set too high; people often do not recognize the need for change until there are disastrous consequences (Tichy and Devanna 1986, p 44). For example, in the 1970s concerns about rising healthcare costs became a national issue, yet nothing was done by the healthcare industry to curb costs; they kept rising. In 1983 prospective payment became a reality, taking most healthcare institutions by surprise and having devastating effects on many. In the 1990s managed care arrangements with their deep discounts are creating further financial crises for many healthcare institutions, particularly those who remain rigid in their organizational process and structure.

Dietetics is facing a similar scenario—change is coming too little, too late. In the 1970s hospital malnutrition was recognized as a major problem (Butterworth 1974). Dietitians had overlooked the nutritional welfare of their patients. They were spending much of their time checking menus, giving inpatient diet instructions, and supervising tray delivery. Their services were not considered important enough to warrant coverage in new

Medicare guidelines. To cope with the apparent problem, role delineation studies were completed. New assessment procedures were developed and instituted. A number of institutions created positions for dietetic technicians who could perform many routine tasks in the department, freeing dietitians for professional roles. Screening for nutritional risk, however, remained a rarity. Steps were not taken to obtain reimbursement for medical nutrition therapies or to mandate nutrition as a standard of high-quality medical care. The work roles of many dietitians remained the same; jobs in clinical dietetics began to decline. Furthermore, the role and utilization of dietitians and their dissatisfaction with their practice and salaries are still not being aggressively addressed.

Other changes must be made in dietetics, including recognition of the dietitian's role as a vital member of the medical team, documentation of the cost-benefit of nutrition services, team decision making, the empowerment of staff, and an improved image of dietitians. To compound the problem, other professionals have been stepping in to assume responsibility for nutrition, including nurses, pharmacists, and chiropractors. In the past the threshold of awareness about the need for fundamental change was set too high. However, the jolt of present-day healthcare reform has triggered the recognition of the need for change in the practice of dietetics and in the organization and delivery of nutrition services.

Model of Organizational Change

The model for understanding the process of organizational change in nutrition departments is illustrated in Fig 4-1. First, the leader recognizes the need for change, then helps followers recognize this need by raising their level of dissatisfaction. Dissatisfaction is a result of followers recognizing that the present situation does not meet their needs or that it conflicts with their values. Next, the dietetics leader depicts a future that appeals to the values, needs, and aspirations of the followers. This is called defining a vision. Third, the social architecture is redefined and revised. This is when behaviors are changed to reach intended outcomes.

Managing Dissatisfaction

In the experience of most big corporations that have undergone major transformations, it was the external environment that caused the leader to become dissatisfied, to arouse dissatisfaction in others, and to mobilize a commitment to a new vision (Oakley and Krug 1991, p 28–42). Similarly, external environmental factors are providing the climate for transformational changes in nutrition service departments. These factors include the transformation to an information society, the need to control healthcare

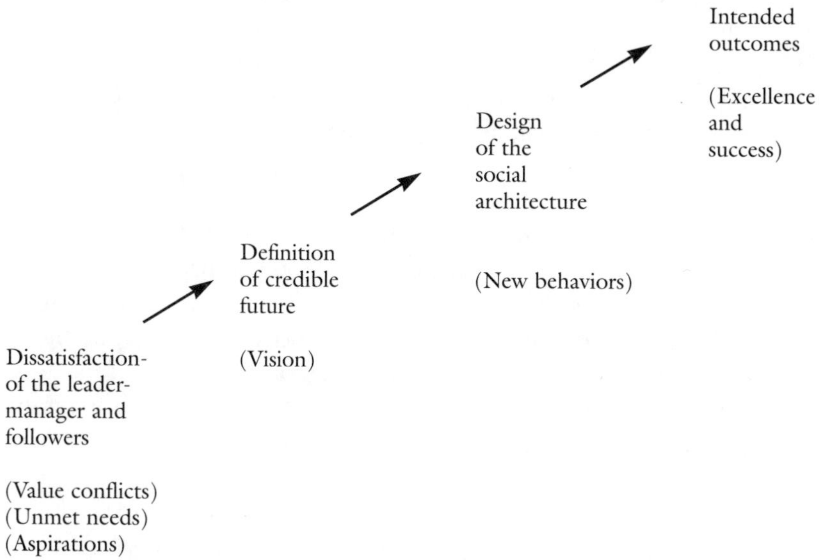

Figure 4-1. Barker's model of organizational change.

costs, and the dissatisfactions of dietitians and dietetic technicians with their practice. Now is the time for dietetic professionals to exert their leadership, respond positively to the external environment, and use these factors to transform their organizations.

The effort a transformational leader needs to spend in convincing others in the organization that it needs to change is inversely proportional to the urgency about the need to change (Tichy and Devanna 1986, p 47). For example, until recently, most nutrition counseling occurred while patients were hospitalized, even though patient adherence to these instructions was quite low. Patient stay was sufficiently long to include nutrition counseling; before hospital discharge, most patients were well enough to focus on needed dietary changes; and many patients preferred this free service to additional outpatient visits for which a fee was likely to be charged. Thus, at that time, there was no urgency to change. Now that patient stays are shorter, patients are sicker at discharge, research shows that patient adherence improves with several counseling sessions, and patients sometimes are charged for inpatient counseling, a sense of dissatisfaction is more apparent. Thus there is a move to conduct all nutrition counseling in outpatient settings.

To create a sense of urgent dissatisfaction is not easy. Some practical techniques, however, are available (Tichy and Devanna 1986, p 53–57).

Creating an Environment Conducive to Interchange. Creating an environment in which people can challenge one another and explore issues can foster a sense of dissonance. When people feel comfortable enough to ask questions, they are then able to think and consider various sides of the issue. People, including the leader, may become dissatisfied with their own thinking and actions. The leader is the person who sets the tone for this environment by asking questions, asking for advice, listening, and allowing discussion.

Broadcasting Pertinent Information. Sharing information widely about the internal and external environments can help people appreciate the challenges they face. The leader should share specific information, such as internal problems, intended strategies for the future, and what is happening in other healthcare facilities that are considered the competition. Publicizing quantitative data such as salaries and patient satisfaction scores is important and helpful if used to help increase dissatisfaction and a sense of dissonance.

Discussing Future Goals. Discussing the future can arouse excitement in an organization, increase people's motivation, and stimulate the development of teamwork. For example, many hospitals are considering the implementation of patient-focused care. The dietitian should discuss what this means and how it can positively affect nutrition services in the future. This can help people work together toward a desirable future goal.

Interacting With Similar Organizations. By using external networks and interacting with people outside the organization, key staff can become aware of problems that could also be present in other organizations. Thus people can become aware that the dissatisfaction they are feeling is not limited to their organization. The issue takes on a wider significance—"This is not a unique problem at our institution, but is a problem faced by all dietetics practitioners." Furthermore, people may become increasingly dissatisfied by seeing what is happening in other settings—for example, seeing other departments initiate effective nutrition screening programs or seeing increased positive recognition for nutrition services in other organizations.

Altering Management Processes. By intentionally altering management processes, the leader can increase the level of staff dissatisfaction. For instance, the performance appraisal system can be used to create dissatisfaction. If a new expectation is created, people may become dissatisfied with the ability of environmental support to fulfill the expectation. If the evaluation system is changed to evaluate staff on their use of the nutrition care process rather than on punctuality, the staff may become dissatisfied with the organizational elements that hinder their ability to deliver high-quality nutrition services. Thus a sense of dissatisfaction is created and change becomes possible.

Managing Dissatisfaction in the Individual

During this phase of engendering dissatisfaction with the past, the individuals in the organization are undergoing psychological changes. Lewin (1958) calls this stage "unfreezing" and Bridges (1980) calls it "endings." The individual is letting go of past beliefs and behaviors. This process must happen first so that people can adopt new beliefs and behaviors (Oakley and Krug 1991, p 92). In this situation the leader's role is to make the future appear brighter and better than the "good old days." At the same time, the successes and failures of the past must be acknowledged.

Complexities of the Change Process

As stated previously, prescriptions for planned change are fraught with difficulties and uncertainties. Understanding the change process is complex for a variety of reasons. It is almost impossible to have a clear understanding of change, because three interacting forces make change elusive: paradoxes, resistance, and distortion.

The Paradoxes of Change

Tichy and Devanna (1986, p 27–28) present four paradoxes of change that shed light on the complexities of organizational change.

Paradox 1. There is a conflict between the forces of stability and the forces of change. It is human to want adventure, variety, and change, and at the same time to yearn for safety and security. Organizational leaders have to balance holding on too tightly to the old ways of doing things with moving too quickly, going out of control, and thus failing.

Paradox 2. The tension between denial and acceptance of reality portends failure if the tendency toward denial is stronger.

Paradox 3. A conflict between fear and hope exists in the hearts of people. In dietetics, this paradox is evident every day. Generally, the dietetics profession views the future optimistically. The changing healthcare environment provides opportunities for new roles for dietitians and dietetic technicians, both in the workplace and in the nation's policy-making arena. However, fear for the actual survival of the profession is expressed daily.

Paradox 4. The leader must often grapple with being both a manager and a leader. The manager wants to protect the organization from experiencing the turmoil of change, whereas the leader yearns for change and movement toward goals.

To illustrate these paradoxes in dietetics, consider the clinical nutrition manager who wishes to move from unit-based practice to a consult-based role for dietitians. First, the clinical nutrition manager and the staff will struggle with the desire for the stability of unit-based practice. In this system, everyone is familiar with their roles and expectations. However, the staff is also aware of the disadvantages of medical nutrition therapies affiliated with the foodservice system. Dietitians and dietetic technicians may desire a different patient care approach that can improve their self-image and job satisfaction. The clinical nutrition manager in this instance will need to walk the line between implementing the change too quickly with not moving fast enough.

During this time of change, the clinical nutrition manager and the staff may deny the need for change. This is similar to the previously discussed phenomenon, in which a threshold for change was set too high. Each day, however, the staff may be confronted with evidence that change is necessary.

The third paradox may also be operating in this example—that is, the staff and clinical nutrition manager may fear letting go of the past and fear that the new system will not work. At the same time the clinical nutrition manager may hope that the new system will improve the quality of work and the satisfaction of staff. Last, as the clinical nutrition manager works with others to implement a consult service, it will be necessary to struggle with the tasks of implementing a new system in an organized, controlled manner. Yet in being too organized and managerial, the clinical nutrition manager may stifle staff creativity.

Resistance to Change

Resistance to change is a well-recognized phenomenon in organizations. In fact, resistance to change and techniques to overcome it are the subjects of most of the management literature about change. Understanding resistance to change helps leaders and managers cope with the complexities of the change process. There are many forms of resistance:

- Rejection of the leadership in the organization
- Low performance levels and productivity
- Clinging to old ways of doing things
- Passivity and avoidance of responsibility

Resistance is harmful. One of the basic laws of physics is that energy will travel along the path of least resistance. Thus, when faced with organizational resistance, the energies of most people will not be directed toward change to actualize the vision. Resistance to change comes from several sources, including people in the organization, the individual leader, and organizational norms and values. Tichy and Ulrich (1984, p 61) describe nine causes of resistance.

1. *Habit and inertia.* Occasionally, resistance occurs because people are comfortable with the routines related to the tasks they perform. In dietetics, an example of this type of resistance is seen when implementing a computer system for tracking such things as clinical productivity, reimbursement patterns, and patient acuity. Such a system can have a radical impact on daily activities and data-based performance evaluations. Staff may raise many barriers to the process of implementing a computerized system, although in reality the system will enhance clinical productivity.
2. *Fear of the unknown.* Not knowing the future and not being able to predict organizational behavior can cause anxiety among the staff. This may result in resistance.
3. *Sunk costs.* Organizations are sometimes unable to implement a change because of costs already spent in doing things in a particular way. Thus there are no available resources to try new approaches.
4. *Threats to powerful coalitions.* With the onset of change, power relationships often shift along with the status of some people. Or there may be a conflict between the "old" guard and the "new" one. One of the difficulties in implementing an environment that empowers everyone is that power and status become dispersed. For example, as hospitals move toward patient-focused care, nurses and other licensed health professionals may be asked to provide oversight for enteral tube feedings, a task many dietitians believe is uniquely theirs. Alternatively, dietetic professionals will be asked to take over some responsibilities, such as phlebotomy, incentive spirometry, and patient care unit management, that were previously assumed by other health professionals. As departmental barriers within institutions dissolve, cohesion among professional groups will be diluted.
5. *Limited resources.* In today's healthcare environment, change almost always means learning how to do more with less. Because there are fewer resources to distribute, someone or everyone is going to lose. This is not easy to sell to people; thus they resist the change.
6. *Indictment of leadership.* When managerial leaders lament the problems facing their organizations, they are also recognizing that they are part of the problem. Thus recognizing the need for change is an indictment of their past behaviors and decisions.
7. *Selective perceptions.* Organizations have certain values and norms of behavior. Thus people in the organization may only see issues from this perspective. They see limited possibilities for making changes. This is why outsiders and consultants can more readily recognize the organization's opportunities and need for change.
8. *Security based on the past.* The past frequently seems more secure than

the future. There are people who resist change, hoping for the return of the "good old days." All organizations are growing ever more turbulent as they scamper to adjust to change in the outside world (Conner 1993, p 3). Healthcare is not exempt from these changes. There is a strong temptation for dietetics professionals, however, to persist in their desire to maintain previously comfortable organizational structures and modes of practice.

9. *Limited climate for change.* Organizations vary in their conduciveness to change. Some require a great deal of conformity and do not support their members in implementing changes. Note, for example, the difficulties many dietitians have had in attempting to establish fees for nutrition services provided to hospitalized patients, or in obtaining institutional approval to document patient care in progress notes. These initiatives have been implemented in some institutions, but not approved at other sites.

Distortions: The Elusiveness of Change

Change, as has been stated previously, is elusive, and therefore the processes of change are not easy to understand. Kanter (1983, p 282–284) provides an interesting approach to the study of the change process in organizations. She suggests that in the attempts to describe organizational change, distortions occur. It is through the distortions that one can learn some of the "truths" about change and gain a fuller appreciation of its complexities.

The major distortion is time. When relating the process of change to others, the "changer" will label some event as the beginning of the change process. This may be the time the changer became consciously aware of a problem, decided to establish a new goal, or began to seek alternative courses of action. However, there is a "prehistory" for change that lays the groundwork for the events to come. Something occurred before the changer became aware of the need for change. Because these events are generally unknown to the changer, any conclusions that are made about the change process are suspect and any attempts to replicate a change are impossible. In other words, recognizing the need for change is not the beginning but some midpoint in the process.

It can be seen, then, that the history of the organization and the dietetics department, which can either assist or block changes, is important. Dietetics leaders who are aware of the past will be able to capitalize on it for the future. This helps to provide security and stability within the department.

Most nutrition services departments have a history of strengths and weaknesses. The dietetics leader needs to be aware of both. For example, in some nutrition services units, the past is characterized by a high degree of respect throughout the organization. Thus an awareness of the past can support future efforts in ensuring that dietetics professionals play a significant role in decision making in the organization. In contrast, some elements of the past could negatively affect plans for the future. In the same organization, a history of ineffectiveness may permeate the dietetics department. The leader would then need to first demonstrate high performance and cost-effectiveness before proceeding with other programs.

Other distortions can occur, besides those related to time. Kanter (1983, p 284–289) explains them as follows:

1. *One person initiates change, not the group.* Generally, one person may be the "shaker and mover" who initiated the change. However, for change to be truly change, it must involve the entire organization. In fact, part of the success of the initiator is getting the team to buy into the innovation and to become part of the process. Thus initiators often keep their leadership roles invisible, with the cooperation and the power of teams in the forefront.
2. *Early events and people are just as significant as later ones in producing change.* When relating a change that is occurring or has just happened, the people and events that are currently in the forefront are the ones credited with the change. In reality, many past events and past people have contributed to the state of the organization.
3. *After a consensus is reached, conflict is forgotten.* During the process of transformation, conflict may be intense. Once a decision is made, however, and a course is charted, those who were on the "winning" side generally forget the conflict, disagreements, and negotiations and they avoid holding grudges. They do this in the interests of organizational harmony. Those opposed to the change may, likewise, choose to forget the conflict and may even benefit from the new events.
4. *There were many workable courses of action available.* To sell a course of action to others it is presented as the best, most obvious choice. Although equally good and plausible choices existed, they are now forgotten.
5. *Periods of uncertainty, confusion, and experimentation often precede a clear-sighted strategy.* When selling a strategy, the uncertainty that often precedes the consensus is discounted. Once a decision is made, people want to take pride in its rationality; thus its elements of confusion are minimized.
6. *Only significant events are remembered.* A large number of happenings that are important to the change process become reduced into one or two significant events. These events are then thought to be the most important and are the only ones that are used to explain change to

others. This occurs, not purposefully, but because people often naturally forget events.

All these distortions make change a difficult phenomenon to understand. To achieve success, individuals must be appropriately supported during each distinctive stage of the process. Furthermore, the "stories" about change frequently omit important data about the timing of events. The actions and ideas of one or two people become credited to the entire group. Confusions, conflicts, diversity, and uncertainty fade when one course of action is chosen and implemented. Thus, when the discerning leader-manager is confronted with the muddling events that accompany change, the supposedly clear-sighted prescriptions for dealing with change seldom appeal or appear useful. In addition, the leader must be prepared to deal constructively with the negative response to change. As Conner (1993, p 131–135) explained, negative response to change is an eight-stage process of stability, immobilization, denial, anger, bargaining, depression, testing, and acceptance.

Strategies for Change

Peters (1987, p 8) suggested tools for change, which he divided into four categories (Fig 4-2) using speed of effect and control of outcomes as his two variables. These include low control, low speed (cell 1); low control, high speed (cell 2); high control, high speed (cell 3); and high control, low speed (cell 4).

The first category, cell 1, includes complex planning schemes, project management teams, structural considerations (eg, matrix organizational designs), and bottom-up team building. Although intended originally to be high-control, low-speed change techniques, they have not realized their intended effect despite years of use in a variety of organizations. They are now labeled as low-control, low-speed techniques. These tools have failed for three reasons. First, they take too long to be implemented and for people to see the effects of their use. There is a significant time lag between when a matrix design, for example, is implemented and when behavioral changes are obvious in the organization. Furthermore, once these tools are used, their use cannot be easily reversed. Thus they often outlive their usefulness. Third, some tools tend to overorganize and produce rigidity, while others, such as bottom-up team building, are too loosely structured.

A low-control, high-speed tool is used to implement change for change's sake (cell 2). The form may involve a wide range of alternatives (eg, a "shake-up" of dietitians) or a new structure (eg, nutrition care teams). The change can occur rapidly, but it seldom has the intended effects. Its use is limited and rarely recommended for situations characterized by confusing,

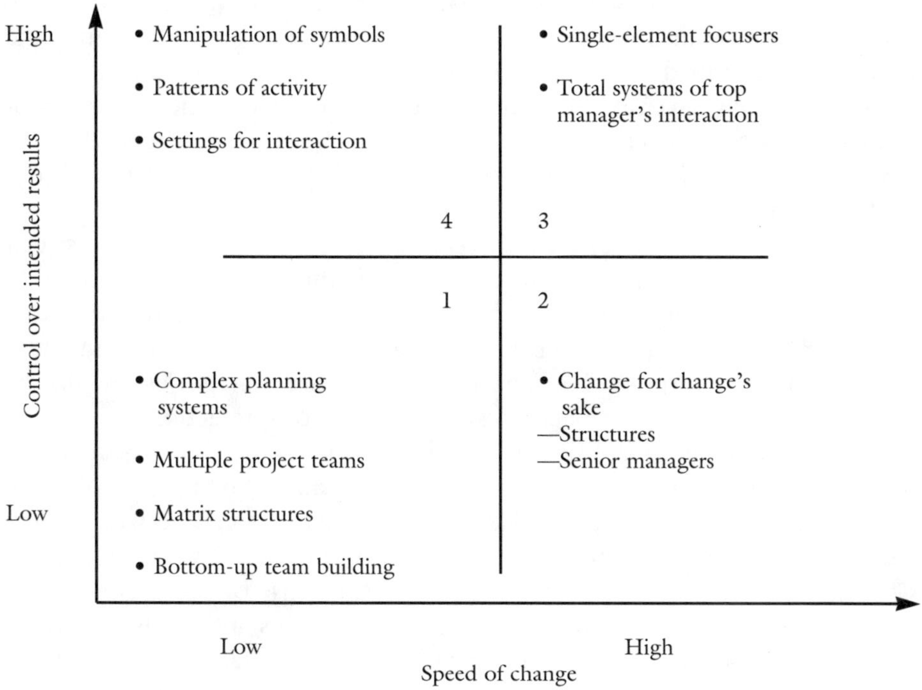

Figure 4-2. Tools for change.

muddling problems. The main outcome of the use of this tool is a sense of novelty that may provide an opportunity to see things in a new, fresh way.

For change that is needed *now,* high-control, high-speed changes are recommended (cell 3). These include using temporary systems to redirect the organization's attention and energies. Examples of these approaches are *single-element focusers* and *systems of interaction*. Single-element focusers are limited, temporary organizational designs such as pilot projects. Pilot projects are successfully used in dietetics to implement new practice modes such as new screening procedures, consult-based medical nutrition therapy, quality improvement programs, and patient-focused care. The entire department watches the pilot project and focuses attention on it. A second approach is to use new systems of interaction. These systems can range from formal mechanisms, such as retreats and forums, to informal mechanisms, such as social activities. By designing situations in which people interact differently than in the past, organizations can help shift people's attention to new directions.

For high-impact, low-speed change (cell 4), Peters recommended the use of what he called "mundane" tools. These are the appropriate tools for the slow, deliberate transformation of a department. They are called mundane because, as described below, they are simple occurrences that managers are involved in each day. Yet the leader seldom thinks about these as tools of change. It is these occurrences and events that can be managed daily to effect change by sending out and receiving messages that direct the energy in the organization.

Change occurs slowly as a result of the use of many of these tools (cell 4), not just one. In view of the fact that the organizational focus of today is temporary, will change, and may be greatly different in four to five years, these tools are not rigid or overorganized and are sensitive to the organization's vision and purpose. They are grouped in three categories: manipulation of symbols, patterns of activity, and settings for interaction.

Manipulation of symbols includes calendar behavior, reports, agendas, public statements, physical settings, and staff organization. These tools have the power to reshape beliefs and expectations over time. The way leaders and managers spend their time is the single most important statement about what is important to them. Review of reports, the use of agendas, minutes of meetings, and public statements shape expectations and focus attention. They place importance on or ignore particular themes and issues. Physical settings, such as operating out of one's office vs operating in the worksite, provide further evidence of concerns and focus. The use of support personnel and layers of management also sends messages about leadership style. Things such as staff authority and responsibilities send important messages.

Patterns of activity include positive reinforcements and the frequency and consistency of the leader's behavior. Frequent, consistent, positive reinforcement shapes expectations and induces change better than any other technique. People need to know directly from the leader or manager that their behaviors and accomplishments contribute to organizational success. By acting consistently and in concert with the defined vision, the leader can reinforce this vision every day and in every situation.

The third category of mundane tools is *settings for interaction*. The presence or absence of the leader at particular functions and the leader's minor activities can shape points of view. Where meetings take place, how the agenda is controlled, who attends and participates, the presentation format, and what questions are asked can focus attention and signal new directions.

Responding to Change

> Thus, a branch floats peacefully down a river whose waters are high with the spring runoff. Although the branch is floating rapidly and occasionally bumps gently into a rock, it is almost effortlessly motionless in relation to the water it floats on. A similar branch has become wedged between some rocks, and is

> thus resisting the swift flow of water around it. This branch is buffeted, whipped, and battered by the water and debris floating past it, and will soon be broken by the pressure against it. If branches could experience, the one wedged into the rocks would be experiencing change with intense pain and distress; the floating one would experience ease and, paradoxically, comfortable stability even in the midst of rapid motion (Enright 1986, p 60).

The dietetics professional has one of two choices when responding to the rapid changes of today's world. One is to be the wedged branch, forcefully and painfully resisting changes that have been thrust upon us; the other is to be the floating branch, comfortably adjusting to the turbulence of these times.

Change can be distressing for people because it affects their levels of need gratification and deprivation. As has been discussed, people have needs for belonging, self-esteem, and self-actualization. Because people have different life experiences, these needs are met through the attachment to specific people, specific jobs, and so forth (Enright 1986, p 60–61). For example, a foodservice worker may meet his or her need for belonging and self-esteem through his or her work on a particular patient unit, with a particular group of people, and by mastering a particular task.

When something happens that threatens the way a person gratifies personal needs, one of two reactions can occur: solidity or resilience. Solidity means holding onto the current situation and those things that satisfy needs. Resilience, however, is the ability to absorb high levels of change while displaying minimal dysfunctional behavior (Conner 1993, p 219). To do this, one keeps in mind the purpose and vision of the dietetics department and the organization. For example, staff in all units of food and nutrition service departments are assuming responsibility for continuous quality improvement in their areas. To do this, they had to break from the past when these activities were performed by a centralized quality committee. Staff did not have to worry about quality performance except for occasionally responding to negative feedback. When all the staff became involved in quality improvement responsibilities, they had two choices: to respond with resilience or with solidity. By responding with resilience, the staff would concentrate on deeper purposes—in this case, high-quality patient care. Thus a sense of achievement can now be obtained not only from care delivery but also from performing quality improvement activities.

By reacting to events with resilience, a person maintains an attitude and belief that things turn out for the best. This is not easy to do when one is threatened by change and adversity. By remembering past difficult situations that were resolved positively, the leader can see hope in times of uncertain change.

When people react to change with solidity, they rely on procedures and policies of the past or they attempt to plan and control the situation. For example, to respond to clinical staff downsizing, a clinical nutrition manager might develop a comprehensive, written plan to force the remaining staff to provide the same services in the same modes as previously, but for more patients. A leader who responds with resilience would see the opportunity to redefine the roles of all clinical nutrition staff to provide long-lasting change that would satisfy people's needs for belonging, esteem, and self-actualization.

Reynolds (1994, p 126) listed several things the leader can do to facilitate change. He or she can:

- Support and promote positive change by example and explanation. Describe what is causing the change, why it is important, and how it can be made beneficial. Channel anxiety into creative thinking.
- Emphasize the values providing stability more than the processes that contribute to instability.
- Tolerate performance short of perfection for high command decisions, recognizing that the appearance of a bad managerial decision could well be the root of lowered performance among subordinates.
- Communicate what the change will require, and help followers to develop the skills to meet new requirements.
- Provide caring during the adjustment period, and discipline if the follower refuses to adjust.
- Demonstrate an appropriate use of humor.
- Refuse to let ideals become expectations.

Implications for Dietetics

Change is elusive, difficult to manage, and rarely fully understood. Knowing this gives the dietetics leader better control over change and the transformation of nutrition services. It also makes change less threatening and the challenges less frustrating.

Exactly what changes are necessary in dietetics? The answer to this question can be found by reflecting on the dissatisfactions facing dietetics professionals and the profession (chapter 1) and understanding societal and healthcare trends (chapter 2). Table 4-1 suggests some necessary organizational changes. Dietetics needs to move from traditional organizational hierarchies to flexible organizational structures. Power should be vested in all. Esteem, versatility, innovation, and creativity are desirable characteristics of transformational nutrition service organizations. Paradoxically, both the individual and the team should be promoted. These ingredients form the conceptual framework of the remaining chapters of the book.

Table 4-1. Necessary Transformations for Dietetics Departments

Past	Transformed Future
1. Traditional hierarchical structures	1. Flexible structures
2. Power vested in management positions	2. Power vested in each professional
3. Poor self-image	3. High positive self-image
4. Solidity/rigidity	4. Versatility; resilience
5. Low salaries; equity in pay	5. Increased salaries; performance-based
6. Quantitative productivity management	6. Development of human resource potential
7. Predominance of rational decision making	7. Intuition and creativity
8. Department as a team	8. Importance of the individual as a member of the team
9. Formal communication	9. Informal communication
10. Depersonalization	10. Respect and caring for the individual
11. Striving for survival	11. Striving for excellence
12. Finding problems	12. Defining opportunities
13. Increasing leadership knowledge	13. Taking leadership action
14. Perfecting policies and procedures	14. Innovation
15. Focusing on the process	15. Focusing on outcomes and results
16. Dependency	16. Self-direction

Application to Dietetics Practice: Case Study

The Setting

The medical center is a four-hundred-bed, not-for-profit facility in an urban area. It offers a wide range of services and is a tertiary care center. A new ambulatory care center and a hospital-based home care program were recently opened. Food and nutrition services were consolidated, with middle managers reporting to one of three assistant directors. The current department director has been in the position for slightly more than two years. When the director assumed the position, the management systems, policies, procedures, budget, and so on, were well organized. The nutrition and dietetics department enjoyed a good reputation within the hospital community.

As with any large nutrition services organization, however, a variety of problems existed, including a high (38 percent) staff turnover rate at both the first-line and professional levels and a low level of job satisfaction, which was explicitly talked about by everyone in the department, other health professionals, and the chief executive officer.

The department director's overall objective was to improve morale in the department. She determined the following goals for her first year in the position:

1. Build self-esteem
2. Give individual professionals greater autonomy within their work units
3. Stabilize staffing by permitting job sharing, instituting flexible scheduling, and creating positions for dietetic technicians
4. Initiate an internal reward system to improve job satisfaction
5. Develop a system for third-party reimbursement of nutrition services, starting with development of a vision and mission statement

Within the first year the department director achieved several of her goals. Although still tentative, morale showed substantial improvement. Job sharing had been instituted, and a plan for flexible scheduling had been developed but not yet instituted. Staff turnover had decreased from 38 percent to 21 percent. One goal was not realized: creation of positions for dietetic technicians. Negotiations with the personnel department for these new positions proceeded slowly and eventually were not approved.

Current Situation

The nutrition services department is now experiencing a significant increase in nutrition consults, resulting in substantial overtime for dietitians, who must oversee all aspects of patient foodservice in addition to routine nutrition screening, assessments, and diet instructions. The increased workload has also resulted in increased job stress and turnover.

Recently, the clinical nutrition manager led a staff retreat with the dietitians to discuss overtime and job stress issues and to develop a plan for dealing with both. This strategy arose out of the clinical nutrition manager's desire to increase the involvement of dietitians in medical nutrition therapy and to enhance the image of the dietitians among physicians and other health professionals. The food and nutrition department head, however, was concerned about excessive overtime and a decline in the role clinical dietitians played in supervising patient foodservices. The question posed for the retreat was this: "What can we do about reducing overtime and getting better supervision of patient foodservices?" The clinical nutrition manager proposed that the answer should come from the staff itself, because she felt that the final recommendations would be considered more seriously if direct input from the staff was attained. All dietitians and foodservice managers attended the retreat; staff dietitians, however, had the largest representation.

At this retreat, many recommendations were prepared. Priorities were determined and later presented to the department head. Dietitians agreed they could save time if they changed documentation methods and shortened the time given to diet instructions. The second major concern was supervision of patient foodservices, including menu management, diet changes, and so on. The clinical nutrition manager and clinical dietitians presented several staffing options that included dietetic technicians. Their primary concern was that they needed more time for conducting nutrition consults, and they proposed developing a system of medical record coding and reimbursement to generate revenue for the department.

The recommendation and plans derived from the retreat were shared with the department head and all professional and management personnel through a written summary distributed shortly after the retreat and through discussion at all meetings. Several follow-up reports were written as recommendations and were accepted and implemented. Follow-up meetings with the staff attending the retreat occurred monthly for six months.

Case Study Discussion

1. Did the department head, associate director, and clinical nutrition manager recognize the need for change? On what evidence do you base your conclusions?

2. Why was the clinical nutrition manager unsuccessful in obtaining approval for dietetic technician positions the first time? What contributed to subsequent goal achievement?

3. What high-control, high-speed tool of change did the clinical nutrition manager employ?

4. What "mundane" tools of change were used?

5. How would you classify the department head's response to the lack of time clinical dietitians spent supervising patient foodservices? Why?

References

Bridges W. *Transitions: Making Sense of Life's Changes.* Reading, Mass: Addison-Wesley Publishing Co; 1980.

Butterworth C. The skeleton in the hospital closet. *Nutrition Today.* 1974;9:4–8.

Conner DR. *Managing at the Speed of Change.* New York, NY: Villard Books; 1993.

Enright J. Change and resilience. In: Williamson JN, ed. *The Leader-Manager.* New York, NY: John Wiley & Sons; 1986:59–73.

Kanter RM. *The Change Masters.* New York, NY: Simon & Schuster; 1983.

Lewin K. Group decision and social change. In: Maccoby EE, ed. *Readings in Social Psychology.* New York, NY: Holt, Rinehart & Winston; 1958:197–211.

Oakley E, Krug D. *Enlightened Leadership: Getting to the Heart of Change*. New York, NY: Simon & Schuster; 1991.

Peters TJ. Symbols, patterns, and settings: an optimistic case for getting things done. *Organizational Dynamics*. 1987;7:3–23.

Reynolds J. *Out-Front Leadership*. Austin, Tex: Mott & Carlisle; 1994.

Tichy NM, Devanna MA. *The Transformational Leader*. New York, NY: John Wiley & Sons; 1986.

Tichy NM, Ulrich DO. The leadership challenge: a call for the transformational leader. *Sloan Management Review*. 1984;25:59–68.

5

Organizational Vision

Chapter Objectives

1. Define organizational vision.

2. Discuss the positive impact that a vision has on organizational functioning.

3. Describe the envisioning process.

4. List the elements of a vision statement.

5. Discuss practical ways to engender commitment to a vision statement.

Introduction

Providing a vision for nutrition services is the first strategy of transformational leadership. A vision makes plain the invisible element of collective purpose. In doing this, it can stimulate the dietetics organization toward desired goals. Authors have described organizational vision using phrases like these: *picture of a desired future* (Senge 1990, p 149); *the deepest expression of what we want* (Block 1987, p 108); *a target* (Snyder et al 1994, p 74); *central belief system* (Britton and Stallings 1986, p 21). For this book, the term vision is used because it best denotes a futuristic approach to values and beliefs.

Definition and Characteristics of Vision

Vision is an image of a possible and desirable future state for an organization. It is an articulation of a realistic, attainable, credible, and attractive future (Nanus 1992, p 8). Visions that have proven to be successful in transforming organizations have several common characteristics. They reflect the core purposes of the organization; they are feasible, yet challenging; and they have a significance that transcends the organization and affects society as a whole. Furthermore, these visions appeal to the values, emotions, and imaginations of the people in the organization (Addleman 1994). Since the goal of leadership is to have people invest their talents and skills toward organizational success, having vision is vital. In dietetics, the vision should have at least two dimensions: the services provided to patients or clients and the management and organization of these services.

Visions should be developed for the overall organization. Flowing from this, visions should be articulated for each department and even each unit. Therefore, dietetics professionals, in any setting and at all levels, can have a vision statement for their area(s) of responsibility. This vision cannot conflict with the explicit or implicit mission and vision of the overall organization. Yet one's vision for nutrition services is more than a restatement of organizational purpose. A vision statement for nutrition services entails distinct, unique statements and goals (Rinke 1989, p 180–182). These statements are suited to the organization, the profession of dietetics, and the individuals working in nutrition services. For instance, the mission of a healthcare facility may or may not be explicitly described. Often, a mission statement may vaguely describe a primary mission of patient care and a secondary one of medical education. The vision of the nutrition and dietetics department in such a medical center, therefore, would include a statement about the dietetics professional's contribution to patient care and to the education of physicians, nurses, dietetics students, and others.

To understand why vision is important it is necessary to look at why organizations exist. People join organizations for rewards—both economic and psychosocial. The financial rewards include profits, prestige, power, and status. The changing values of people and of organizations can serve as guidelines to determine exactly what psychosocial rewards people are seeking in their organization. For example, a successful vision statement would appeal to the need to belong to a group that does challenging, creative, and meaningful work.

People also seek psychosocial rewards through their position in the external environment. When the organization has a widely shared, clear sense of its purpose, direction, and desired future state, people in the organization are able to define their own roles in the organization and in society (Bennis and Nanus 1985, p 90–91).

If vision is such an important element in effective, successful organizations, why isn't it more widely used? The answer lies in the inherent complexity of organizations. Organizations have a diversity of people who have varying and conflicting purposes and values (Bennis and Nanus 1985, p 94). For example, in a hospital, dietetics professionals, social workers, nursing staff, physicians, administrators, and so on, view the mission and goals of the organization from different yet equally important perspectives. Within foodservice and nutrition departments, a similar disparity may exist between staff and managers, educators and administrators, clinical nutrition personnel and foodservice staff and managers. Developing and maintaining an organizational vision is difficult because of this diversity.

Functions of Organizational Vision

A simple model elucidates the importance of vision:

Vision	→	Energized action for change	→	Success and excellence

In this model, vision is necessary to generate energy in organizations. This energy results in action, and action can lead to organizational success. By having an optimistic, credible vision, the organization functions more smoothly and in a unified direction.

Organizational Alignment

Another major function of the vision is to provide a framework for team building in today's healthcare environment. When the members of the team are committed to a shared vision, the relationship among team members and even one's self-concept may change. *Organizational alignment* is a situation

> in which the members operate as a whole, knowing that the actions taken will allow each of them to be true to themselves as well as to the organization. They see that the purpose and vision of the organization is worthy of the commitment of their life-spirit. And they, in effect, expand their definition of self, to enjoy a sense of unity with every other person in the organization (Kiefer 1986, p 191).

Alignment pulls together a disparate, heterogeneous work force. At the same time, however, each person can feel that his or her contributions are important. A dietetics team that is noted for its superb patient care, teamwork, and low staff turnover is most likely composed of an aligned staff.

Empowering people—that is, giving them the resources and power to be creative and innovative—works best when people in the organization are aligned. When there is no alignment, empowerment may be difficult to manage. Everyone may wish to do their own thing without regard to others and organizational goals. This creates organizational disharmony and dysfunctional conflict.

Performance

Studies have shown that organizations that have a strong vision and a strong sense of values and beliefs outperform those that do not (Nanus 1992, Snyder et al 1994). Furthermore, companies with widely shared values are more successful than those without any stated values or those whose visions were expressed in financial terms only. The explanation of the latter phenomenon is that financial values alone may motivate the top administrative group, but do not filter down and motivate the entire work force (Peters and Waterman 1982, p 281).

Vision can provide a stimulus toward excellence and quality improvement by setting goals and thresholds that exceed current performance levels and by challenging staff to stretch and reach. It can alter the nature of the leader-follower relationship with the impetus for performance being attainment of goals and quality standards rather than a system of rewards and punishments.

Change and Adaptability

Employees are more likely to adapt to and respond to change with versatility and resilience if there is a commonly held belief system. This may seem contradictory. People with firmly held beliefs are sometimes thought to be rigid and inflexible. But in reality, with a firm vision, employees are more willing to adapt to small, short-term changes that are consistent with their vision and belief system (Oakley and Krug 1991, p 167–190). Furthermore, the vision serves to describe what can be and serves as a guide to overall renewal within the organization and its services.

Decision Making

Providing a vision facilitates decision making at lower levels in the organization. People do not have to appeal to higher levels of authority when the vision provides a frame of reference for decision making (Bennis and Nanus 1985, p 92). Personal empowerment is particularly important in units dedicated to continuous quality improvement. Furthermore, the vision provides a framework for making decisions about the future because of its focus on long-term vs short-term gains.

Commitment and Meaning

By explicitly articulating a concrete picture of a desired future, the organization creates an environment in which commitment is the norm not the exception. Commitment is a way to empower people in the organization, because committed individuals have the emotional resources to be creative and to innovate.

Conflict Resolution

By focusing on a clear vision, the members of the organization can resolve conflicts more easily. The vision provides the framework for conflict resolution rather than through the use of power plays, game playing, and personal idiosyncrasies.

Envisioning: The Role of the Leader-Manager

Developing a vision for an organization, department, or other unit is a dynamic process. It involves the art of discovery and requires a profound knowledge of both oneself and the organization. The vision that is ultimately articulated should be realistic and feasible. This means that the skills and resources of the organization or subunit must be considered. In a bureaucratic organization (which characterizes the majority of healthcare organizations and nutrition service units), the act of envisioning is necessarily limited by organizational constraints. Rules, procedures, historical decisions, and contracts among the parties may limit the leader's freedom to act. Thus the vision that emerges is organizationally feasible, not merely an expression of the leader's dreams (Mintzberg and Waters 1983, p 70).

To envision, the leader-manager uses the skills of foresight, worldview, hindsight, depth perception, peripheral vision, and revision (Bennis and Nanus 1985, p 102). Each of these skills is described below along with sample questions dietetics leaders might ask while developing a vision for their respective organizations.

Foresight

Foresight involves exploring how the vision will fit into the way food, nutrition, and dietetics services or education may develop. In other words, the leader must have a sense of a possible future for the program, the unit, the department, the organization, and society. To do this, the dietetics professional needs to be aware of trends in healthcare and dietetics. Predicting the future is, of course, not possible. However, the leader's awareness of what is likely to happen is important:

- What are the long-range opportunities and risks for the department or nutrition services?
- How will healthcare reform at both the state and national level affect nutrition services?
- What are the likely outcomes of reimbursement or coverage for medical nutrition therapy? Expansion of WIC programs? Interest in work-

site wellness initiatives? Increased numbers of dietetics students?

- What are the characteristics, both qualitative and quantitative, of dietetics professionals in the community?
- What will be the role of dietitians and dietetic technicians in managed care environments? Home care services? Primary care clinics?

Worldview

A worldview involves awareness of the impact of new trends, not only in healthcare but also in society as a whole. This perspective will enhance the leader's envisioning:

- What societal trends, such as demographics and cultural diversity, will affect healthcare and dietetics practice?
- How will the information age and other changes in technology affect healthcare in general and dietetics in particular?
- What values will people be bringing to their work?

Hindsight

Likewise, to envision, the leader uses hindsight—an appreciation of the traditions and cultures of the profession as well as the organization and its mission. To develop an appreciation for the organizational history, the leader might ask:

- What is the current mission of the organization?
- Has it changed recently as a result of growth, restructuring, or downsizing? Or does it have a stable presence in the community?
- What is the history of the food and nutrition services department? Is it stable or constantly changing?
- What are the past and current strengths of the staff?

Depth Perception

Depth perception means that the leader must survey the entire picture—both the internal and external environment. This should be done in appropriate detail and with the correct perspective:

- What does the dietetics department contribute to the organization, the profession, patients, and society?
- What are my own interests, skills, and dreams?
- What are the internal resources of the department or subunit?
- What is the match between the internal strengths and external needs?

Peripheral Vision

Peripheral vision refers to the leader's awareness of competitors and stakeholders and their futures. The leader might ask:

- What is happening to other professions (eg, pharmacy, nursing, and medicine) that may affect dietetics or place the disciplines in competition?
- How will patient-focused care and the use of cross-functional teams change the practice of dietetics?
- How will the shift of physician demographics from specialists to family practitioners affect nutrition referrals and the role of dietitians?
- What is happening in dietetics at other institutions and what are the current standards of practice?
- What dietetic services do patients value? What are their needs and expectations?

Revision

The leader reviews and reassesses the vision as the environment changes (Brylinski 1993). This is necessary because one risk of a shared value system is that the external environment can change and then the vision becomes no longer helpful to organizational success (Nanus 1992, 157). Periodically, the leader-manager should assess the vision by asking: Where were we? Where are we now? How well have we done? Where do we go and by when?

Developing a Vision Statement

Philosophy Statements

Unlike nursing, dietetics and most other departments in healthcare institutions and other organizations do not have written philosophies of their professions and their places in society and healthcare. These philosophical statements delineate a common belief system (Rinke 1989, p 183–184). Common elements of a foodservice and nutrition care philosophy might include beliefs about personnel, food, and service; taking care of the customer; health and wellness; innovation; and the benefit of medical nutrition therapy. Dietetics leaders would do well to begin the formulation of a philosophy to help guide the visioning process. One place to start would be to reflect on the mission and vision statements established for the profession by The American Dietetic Association.

Mission Statements

Healthcare organizations generally have mission statements. A mission statement describes in broad terms the reason for the organization's existence. It also describes the patient or client population and lists the services provided. It is oriented to the present rather than the future. A hospital mission statement might be as short and concise as the following:

> The mission of General Medical Center is to care for patients in Greater County. It is a private, not-for-profit organization. The medical center offers a wide range of primary, secondary, and tertiary services for both homebound and hospitalized patients. The Medical Center has a tertiary emergency room and is the only trauma facility in the county. In addition, the Medical Center offers a full range of diagnostic, medical, psychiatric, surgical, and rehabilitative services for both outpatients and those admitted to the hospital. Pediatric and obstetric services are also available. The Medical Center is a referral center for pediatric and neonatal intensive care.

The dietetics department should have a mission statement as well (Schiller et al 1991, p 35–36). It would reiterate the general mission statement of the overall organization and expound on the available nutrition services.

Vision Statements

A similar but different approach for organizations is to write a vision statement. The vision statement is more futuristic than either the philosophy or mission statements. It describes a desirable future and a statement about where energies should be focused. This statement provides a written, concrete guide that the people in the organization can use to reach for the future. The terms used in a vision statement, though, are subjective rather than precise objective statements.

Generally, the vision statement includes information about patients or clients, nutrition services staff, management systems, and the relationship of the department to the organization, community, and society. Nanus (1992, p 28–29,121) delineated the desired properties of a vision statement. The vision should:

- Be future-oriented
- Be utopian, thus leading to a clearly better future for the organization
- Be appropriate for the organization and for the times, reflecting the uniqueness of the organization, its distinctive competence, what it stands for, and what it is able to achieve
- Set standards of excellence and reflect high ideals

- Clarify purpose and direction
- Inspire enthusiasm and encourage commitment
- Be well articulated and easily understood
- Be ambitious, expanding the organization's horizons

The case study at the end of this chapter includes sample statements from a vision statement.

Longer vision statements often have a logo or slogan that captures the essence of the message. The most popular examples of these slogans are found in corporate settings (eg, Du Pont's "better living through chemistry" or Delta Airline's "family feeling"). Slogans are becoming commonplace in healthcare settings. The Ohio State University Medical Center uses "intensive caring"; Nova Care uses "helping make life a little better." For many companies, the use of slogans may be meaningless. In excellent organizations, however, the leader believes deeply in the vision for the organization and reinforces it through management actions, systems, and communications.

Communication of and Commitment to the Vision

Once the vision is developed, the work of the leader shifts to communicating and building a commitment to the vision. The written vision statement should be published and widely distributed. In meetings with staff, leaders can discuss the statement. They should openly and honestly explore feelings and reactions to it. This process is educative since the articulation of a vision for a department or work group is most likely new to everyone involved.

The discussions can include other aspects of the vision. First, they can be focused on the values inherent in the vision statement. For example, people can explore their definition of high-quality patient care or their use of the nutrition care process. Second, the human needs and aspirations of people can be examined. Concepts such as self-esteem, belongingness, a sense of importance, and meaningful work are generally not recognized and openly discussed. These meetings with staff provide the transformational leader the opportunity to discuss these values explicitly and to increase the staff's consciousness of them.

The words used to communicate and sell the vision are also important. Bennis and Nanus (1985, p 107) found that effective leaders used metaphors to clarify the vision and to keep people focused. For many dietetics leaders, this is a new skill. Learning to communicate the vision metaphorically and with enthusiasm will take time and a conscious effort.

Explaining how the vision statement differs from past management techniques and directives is important for building staff commitment. Specifically, the staff needs to learn that a vision statement focuses on the future. It is a hope rather than a truth. The leader may want to compare the vision statement to a past practice with which staff is familiar. For example, unlike in a system such as management by objectives, the vision statement promotes values and humanness, not tasks and processes. The staff should understand that a vision statement involves the entire organization, not just the managers. It has implications for everyone (Tregoe et al 1989, p 152).

Communicating openly about one's own feelings and beliefs about the vision is another important strategy leaders can use to gain commitment to the vision. This, also, may be a new behavior for some leaders. Many dietetics professionals have been taught to be logical and to keep feelings out of the work environment. It is important, however, for the followers to have a true sense of the leader's feelings. One way to do this is to admit that the visionary process is new. The leader can acknowledge that it may not be a comfortable process personally, or that mistakes are likely. Furthermore, the leader can ask the staff to challenge and question decisions and actions so that all can grow and learn together.

After these initial meetings, the leader continues to communicate the vision persistently, consistently, and enthusiastically. Gaining the commitment of the dietetics staff for a vision is a long, sometimes tedious, process. The leader must be patient and persistent to sustain the necessary momentum. Face-to-face interactions between the leader and staff are also desirable. People need to test the sincerity and commitment of the leader, and only personal discussions afford this opportunity. However, personal interactions are not always possible in large foodservice departments. Thus the department head relies heavily on leaders in midlevel positions. They, too, help spread the message, both in words and in deeds. Thus leaders in large departments need to gain a commitment for the vision first from middle managers.

It is the first-line supervisors and staff who translate the vision into action. Therefore, they are the most important group from whom to secure commitment. Middle managers must be viewed as leaders also, and given freedom to develop a corresponding vision for their own work groups (Nanus 1992, 155). Using other media, (eg, videotapes, audiotapes, and newsletters) to tell success stories is another way to build commitment for the vision.

Gaining commitment for a vision has many difficulties. One is that the vision statement is a "leading-edge" document. It does not describe what is, but rather what can be. Although it makes visible what was previously invisible, by its nature it is ambiguous. The leader, by accepting and acknowledging this ambiguity, can help followers to accept and tolerate it as well.

The leader-manager should accept criticism of the vision statement. One hundred percent commitment of a large, diverse dietetics staff is not realistic. It is very easy for a leader who has developed a vision statement and who is personally committed to it to overlook and ignore the reactions and feelings of others. To build true commitment, however, the leader listens to, reacts to, and openly explores criticisms and negative feelings about the vision. Furthermore, the leader, recognizing that people will resist change, handles the resistance so the vision is not abandoned as too difficult or impossible.

Implications for Dietetics

By developing, adopting, and maintaining a visionary approach to leadership, the dietetics leader significantly changes his or her role. Where once all energy and time were devoted to crisis management and daily problem solving, new approaches are adopted. The actions of the leader are vital to success in developing a vision and gaining commitment to it (Richard and Engel 1986; Nanus 1992, p 138–156). Some practical techniques to ensure consistency of action and vision follow:

- When making decisions, each alternative should be reviewed to see how the solution is related to the vision.
- In times of crisis, the action taken by the leader must be consistent with the vision. For instance, if the vision is the incorporation of medical nutrition therapy as an integral part of all healthcare services delivered by the organization, strategies should be implemented to ensure that dietitians are involved in cross-functional care-mapping teams.
- People in the organization should understand how specific tasks connect to and move toward the vision. Routinely, the leader could spend a short time reviewing how planned activities relate to the vision.
- Producing "a miracle" or a sign (eg, the successful negotiation of a special benefit for staff) can demonstrate a commitment to them.
- Task forces should be formed to study various items of the vision statement, such as creativity and innovation.
- Demonstration projects can be developed that are aligned with the vision.
- Successes should be shared during formal and informal meetings.
- How one's own actions and the vision are consistent should be explained. Sometimes what seems consistent to the leader may not appear that way to the followers. By setting up an environment in which people can challenge perceived inconsistencies, any apparent lack of consistency will emerge and can then be clarified.

Application to Dietetics Practice: Case Study

The Setting

The current director of nutrition services for a health maintenance organization (HMO) has been in his position just over two years. Since his arrival, he has increased referrals for nutrition counseling by 60 percent, expanded the staff by two full-time equivalents, attained competitive salary and benefit packages for dietitians, and has established procedures to ensure the inclusion of nutrition in all health fairs and public programs sponsored by the organization. He is very interested in contracting with local industries to provide worksite nutrition services. He feels that this is his top priority, yet is frustrated because the staff dietitians do not express a similar concern. These dietitians believe they are already working at full capacity and they resist the changes in scheduling and work patterns necessitated by worksite nutrition services. The director believes that although there are things he can do to expand nutrition services, the major responsibility for success rests with the professional staff.

In the past, the director has independently established annual goals for HMO nutrition services. There has never been a philosophy of nutrition care at the institution, and the mission statement for nutrition services has not been revised for several years.

Current Situation

The director of the HMO nutrition services has decided to deal with resistance to pursuing worksite nutrition contracts in two ways. He has arranged for a one-day retreat for dietitians in nutrition services to identify issues and to develop productivity targets for each dietitian. Prior to the retreat, he and the director of education at the institution write and issue a vision statement for the department. Table 5-1 contains excerpts from the vision statement.

Case Study Discussion

In view of the vision statement in Table 5-1, certain questions arise:

1. How will the HMO nutrition service department ensure excellence and success?

2. How will the HMO dietitians provide nutrition education and other nutrition services?

Table 5-1. Sample Vision Statement (Excerpts)

1. The mission of nutrition services is to provide nutrition education, preventive care, and medical nutrition therapy that assist patients and other clients make appropriate food choices for optimal health, preventing disease, maintaining nutritional status, or regaining health. This mission is accomplished through cost-effective and outcome-oriented programs that ensure effective patient care and provide dietetics personnel with opportunities for professional satisfaction and growth.
2. Nutrition services provides a practice environment that fosters excellence in practice by encouraging and supporting each employee's efforts to contribute to patient care and nutrition programming to the maximum capacity possible and by maximizing the job satisfaction of individual staff members.
3. In an era of resource constraints, the dietitian is challenged to establish priorities in the delivery of nutrition services to ensure that the optimum quality and quantity of services are provided, given existing resources. Thus the dietitian continuously assesses the appropriateness of nutrition services and the adequacy of available resources, determines priorities, selects and implements those nutrition care activities that make best use of available resources, and evaluates outcomes in terms of established standards of care.
4. Nine key concerns—professional standards, quality improvement, patient satisfaction, management systems, productivity, staff empowerment, research, education, and image—form the basis for the identification, prioritization, and evaluation of nutrition services goals and objectives and the activities designed to achieve them.
5. Registered dietitians (RDs) and dietetic technicians registered (DTRs) are identified as professionals who have selected dietetics as their lifework and are committed to the profession and their own growth within it.
6. Nutrition services recruits the highest caliber of professional and nonprofessional dietetics personnel available; places those personnel in positions appropriate to their knowledge, expertise, and qualifications; and fosters individual growth and development in the employment setting.
7. Always cognizant of the ultimate goal of providing comprehensive nutrition care for every patient, the dietetics staff recognizes that flexibility and creativity are essential in selecting appropriate and achievable goals based on the patient's abilities and preferences and available time, materials, and personnel.
8. As healthcare providers responsible for the delivery of comprehensive nutrition services in a setting that is on the leading edge of technological advancement, dietetics professionals anticipate the need for and create the innovative care approaches necessary to respond effectively to the constantly changing nutritional and dietary needs of patients and the public.
9. As the leaders of nutrition care delivery, dietitians set the tone and standards for patient care.
10. Management systems within nutrition services facilitate the work of patient care and nutrition education; these systems create and maintain a climate that promotes effectiveness and job satisfaction.

3. What is the overall purpose of this nutrition services department?

4. How does the department ensure self-direction and fairness?

5. What is the management system of this department?

6. How does the department involve employees?

7. Is the system relatively flexible?

8. What does the vision statement say about creativity and innovation?

References

Addleman R. The power of vision. *Trustee.* 1994;47:4–5,26.

Bennis W, Nanus B. *Leaders: Strategies for Taking Charge.* New York, NY: John Wiley & Sons; 1985.

Block P. *The Empowered Manager: Positive Political Skills at Work.* San Francisco, Calif: Jossey-Bass Publishers; 1987.

Britton PR, Stallings JW. *Leadership Is Empowering People.* Lanham, Md: University Press of America; 1986.

Brylinski C. Strategic planning: an overview. *Clinical Nutrition Management Newsletter.* 1993;12:1–4.

Kiefer C. Leadership in metanoic organizations. In: Adams JD, ed. *Transforming Leadership: From Vision to Results.* Alexandria, Va: Miles River Press; 1986:185–198.

Mintzberg H, Waters JA. The mind of the strategist. In: Srivastva S & Assoc, ed. *The Executive Mind.* San Francisco, Calif: Jossey-Bass Publishers; 1983:58–83.

Nanus B. *Visionary Leadership: Creating a Compelling Sense of Direction for Your Organization.* San Francisco, Calif: Jossey-Bass Publishers; 1992.

Oakley E, Krug D. *Enlightened Leadership: Getting to the Heart of Change.* New York, NY: Simon & Schuster; 1991.

Peters TJ, Waterman RH. *In Search of Excellence: Lessons From America's Best-Run Companies.* New York, NY: Harper & Row; 1982.

Richard D, Engel S. After vision: suggestions to corporate visionaries and vision champions. In: Adams JD, ed. *Transforming Work: A Collection of Organizational Transformation Readings.* Alexandria, Va: Miles River Press; 1986:199–214.

Rinke WJ. *The Winning Foodservice Manager.* Gaithersburg, Md: Aspen Publishers; 1989.

Schiller MR, Gilbride JA, Maillet JO. *Handbook for Clinical Nutrition Services Management.* Gaithersburg, Md: Aspen Publishers; 1991.

Senge PM. *The Fifth Discipline: The Art and Practice of the Learning Organization.* New York, NY: Doubleday; 1990.

Snyder NH, Dowd JJ, Houghton DM. *Vision, Values, and Courage: Leadership for Quality Management.* New York, NY: The Free Press; 1994.

Tregoe BB, Zimmerman JW, Smith RA, Tobia PM. *Vision in Action: Putting a Winning Strategy to Work.* New York, NY: Simon & Schuster; 1989.

6

Social Architecture

Chapter Objectives

1. Define social architecture.
2. Discuss the purpose of social architecture.
3. List the three types of social networks found in nutrition care organizations.
4. Explain how norms affect organizational behaviors.
5. Discuss three types of social architecture.
6. Describe a situation in which participatory management should be used and one in which it should not be used.
7. Describe various methods for enhancing the social architecture of food and nutrition organizational units.

Introduction

> Social architecture is an intangible, but it governs the way people act, the values and norms that are subtly transmitted to groups and individuals, and the construct of binding and bonding within a company (Bennis and Nanus 1985, p 110–111).

Providing a vision for nutrition service units is not enough. As an even more challenging task, the leader provides structure and processes so that the vision can be implemented and sustained (Belasco 1990, p 17–30). A leader who only has a vision and does not support it with structure is merely wishing for change. Hoping dreams will come true without working toward a goal is unrealistic. Similarly, structure without vision is useless.

A popular synonym for social architecture is *organizational culture,* a term widely used in management literature. Deal and Kennedy (1982, p 4) are perhaps the most cited authors on this topic. They have adopted the definition of culture from *Webster's New Collegiate Dictionary:*

> The integrated pattern of human behavior that includes thought, speech, action, and artifacts and depends on man's capacity for learning and transmitting knowledge to succeeding generations.

Deal and Kennedy then defined organizational culture as the way things are done in an organization.

The term *social architecture* is being used in this book because it is less vague than *culture.* The former includes the structural elements of human resource management and implies having the ability to change the organizational environment. Furthermore, it is a good metaphor. As the social "architect" of the nutrition services unit, the dietetics professional is not building a new structure from raw materials and an ideal design. Instead, the leader is undertaking a major renovation. New additions can be made and some "rooms" can be deleted. Some "walls" can be rearranged, but not the weight-bearing ones. The "electrical wiring" and "plumbing" can be updated. However, the basic foundation and the frame remain. In other words, the blueprint for remodeling social architecture within the food and/or nutrition service department is constrained by the past. However, the prevailing culture influences how people become leaders and how leadership affects organizational climate (Pheysey 1993, p 142–163). Tools used by the leader include an understanding of and ability to redesign social networks, norms, and organizational structures.

The Function of Social Architecture

The purpose of building the social architecture is to generate commitment to the established vision and organizational identity. Social architecture also provides meaning to its members and presents a shared interpretation of organizational events so that people know how they are to act. Furthermore, the social architecture provides a system for informal control. The traditional theories and prescriptions of management and leadership are largely focused on the methods of control. These methods include the budget; management information systems; the formalized, technical aspects of the reward and punishment systems; a system for performance appraisal; methods for division of labor; and job descriptions. However, none of these systems alone is capable of controlling organizational functioning. In fact, their overuse leads to rigidity and stifles creativity and innovation. In contrast, building and maintaining a social architecture provides "informal control" that ensures bringing to reality a shared vision of the future (Nystrom 1993).

Social Networks

Tichy and Devanna (1986, p 186–202) describe social relations in organizations as networks. Organizations are a cluster of people joined by a variety of links. Social roles define who people are (dietitian, diet clerk, food-service manager), as well as who they are in relation to others in the organization (superior, subordinate, peer). People in the organization exist in networks. For example, there are networks of bosses, peers, subordinates, and friends. All these people expect certain behaviors of each other, depending on the assumed role. These expectations may, of course, conflict with one another, and leaders in food and nutrition departments constantly face these conflicts. Staff dietitians balance the demands of patients, staff, and superiors. The department head often must manage a similar disharmony of expectations. The facility's chief executive officer may frequently look for ways to contain costs while dietetics personnel ask for increased salaries and benefits.

Each person in his or her social life is a participant in another network, thus connecting the networks with one another. Communications, influence, and affection flow among these networks. In roles as the social architects of food and nutrition units or departments, dietetics leaders develop an understanding of these networks in the organization. They manage them and, if necessary, reweave the system of social relations and the flow of communications to realize meaningful change.

Formal and Informal Networks

Networks can be categorized into two groups. *Formal* or *prescribed* networks are clusters of people who relate to one another as defined by the organizational design. They are easily identified by the organizational chart, policies and procedures, committee structures, and work groups. *Informal* or *emergent* networks are those that have no organizational sanctions. They simply emerge out of the everyday activities of the organization. They have often been called the "informal organization" and have had a negative connotation, at least for managers. In fact, they are neutral. They take on desirable or undesirable characteristics depending on how they are managed.

Both prescribed and emergent social networks can have three purposes: *information, influence,* and *friendship*. Information networks determine the flow of information regarding the organization and its environment. They determine who exchanges information with whom. *Influence* networks describe who influences whom about what, using both formal orders and informal persuasion. *Affect* networks determine feelings of friendship among people. It is largely through the friendship networks that values and norms are disseminated and reinforced.

Management by Wandering Around

By having an understanding of the networks in the organization, the dietetics leader can then influence them. Obviously, it is easier to rearrange the formal networks than the informal ones. "Management by wandering around" (MBWA), a term coined by Peters and Waterman (1982, p 122), is an essential tool for assessing and managing the social networks. Talking to the right person in the hallway, providing on-the-spot positive reinforcement, and giving information are behaviors that can affect a variety of networks. This is true for both formal and informal networks.

The purpose of MBWA is to find out what is going on in the organization. It allows the leader to observe what is causing problems for people—staff, patients, and visitors. It is also an opportunity to guide and direct others by posing questions that convey the leader's values and vision. The first technique of MBWA is to listen to others and get firsthand information. Since the sharing of values can only happen in face-to-face interactions, the second technique is to use the interaction as a time to teach and share values and to build the self-esteem of others. Third, MBWA provides the opportunity for the leader to facilitate work. Frequently, a problem that is currently hampering the productivity of the day can be brought to the attention of the leader. A quick resolution may be possible. One shortcoming of giving on-the-scene advice and guidance is the tendency for employees to act on what the leader says because the leader is "the boss." This may result in lowered employee self-esteem. The leader can help reduce this tendency by talking last, asking people what they think, and asking people for detailed information to examine their reasoning (Peters and Austin 1985, p 447–465).

Because institutional food and nutrition departments are not geographically contained, MBWA is an essential technique for department heads and other dietetics leaders. The technique is also useful for dietetics professionals in self-contained units, such as counseling centers, home care agencies, and public health departments. Historically, when hospital foodservices were decentralized, administrative dietitians made frequent, probing rounds of the floor kitchens. They supervised and evaluated patient foodservices. A few remnants of this approach remain today, and some institutions, once centralized, are going back to a decentralized foodservice system. There may be some bad feelings among staff regarding the issue of supervisory rounds in dietetics departments. Most foodservice managers, however, maintain that making rounds is an effective supervisory technique.

Visiting nutrition care units or other stations in the network to see what is happening and to be accessible to staff is important. It conveys a message of caring and support. Unless presented with a dramatic problem, the dietetics leader should withhold criticism. If a problem is discovered, it can be dealt with later and on more general terms. The leader who makes rounds of the galleys and clears refrigerators of outdated items is not nearly as successful as the one who ignores the outdated items. Later the leader analyzes why unused items have accumulated and what obstacles in the environment led to this problem. The leader can use rounds to facilitate change for staff, not to take a punitive approach, which engenders guilt and lowers self-esteem.

Norms

Norms are habits of the organization. Like social networks and organizational structure, they have a strong influence on the behaviors of everyone in the organization. Norms are intangible. Without an attentive, objective analysis of norms, most people are not aware of them. The best way to understand norms is by example.

In some organizations, it may be acceptable behavior to point fingers and blame others. Doing this may result in the person successfully relinquishing responsibility for a task. In dietetics, this can be seen at all levels. Because dietetics departments are usually responsible for all foodservices within the healthcare institution, the success of the department depends on the cooperation of many other departments. Many problems with these other departments may exist and many are left unsolved. Dietetics managers can then blame other departments and not accept responsibility for solutions. A common example is the delivery of patient trays. In many institutions nursing personnel deliver the trays. Patients may complain about food temperatures. In some dietetics departments, it is an acceptable norm to simply blame nursing services, and continue to criticize lack of promptness in tray delivery, rather than conduct a quality probe to determine the root of the problem. In other dietetics departments, it is not acceptable to blame others, and the dietetics department takes the lead in addressing the problem (Lathrop 1993, p 153).

Norms may at times conflict with the organizational/departmental vision. The vision of the dietetics department may be that continuous quality improvement (CQI) is expected of everyone. It is then everyone's responsibility not only to provide high-quality care and services to patients and other "customers" but also to participate actively in the quality improvement program. However, the norm might be that quality improvement is viewed as the problem of the CQI coordinator and dietitians on each unit.

Organizational Structure

The use of the term *structure* here will mean:

> the underlying interacting variables in a system that organize it in a particular and unique manner. This underlying structure consists of the prescribed organization (its stated goals, policies, procedures, and formal hierarchies), and the collective human attitudes (expectations, motivations, talents, and interpersonal relationships). It is the interaction between the prescribed and the human elements of structure that tend to drive organizations toward or from their desired destination (Shandler 1986, 124).

Structure affects how people in the organization behave; thus it can accelerate or inhibit movement toward organizational goals. Human behaviors (in dietetics) are affected by a number of organizational variables, including recruitment and hiring practices, staff development procedures, the appraisal and control system, the nutrition care delivery system, and the financial system. These variables may have either positive or negative influences on behavior.

Types of Social Architecture

Three types of social architecture classify 95 percent of all organizations (Table 6-1) (Bennis and Nanus 1985, p 118–138). *Formalistic* organizations, the major organizational model of the industrialized world, combine decentralized operations with centralized policy and financial control. Decisions are made by people in positions of authority. Control is exerted by written rules, regulations, laws, and a formalized system of rewards and punishment. Power is vested in superior positions in the hierarchy. Employees are expected to comply with authoritative decisions. Promotion and growth are based on loyalty, following the established order, and fitting in.

In *collegial* organizations, group discussion and agreement form the method of decision making. Controls occur through interpersonal relationships and commitment to groups. Power, influence, and status exist through peer recognition, not hierarchical position. Information exchange is verbal and face-to-face. In decision making, the group values consensus and avoids failing to reach consensus. Personal growth occurs through peer group membership.

Personalistic social architectures are found primarily in "young," high-growth organizations. They place emphasis on the individual. In personalistic organizations, decisions arise from within the individual. Control occurs from within the person; power is derived from the person. The desired end is self-actualization, with growth occurring through acting on self-awareness.

Table 6-1. Three Styles of Social Architecture

Values and Behaviors	Formalistic	Collegial	Personalistic
Basis for decision	Direction from authority	Discussion, agreement	Directions from within
Source of power	Superior	What "we" think and feel	What I think and feel
Forms of control	Rules, laws, rewards, punishments	Interpersonal, group commitments	Actions aligned with self-concept
Desired end	Compliance	Consensus	Self-actualization
To be avoided	Deviation from authoritative direction; taking risks	Failure to reach consensus	Not being true to oneself
Position relative to others	Hierarchical	Peer	Individual
Human relationships	Structured	Group-oriented	Individual-oriented
Basis for growth	Following the established order	Peer group membership	Acting on awareness of self

From W Bennis and B Nanus, *Leaders: Strategies for Taking Charge* (New York: Harper & Row; 1985), p. 135. Copyright by Warren Bennis and Burt Nanus. Reprinted by permission.

Foodservice departments are most often characterized by the formalistic type of social architecture. Gilbert and Sneed (1992) found in a study of 423 foodservice employees that the predominant culture was bureaucratic. Among these employees, job satisfaction and organizational commitment were higher in organizations with collegial and innovative cultures. There was no correlation between the organizational culture and absenteeism, turnover, or productivity. The findings, however, support the idea that a change in workplace social architecture can have a major influence on employee behaviors and outcomes. Such changes are important at a time when dysfunctional hospital cultures exist in many healthcare institutions. A new social architecture is needed in healthcare organizations to achieve the new vision embodied in such approaches as "continuous quality improvement, benchmarking, outcome management, employee participation, project and work teams, and systematic staff and management development" (Sovie 1993).

Foodservice and nutrition departments most often exist within a healthcare facility with the same style. Thus, designing a new social architecture for an entire dietetics department would be constrained by the entire organization's willingness to change, not just the department's. The identification of nutrition services as separate departments and the movement of many nutrition services to nonhospital settings provide opportunities to design new social networks for foodservice and nutrition services personnel. These new networks combine elements of both collegial and personalistic social architecture with a new concept: the semiautonomous work group.

The Semiautonomous Nutrition Team

Healthcare executives are encouraged to foster integration throughout the organization. One aspect of such integration is autonomous work teams (Beckman 1993). Lashbrook (1986, p 127) succinctly described the "positive work culture" that emanates from the redesign of the social architecture and creation of semiautonomous work groups:

> A positive work culture is characterized by members of a work unit perceiving themselves to be satisfied with themselves, their jobs, their co-workers, and the way they are managed, and by using as evidence for their levels of satisfaction the norms of the work unit with respect to communication about mission, goals, feedback, rewards, and support.

In a positive work culture, the leader wants to build a climate of success and excellence. In redesigning a nutrition service department's social architecture, the leader considers not only what is good for the department but also what is good for the overall organization. Permeating the entire design is a firm belief in the value of the nutrition care services rendered. This is true within the institution and is perceived by patients.

The elements of the following design may seem like a brave new world to some. The design is presented as a vision—one that is realistic and credible over time. It is hampered by many organizational and political constraints. On paper these constraints may seem simple and straightforward. In the real struggles to achieve this vision, however, they are not. Nevertheless, examples of such transformational leadership can be found in the literature (Stout-Shaffer and Larrabee 1992).

In the proposed design, each nutrition care unit is a semiautonomous work unit with its own unique vision and goals, which are consistent with and contribute to the vision and goals of the overall department and organization. Each unit is given as much freedom as possible to make decisions for itself in a democratic fashion. Foodservice managers, staff dietitians, dietetic technicians, and other dietetics personnel discuss and reach consensus on decisions affecting their practice and the services provided to patients and others. The decentralized designs currently in place in many dietetics organizations do not embrace this form of decision making. Generally, the department head or clinical nutrition manager retains the majority of the delegated decisions in most decentralized designs. Shared governance models have begun to embrace democratic decision making. For the most part, however, these models are implemented on a department-wide basis rather than being unit-based.

The members of the work group can be solely dietetics personnel. However, in patient-focused hospitals, dietetics personnel may belong to work groups that include physicians, pharmacists, nurses, respiratory therapists, social workers, secretaries, and patient care technicians. Certainly, this second design is not as prevalent as the first, but is being adopted in more institutions (Lathrop 1993, p 145–146).

Decentralization vs Semiautonomous Work Units

Dietetics is in a favorable position to design itself around semiautonomous work groups in that it is already organized into discrete units that provide specific functions or care for a select group of clients. The idea of the semiautonomous work group is, in fact, a logical extension of the present movement toward patient-focused care. In the traditional decentralized design, though, nutrition care units are at the bottom of a hierarchical organizational chart (Fig 6-1). As semiautonomous work groups, nutrition care units are better illustrated surrounding a core of centralized leadership and staff functions. They absorb from this core the requisite support and resources. The units and the central core have mutual influence on one another (Fig 6-2). The work units—some that are geographically remote from the organization (such as outpatient nutrition services, satellite primary care centers, and skilled nursing facilities) and some that are near the central core—would interact with one another and the central core as needed via electronic connections. Each nutrition care unit should complement the healthcare team that serves a common patient population.

Figure 6-1. Traditional hierarchical organizational chart of a dietetics department.

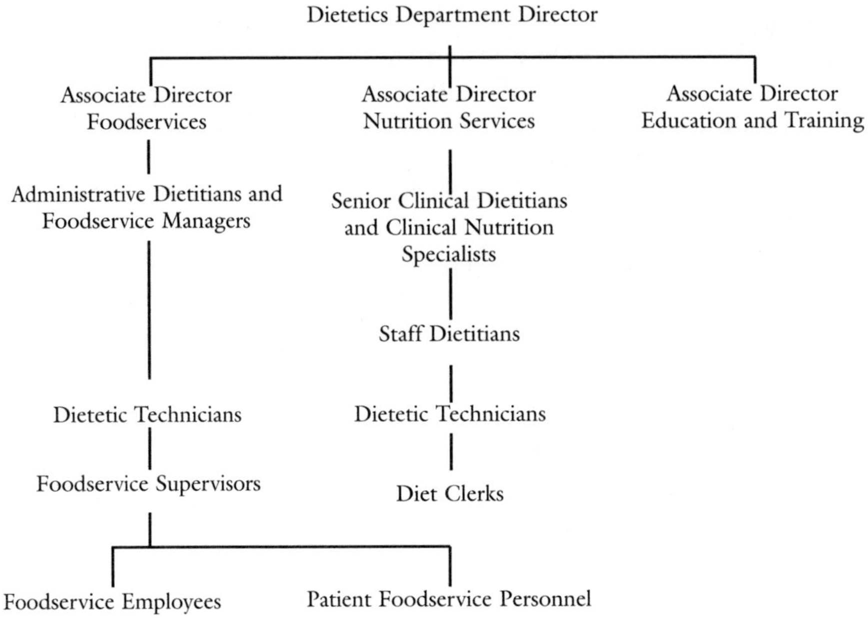

Figure 6-2. Organizational design of semiautonomous work units.

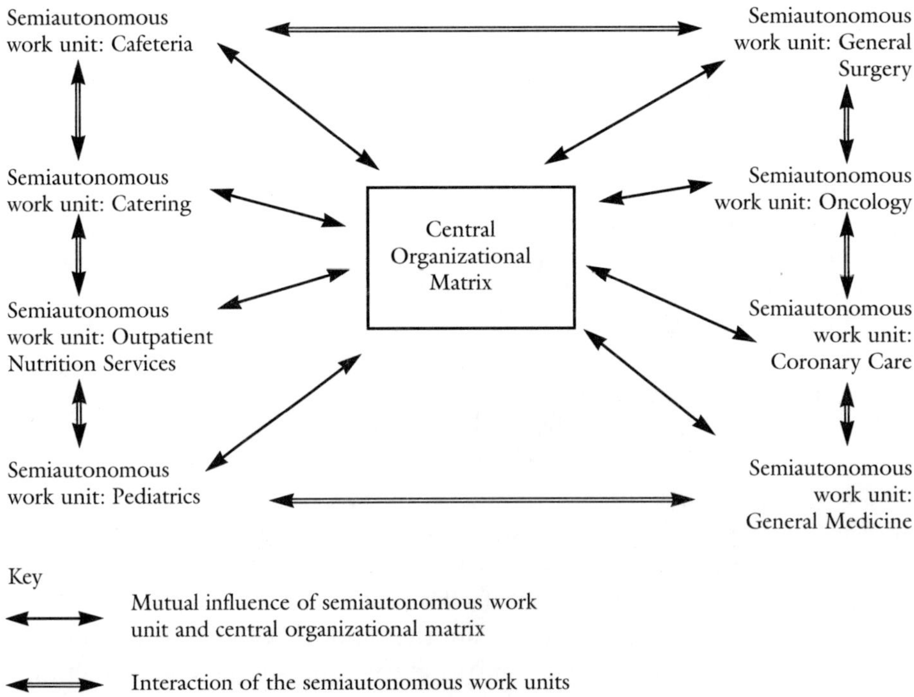

New Role for Managers

Implementation of this design will lead to a reassessment of the number and roles of middle managers, including clinical nutrition managers. Computers and communication links that bind together the semiautonomous work units and the central core will be cheaper than a middle management layer in today's hierarchical organizations. In fact, a number of healthcare institutions have already eliminated clinical nutrition management and other middle management positions. Electronic technology and self-contained patient care units will soon replace many of the communication, processing, and coordinating functions of the traditional clinical nutrition managers. What will be required instead are strong leader-managers for each nutrition care work unit. In many settings, these dietetics leaders will report directly to the patient care unit director and will be part of the decision-making body for issues that affect the respective patient care unit (Lathrop 1993, p 143–157). With this change will come a redefinition of power in the organization. There will be an emphasis on the empowerment of all rather than placing power in the hands of the few managerial elite. This change entails a belief that power is not a limited resource, but one that grows when more people share it.

People occupying staff positions, such as education coordinators, computer support personnel, researchers, and so on, will act as consultants. For example, each patient care unit will be responsible for its own quality improvement initiatives, standards of practice, staff development, and research activities. However, those holding staff positions may be available to consult, to develop personnel, and to pull together statistics and broad policies for all patient care units.

New Roles for Dietetics Personnel

The foremost concern in redesigning a nutrition service unit's social architecture is the role and function of professionals. This relates specifically to the dietitians as well as to others (eg, clinical nutrition specialists and dietetic technicians). It is essential that the value of medical nutrition therapy be recognized and that the talents of all dietetics personnel be used effectively. Although there are no proven formulas for ensuring the best possible use of the talents and skills of all dietetics personnel, there are some important guidelines to consider when redesigning a nutrition service department:

1. Dietitians should be spending as much time as possible in doing the tasks that cannot be delegated to others, such as nutrition assessment, planning, complex nutrition counseling, and evaluation.
2. The daily routine tasks, such as screening and simple diet instructions,

are best delegated to others. However, dietitians should establish systems and protocols and supervise other nutrition care personnel. Dietitians need to retain responsibility for the overall quality of nutrition care provided.

3. Personnel other than the dietitian can participate in the delivery of nutrition care services. In situations where cross-training occurs, the dietitian may train other caregivers to screen for nutritional risk and provide general nutrition education to patients and families.

One of the major challenges in moving toward semiautonomous nutrition service units will be to develop professional dietetics staff. Decisions cannot simply be delegated. Supporting and developing the decision-making skills of all staff will facilitate thoughtful and wise deliberations and decisions at the unit level. Much emphasis has been placed on developing the leadership skills of dietitians, yet in many instances this has failed (Schiller et al 1993). However, even less emphasis has been given to the development of the entire staff to support their decision-making skills. Department heads and nutrition care managers need to look closely at their commitment to the growth and development of staff dietitians and to the entire staff. This means that formal instruction will be needed in topics such as transformational leadership, decision making, change, creativity, and innovation.

How Work Groups Are Paid

Ideally, a semiautonomous nutrition team receives pay and rewards based on the revenue generated by the work group. In some situations outside of hospitals, such as the sales department of a medical nutrition products industry, this is possible. However, it is not possible in healthcare given the current financial management systems; in most cases dietetics services are still viewed primarily as expense centers. Major changes in healthcare financing would be needed for each work unit to be paid independently. However, a system of rewards could be based on revenue generation, improvements in quality care, and/or reduced length of stay.

Table 6-2 summarizes the elements of the social architecture of semiautonomous work units. Comparing this to the elements of the three most commonly found social architectures (Table 6-1) further exemplifies how semiautonomous nutrition care will function in the future.

Specific Organizational Designs

In this section, three specific organizational designs will be considered. The first is participatory management, which is becoming more popular in healthcare organizations. This popularity mirrors a similar move in other

Table 6-2. Social Architecture of Semiautonomous Work Units

Values and Behaviors	Semiautonomous Work Unit Style
Basis for decisions	Discussion, agreement, democratic, consensus, decentralization
Source of power	Empowerment of the work group
Forms of control	Interpersonal, group commitments; individual and group rewards
Desired end	Alignment, creativity, innovation
To be avoided	Poor team functioning
Position relative to others	Peer, value of the individual within the work group
Human relationships	Group- and individual-oriented
Basis for growth	Peer group membership Acting on awareness of self

organizations toward the involvement of workers in decision making. The second design is a particular form of participatory management in which the dietitian functions as a member of cross-trained, patient-focused teams. The third design considered is parallel organizations.

Participatory Management

Participatory management has many definitions, but most of these definitions have a common element; that is, participatory management involves joint decision making by a team of two or more people. Decisions made by the team can include setting goals, solving problems, making recommendations, planning, generating alternative courses of action, making changes, or producing a unit of work. Kanter (1982, p 6) emphasized that the team in a participatory approach is fully informed and fully consulted.

Obviously, participatory management is not autocratic decision making. A finer distinction is that it is not delegation. In delegating, the manager keeps control over what is being delegated and the final goals of the delegated activity. Similarly, managers who canvass employees' opinions and consult employees are demonstrating a consultative management approach. But this is not participatory management (Kanter 1982, p 6).

The basic principle of participatory management, regardless of its form, is that employees who will be affected by a decision have some formal way to contribute to the decision. This input is seriously considered and becomes part of the final decision.

Forms of Participatory Management. As stated, there are many forms of participatory management. It is not a single mechanism or a particular program. Programs such as quality circles are popular forms of participatory management (Mullins and Schmele 1993). Quality circles, which were adopted from Japan, provide specific guidance for how employees at all organizational levels can participate in decision making, thus improving the productivity of their work units. Some informal processes, such as the daily or weekly meeting of the management team to make a joint decision, are other examples of participatory management.

In dietetics, participatory management can occur at the unit level. Consulting dietitians can involve dietary managers or other health professionals in the decision-making process. Staff dietitians can form groups of dietetic technicians and other support personnel to make decisions about a variety of issues, including the delivery of nutrition services, quality improvement activities, and scheduling policies. Participatory management can also occur at the departmental level. In this case, it is difficult to have every employee contribute to every decision that is made in a participatory manner. Generally, a representative group of people affected by a decision makes the decision. For example, standing committees may make the decisions about dietetics research efforts, new policies and procedures for employee and patient safety, or the direction of quality improvement programs. Task forces may deliberate about smaller, more discrete, nonrecurring issues, such as a revision of forms, setting goals for the year, or revising the philosophy or mission statement. Although these particular situations are not ideal, they certainly represent an improvement over autocratic decision making. Given the size of many food and nutrition departments, they are realistic approaches.

Propriety of Participatory Management. Participatory management is not a panacea for solving all organizational problems, but it does facilitate employee alignment and empowerment. The leader needs to be sensitive as to when a participatory approach should be used. Daily decisions will continue to be the responsibility of managers. Kanter (1982, p 6–7) suggested that the use of participation is most appropriate in the circumstances in which the leader needs or desires to:

- Gain new sources of expertise and experience
- Get collaboration that multiplies a person's efforts by providing assistance, backup, or stimulation of better performance
- Allow all those who feel they know something about the subject to get involved

- Build consensus on controversial issues
- Allow representatives of those affected by an issue to influence decisions and build commitment to them
- Tackle a problem that no one "owns" by virtue of organizational assignment
- Allow a wider range of discussion/solutions than are available by normal means (eg, to get an unusual group together)
- Balance or confront vested interests in the face of the need to change
- Address conflicting approaches or views
- Avoid precipitate action and have time to explore a variety of effects
- Develop and educate people through their participation

Likewise, there are situations in which participation is *not* appropriate:

- When one person is clearly the expert and those affected by the decision acknowledge this expertise
- When the manager already knows the "right answer"
- When the content of the participation is part of someone's job description and the participatory method was not his or her idea
- When no one really cares about the issue
- When no contribution would be made by a person's involvement in the product;
- When there is a need for quick action
- When people are happier and more productive if working alone (Kanter 1982, p 7)

Managing Participation. Participation needs to be well managed. Most important, there should be a clearly defined structure for participation. This includes the consideration of a number of elements.

1. Appropriate people should be involved; each situation will define who these people are. Leaders should seriously examine who will be affected by the results of the decision and include a representative number of these people.
2. A time frame for completion of work should be determined at the outset. This allows for less procrastination and creates energy for moving toward an outcome.
3. Defining who is responsible for what tasks lessens the possibility of later conflict.
4. To whom the team is accountable needs to be defined. For instance, in some cases a participatory group may report directly to the consul-

tant or to a leader-manager. In another case, they may report directly to a standing committee and its chairperson.

5. Expectations of the group need to be described and adhered to, including the standards for group meetings, expectations for accomplishment of assigned tasks, and the methods of conducting their business.
6. At what point the team will dissolve, how it will be rewarded and recognized for its accomplishments, and how it will communicate its process and final results are best determined at the outset.

Dietetics Personnel in Patient-Focused Hospitals

Little can be found in the dietetics literature about patient-focused hospitals and even less about how dietetics professionals might function in a patient-focused environment. In this section we will first describe patient-focused care. We will then propose two possible models for integrating food and nutrition services in patient-focused units.

The concept of patient-focused care arose from a desire to transform the "fragmented, overly specialized, bureaucratic, delay-prone patient care model to a new paradigm focusing on the patient's perspective and fundamental needs" (Lathrop 1993, p xi). This new paradigm calls for a reorganization of hospitals. It means reducing fragmentation and rigid specialization by cross-training personnel who then engage in a variety of patient care services. It means decentralizing most services, putting equipment and personnel near patient wards, and markedly reducing the need to transport patients to receive various diagnostic tests and rehabilitative treatments. It means limiting the number of healthcare providers with whom the patient interacts in a usual four-day stay. In a typical hospital today, the number drops from more than fifty to less than fifteen in a patient-focused hospital (Lathrop 1993, p 12). Most fundamentally, it means reorganizing healthcare personnel and restructuring the hospital's vision and social architecture so that primary emphasis is happily given to the needs and comfort of the patient (Porter-O'Grady 1992).

One of the most comprehensive books on patient-focused care available to date (Lathrop 1993) describes the deployment of physical and occupational therapists, respiratory care services, and medical and radiological technologists, but alludes to foodservice only in passing and never mentions clinical nutrition services. Thus most administrators, executives, and consultants who will take a lead in organizing patient-focused hospitals are likely to ignore a role for clinical dietitians. Furthermore, they probably will pay little attention to providing medical nutrition therapy to patients. High-quality foodservices may be addressed, because this is a very visible component of "hotel service" for the hospitalized patient. Accordingly, dietitians must take a strong leadership role, educating administrators, nursing leaders, and others about medical nutrition therapy, and demonstrating the cost-benefit of having dietitians as part of patient-focused teams.

One care delivery model is for each patient-focused unit of forty or so patients to have its own dietetics team composed of a dietitian or dietetic technician, diet clerk, and sufficient foodservice workers to assemble, deliver, and retrieve trays and to provide any other food and nutrition services needed by patients on a particular unit. Each dietetics team would coordinate its services with the patient care teams, ensuring that each patient receives oral, enteral, or parenteral nutrition as appropriate and in concert with other treatments and nutrition education as needed. This dietetics team would be under the direction of the appropriate centralized foodservice or clinical nutrition manager.

Another model calls for dietetics professionals to be integral members of patient-focused teams. This would be particularly appropriate for groups of patients for whom complex medical nutrition therapy is warranted, such as pediatric intensive care, burn units, medical and surgical units, and critical care areas. Of course, dietitians who are thus deployed must be cross-trained to do other tasks so that they are fully productive even when not providing nutritional therapies (McKenzie 1994). In this model, foodservice may be centralized and considered as part of the hotel-type amenities provided.

Licensure laws spell out the scope of practice for dietitians. In most states where dietitians are licensed, nutrition assessments, counseling, and treatment may be carried out only by licensed dietitians. Thus even in patient-focused settings, high-quality care demands that dietitians be available to provide these essential services (Schiller et al 1994, p 219).

Parallel Organizations

Parallel organizations (Stein and Kanter 1980) may be another answer to the problem of how to reform organizations. Parallel organizations are flat, flexible, formal problem-solving and governance organizations that serve to supplement conventional bureaucracy. They exist side-by-side with the formal hierarchy but do not replace it. Parallel structures provide a means for managing change, flexibility, and responsiveness. Most important, they provide a source of opportunity and power above and beyond the sources of the bureaucratic structure (Johnson 1992). This source of opportunity and power is particularly important to people such as dietitians and dietetic technicians who are in need of opportunity and power, because these attributes are not generally awarded them in traditional bureaucratic structures.

The committee structure existing in most food and nutrition departments is an example of a parallel organization. However, committees are only effective if they have the power to make recommendations that lead to action and improvement of the service. Vertical and horizontal integration can occur with the use of a defined committee structure. The structure, though, needs an oversight council to act on recommendations of each committee, as shown in Fig 6-3. This structure provides two benefits. First, it ensures that the committee's recommendations are implemented and not "forgotten" within the seldom-read minutes of the committee. Second, it provides horizontal integration. The actions of each committee are known by and can influence the direction and action of other committees. For instance, if the Dietetics Safety Committee recommends the use of a new system for handling trays from isolation units, the Policy and Procedure Committee and the Dietetics Education Committee would need to write policies and procedures and educate staff, respectively.

Implications for Dietetics

Effective dietetics leader-managers understand the concept of social architecture to manage social networks, norms, and organizational structures. They should be aware of how the organization is formally designed to enhance the participation of all dietetics personnel in decisions that affect the staff's work and patient care. Likewise, they should understand the informal networks and how they can positively influence these networks for organizational benefits. This includes understanding the norms of the organization and participating in changing those that negatively affect organizational performance.

In designing the social architecture for today's organization, the leader-manager uses the principles of participatory management to address the needs of employees to be an active part of the organization and to achieve. Many forms of participation can be adopted, depending on the norms and the overall organizational structure. In designing the social architecture for the future, the dietetics leader-manager should consider the proposed design of semiautonomous work units and slowly begin to incorporate elements of the design into today's organizations for the delivery of food and nutrition services.

Application to Dietetics Practice: Case Study

The Setting

The setting is a large medical center in the Midwest that offers a full range of patient services on an inpatient and outpatient basis. Foodservice and nutrition care service compose two different departments, and the head of each department reports to a vice president for patient services. The director of nutrition care services is responsible for nutrition services at the outpatient facility and HMO as well as medical nutrition therapy for

Figure 6-3. Committee structure of a nutrition services department.

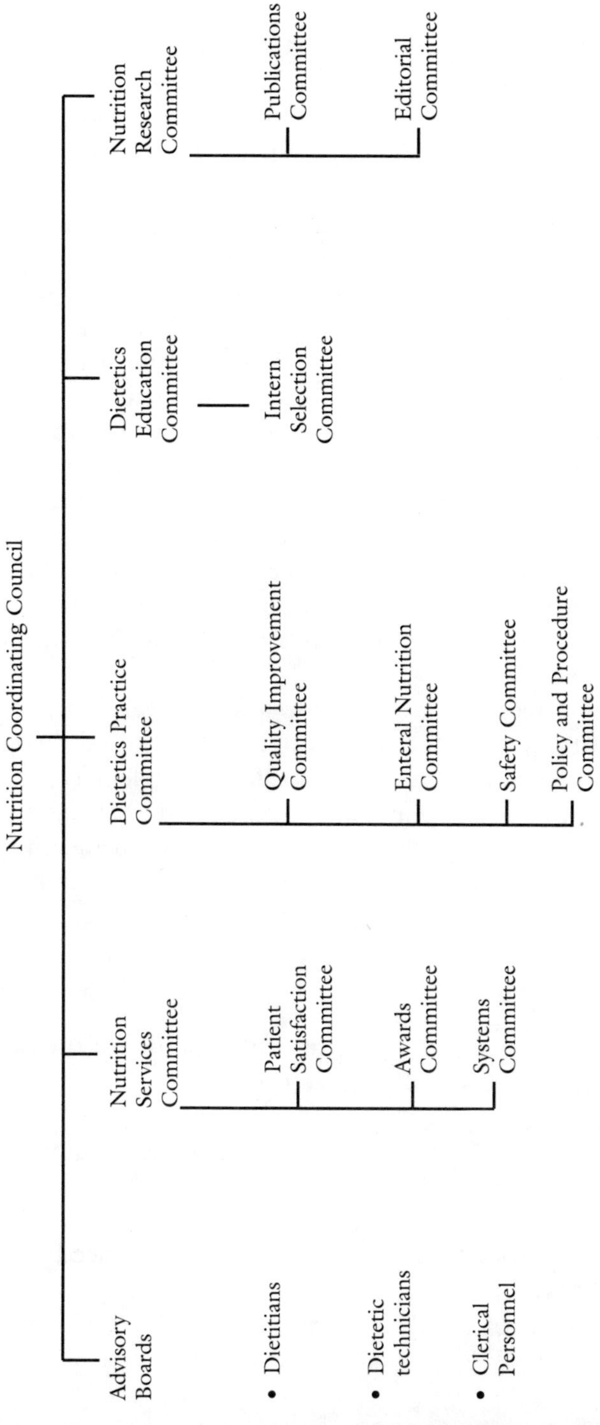

patients on twenty-two nursing units, including three intensive care units, a dialysis unit, acute and intermediate medical/surgical units, and a ninety-bed long-term-care unit. In addition, the director of nutrition care services is ultimately responsible for the hospital's dietetic internship.

Current Situation

The hospital is developing cross-functional teams to deal more effectively with quality improvement and infection control. Dietitians on each unit are taking the initiative to serve as integral members of cross-functional teams and they also work closely with and receive support and direction from the nutrition service department's quality improvement committee and safety committee.

The committee structure is illustrated in Fig 6-3. The membership of the nutrition coordinating council, which the clinical nutrition manager views as the policy-making body of the nutrition services department, consists of the clinical nutrition manager, three associate managers, chairpersons of each of the three advisory boards, and chairpersons of each committee. For the most part, committee chairpersons are dietetics professionals—those considered "the best and the brightest." Therefore, there is a great deal of representation of that group on the council. There are three advisory boards consisting of people in each job classification, including dietitians, dietetic technicians, and clerical personnel. Each advisory board meets monthly with the clinical nutrition manager.

In addition to committees, there are meetings at all levels in the department to share information. Task forces are commonly used to develop one-time programs or to solve a defined problem, such as implementing a new computer system, drafting a new philosophy and annual goals, and implementing professional standards of practice. Issues arising in meetings and the recommendations from task forces are also submitted to the nutrition coordinating council.

Case Study Discussion

1. How would you describe the organizational structure of the dietetics department? What is the social architecture?

2. What are the elements of participatory management found in the nutrition services department?

3. How could participatory management be further enhanced?

4. What are the benefits of the three advisory boards?

5. What norm guides the decision about who chairs committees?

6. Would you describe the committee structure as informal or formal networks?

References

Ackoff RL, Finnel EU, Gharajedaghi J. *A Guide to Controlling Your Corporation's Future.* New York, NY: John Wiley & Sons; 1984.

Beckman JD. The architecture of integration. *Healthcare Forum Journal.* 1993;36:56–63.

Belasco JA. *Teaching the Elephant to Dance: Empowering Change in Your Organization.* New York, NY: Crown Publishers Inc; 1990.

Bennis W, Nanus B. *Leaders: Strategies for Taking Charge.* New York, NY: Harper & Row; 1985.

Deal TE, Kennedy AA. *Corporate Cultures: The Rites and Rituals of Corporate Life.* Reading, Mass: Addison-Wesley; 1982.

Gilbert NM, Sneed J. Organizational culture: does it affect employee and organizational outcomes? *Journal of the Canadian Dietetic Association.* 1992;53:155–158.

Johnson LM. Structures, strategies, and synthesis: the nurse executive as social architect. *Nursing Administration Quarterly.* 1992;17:10–16.

Kanter RM. Dilemmas of managing participation. *Organizational Dynamics.* 1982;11:5–27.

Lashbrook WB. Management as a performance system. In: Williamson JN, ed. *The Leader-Manager.* New York, NY: John Wiley & Sons; 1986:125–136.

Lathrop JP. *Restructuring Health Care: The Patient-Focused Paradigm.* San Francisco, Calif: Jossey-Bass Publishers; 1993.

McDaniel C, Stumpf L. The organizational culture: implications for nursing service. *Journal of Nursing Administration.* 1993;23:54–59.

McKenzie L. Cross-functional teams in health care organizations. *Health Care Supervisor.* 1994;12:1–10.

Mullins D, Schmele JA. Reconsideration of the quality circle process as a contemporary management strategy. *Health Care Supervisor.* 1993;12:14–22.

Nystrom PC. Organizational cultures, strategies, and commitments in health care organizations. *Health Care Management Review.* 1993;18:43–49.

Peters TJ, Austin N. *A Passion for Excellence: The Leadership Difference.* New York, NY: Warner Communications; 1985.

Peters TJ, Waterman RH. *In Search of Excellence: Lessons From America's Best-Run Companies.* New York: Warner Communications; 1982.

Pheysey DC. *Organizational Cultures: Types and Transformations.* New York: Routledge; 1993.

Porter-O'Grady T. Transformational leadership in an age of chaos. *Nursing Administration Quarterly.* 1992;17:17–24.

Schiller MR, Foltz MB, Campbell SM. Dietitians' self-perceptions: implications for leadership. *J Am Diet Assoc.* 1993;93:868–874.

Schiller MR, Miller-Kovach K, Miller MA. *Total Quality Management for Hospital Nutrition Services.* Gaithersburg, Md: Aspen Publishers; 1994.

Shandler M. Leadership and the art of understanding structure. In: Adams JD, ed. *Transforming Leadership: From Vision to Results.* Alexandria, Va: Miles River Press; 1986:123–132.

Sovie MD. Hospital culture: why create one? *Nursing Economics.* 1993;11:69–75.

Stein BA, Kanter RM. Building the parallel organization. *Journal of Applied Behavior Science.* 1980;16:371–388.

Stout-Shaffer S, Larrabee J. Everyone can be a visionary leader. *Nursing Management.* 1992;23:54–58.

Tichy NM, Devanna MA. *The Transformational Leader.* New York, NY: John Wiley & Sons; 1986.

7

Elements of the Social Architecture

Chapter Objectives

1. Differentiate between permanent and temporary objectives.
2. Cite five parameters of feedback and how each is used to ensure successful feedback in the organization.
3. Describe the primary purpose of performance appraisal systems.
4. List ways to manage both a monetary and nonmonetary reward system.
5. Discuss the importance of providing a supportive environment.
6. Discuss why the development of people in the organization is often neglected.

Introduction

To design, shape, and remodel the social architecture, the leader is concerned with specific managerial tasks that are part of the overall social architecture. These elements are relevant to the social architecture of both today's and tomorrow's food, nutrition, and dietetics departments or units. These factors can be viewed as part of human resource management and include vision, goals, selection and placement of personnel, feedback, appraisal, rewards, support, and development.

These elements should be internally consistent; however, internal consistency seldom exists in any organization or department, because each element is usually developed and revised in a piecemeal fashion, over time, and by different players with different philosophies and agendas. For instance, it is common for the appraisal system to be developed according to the guidelines of the human resource department. Thus there may be criteria in the evaluation that do not help foodservice and nutrition departments realize their goals.

The purpose of the following discussion is not to present the technical aspects of each element, such as writing objectives and developing performance appraisal systems. The intent, instead, is to present underlying concepts and beliefs about the need and rationale for and the appropriate design of the specific elements of the social architecture. By using the presented information, leaders can assess the social architecture of their own organizations and see areas for improvement and internal consistency.

Vision

Every dietetics professional is a leader. Dietetics professionals, as leaders, are poised to "achieve greater workplace autonomy, recognition, and professional status" (Parks 1994). Thus all dietetics leaders need to develop a vision for themselves and their services. See chapter 5 for a detailed discussion of organizational vision. It is important to understand that vision is the very foundation of social architecture. Without a firm vision for the organization, the social architecture will crumble.

Goals and Objectives

There has been confusion regarding the terms *goals* and *objectives.* Some people refer to goals as longer-term aims or purposes; written goals are broad statements that are not necessarily measurable. Objectives are then seen as short-term, measurable steps to achieve the broader goal. Some people define them in the reverse, with objectives as the long-term aims and goals as the short-term aims.

Regardless of what terminology is used, dietetics professionals need both a long-term purpose and short-term steps to achieve their purposes. Together they define the ends toward which a nutrition and dietetics unit strives—ends that will contribute to overall organizational success. They are the next steps in the visionary process: concrete short-term and long-term plans for the department. If these plans are appropriately used and communicated, employees can see that their performance contributes to the accomplishment of organizational purpose. Like vision, goals and objectives are held by all members of the work unit to provide a unifying force.

Long-term plans and short-term plans are differentiated in this book as *permanent objectives* and *temporary objectives* (Stevens 1985, p 40). *Permanent objectives* are ongoing, they are achieved over and over again, and they are long-term in nature. Examples of permanent objectives follow:

- Achieve and maintain high levels of customer satisfaction
- Recruit qualified staff who fit into the dietetics unit and possess appro-

priate expertise and a value system consistent with the organization's

- Use nutrition and dietetics research findings to establish standards of practice and to improve patient care
- Provide opportunities for staff growth and development

In contrast, temporary objectives are established to improve an aspect of dietetics practice needing special attention. The improvement or change is usually one needed only temporarily (one year). Examples of temporary objectives might include implementing a reimbursement system for nutrition services or developing a plan for upgrading dietitian salaries.

Determining Objectives

Two opposite approaches to determining objectives are often taken. In the first approach, objectives are written by top management. These are then sent to each department to determine departmental objectives that contribute to the overall objectives of the organization. Next they are sent to each division and unit for objectives that contribute to the department's objectives. Using this approach, each manager in the chain serves to coordinate the objectives of subordinates in the organization. This ensures the fit and appropriateness of the objectives at the lower levels in the organization with those at the top.

An example of this approach is a hospital that aims to be competitive by providing high-quality care at the lowest possible cost. In that case, the objectives might be as follows:

- *Hospital permanent objective:* To deliver high-quality patient care in a cost-effective manner.
- *Hospital temporary objective:* To integrate the quality improvement, guest relations, and marketing programs of all departments.
- *Dietetics department permanent objective:* To deliver high-quality nutritional care in a cost-effective manner.
- *Dietetics department temporary objective:* To revise the nutrition services quality management program to include criteria for evaluating patient satisfaction regarding nutrition services.
- *Nutrition care unit permanent objective:* To provide high-quality nutrition care to the outpatient population within budgetary limitations.
- *Nutrition care unit temporary objective:* To collect data about patients' perceptions of waiting times, dietitian interaction, and usefulness of nutrition/dietary counseling; and to establish and monitor criteria for nutrition care outcomes.

Another approach is to begin at the bottom of the organization, having each unit determine its objectives. Eventually, top management pulls together all the objectives into a common document. For example, a nutrition care unit might want to implement a patient teaching program. The unit, department, and hospital objectives might develop like this:

- *Nutrition care unit permanent objective:* To provide quality nutrition care to cardiac patients.
- *Nutrition care unit temporary objective:* To develop a nutrition education program for cardiac rehabilitation patients.
- *Dietetics department permanent objectives:* To provide high-quality nutrition care to patients.
- *Dietetics department temporary objective:* To support the development of patient nutrition education programs for specific population groups.
- *Hospital permanent objective:* To provide high-quality care to patients in a cost-effective manner.
- *Hospital temporary objective:* To provide resources for the development of patient education programs.

The advantages of the first approach are standardization, consistency, and vertical and horizontal integration. This approach, however, is not consistent with a decentralized philosophy. The major advantage of the second approach is that people at all levels, especially those with the best understanding of the activities of the unit, are involved in goal setting. Without a bottom-up approach to forming objectives in the example above, it would be unlikely that the overall hospital objectives would include a specific commitment of resources to patient education.

The best approach, in most situations, is one that combines both bottom-up and top-down planning. Top management can develop overall organizational goals and expect each unit in the organization to contribute to the goals. At the time of goal formulation, the involvement of as many people as possible improves the process. At the same time, each organizational unit can develop unit-specific and unit-generated goals. These goals are reviewed and approved by higher management, which is then obliged to support the goals of the unit as well as overall organizational goals.

Personnel Selection and Placement

The aim when selecting and placing personnel is to achieve a fit between the technical skills, expertise, and values of the person and those of the organization. This is done with an eye toward the future. To achieve a perfect fit is not easy and most often not achievable (Pheysey 1993, p 84). However, interview techniques (eg, preparing questions in advance regarding the person's philosophies, goals, and aspirations) are important. Involving as many people as reasonably possible in the selection is also an excellent technique for screening and selecting people. This can be done by the use of search committees. A well-selected search committee can bring a variety of perspectives to the selection. For example, the search committee for the selection of a staff dietitian could consist of the clinical nutrition manager, a dietetics educator, a clinical nutrition specialist, a foodservice administrator, and a dietetic technician from the unit. These individuals would bring a broad perspective to the process.

Feedback

Feedback is the information that employees receive about their performance; it contributes to goal accomplishment. Feedback is not reinforcement by reward (the next element); instead, it precedes reinforcement (Lashbrook 1986, p 129–130). Feedback serves to reinforce desired behaviors, helps to instruct employees in the behavioral requirements of their jobs, provides information about what a leader feels is important, influences the content and quality of work-related communications, and can increase job satisfaction. Feedback has five parameters (Fairbanks and Prue 1986, p 338–341):

1. The *recipients* of feedback can be either individuals or groups. It is recommended that both group and individual feedback occur. This appeals to the paradoxical need of each person to be an individual while at the same time belonging to a group. Since so much of the work of foodservice and nutrition relies on group work, it is essential for the group to have feedback. Feedback can be given either privately or publicly. One study found that public feedback is generally more successful than private (Fairbanks and Prue 1986, p 339). However, the leader's judgment should be based on the individuals involved and the content of the feedback.
2. The *content* of the information is characterized by being accurate, relevant (tied to goals), and usable. The focus of the feedback can be on process (how the task was accomplished) or outcome (the results). Providing feedback on several areas of performance, if possible, avoids the tendency to focus too much attention on one area to the detriment of another.

3. *Temporal* characteristics include how often and when feedback is given. This involves two directions (ie, employees should be able to ask for and receive feedback when they need it). Likewise, the leader needs to feel free to give feedback whenever appropriate. Feedback can be provided immediately after an event or there can be a delay. Generally, feedback given as soon as possible after an event is preferred. Less frequent feedback may be given for overall performance of the individual or group.
4. *Mechanisms* of providing feedback can be verbal, written, or mechanical. Again, the use of a variety of feedback is best. Mechanical feedback (eg, computer printouts) will be the wave of the future, although it may not be used widely today.
5. *Sources* of feedback include all levels of managers, co-workers, subordinates, outside consultants, and clients. For feedback to be accepted, the recipient of the feedback needs to respect and trust the person providing the information. The more sources of feedback a person receives, the more likely the feedback will be accepted.

The leader-manager should use positive feedback to a much greater degree than negative feedback. Positive reinforcement is a better motivator and a better reinforcer of behavior because it enhances and protects self-esteem; negative feedback can damage self-esteem. Negative feedback use should be reserved for situations in which there is no other alternative but to give negative feedback and to situations that threaten the safety and well-being of others. Whenever possible, negative feedback should be preceded and succeeded by positive feedback.

Appraisal

The ideal performance appraisal system is expected to accomplish the objectives of making satisfactory workers even better, rid the system of unsatisfactory workers, and improve the distribution of merit pay (Stevens 1985, p 359). However, few, if any, performance appraisal systems achieve these objectives. One reason for this failure is that performance appraisal systems are seen as isolated entities. They are not viewed as one component of the entire social architecture (Dubnicki and Williams 1992).

The failure of performance appraisal systems may rest with trying to achieve too many conflicting objectives, such as both rewards and punishment. The primary purpose of the performance appraisal system should be to develop people. To do this, the transformational leader uses a goal orientation in performing the appraisal. This contrasts with the traditional approach of judging and looking for weaknesses in others. People need goals for developing their knowledge and skills and for contributing to the organization. A goal orientation to performance appraisal has several benefits: goals can hold people accountable, empower them to act, and therefore increase their self-esteem.

Rewards

The successful dietetics leader needs to use the reward system effectively. To do this, it is important to remember that rewards are used to reinforce behaviors. For rewards to work, they *must* be tied to desired behaviors (Rinke 1992, p 209). Behaviors are crucial in that they link the intended vision with actual outcomes. For example, if a foodservice manager is attempting to increase cooperation among staff regarding the coverage of the unit, a reward system should be used for this purpose. People who willingly cooperate with others to stay late or change their time so another staff member can have some special time off should be rewarded. As discussed below, the reward can be either monetary or nonmonetary.

Reward System Failures

To successfully design a reward system, it is helpful to look at why reward systems have not worked. Reward systems fail for three reasons:

1. The links between rewards and behaviors have weakened. Thus organizational reward systems have become a disincentive, rather than an incentive. If everyone in the organization is rewarded the same, whether or not their performance is equal, people think, "Why work harder than anyone else?" In a survey of American workers, approximately 50 percent of the respondents felt there was no connection between their performance and how much they are paid (Yankelovich and Immerwahr 1986, p 413).
2. Managers lack the skills or willingness to use the reward system to motivate others.
3. There is a mismatch between people's values and most organizations' reward systems. The emphasis of the reward systems has been on pay. Pay is important, because it symbolizes material success and provides a higher standard of living. Today's worker, however, brings a pluralistic set of values to the workplace. These values can guide the leader's choice of reward in a given situation (Yankelovich and Immerwahr 1986, p 409–413).

Kerr (1986) suggested other reasons why the reward systems in organizations are not effective. His basic premise was that some systems reward a particular behavior while apparently hoping for an entirely different one. In other words, the professed desire to accomplish a goal or vision is not structured into and sustained by the reward system. In fact, the reward system may be directing behaviors in a different way. For example, the reward system in dietetics might be based on the delivery of care in an efficient, cost-effective way—a worthy goal. Yet the transformational leader may be hoping for not only cost-effective delivery of care but also assessment, planning, and evaluation of that care. If the reward system does not reinforce these behaviors, they will not occur.

Kerr (1986) believed that the causes of this problem are threefold. First, there has been an overemphasis on objective, simple, quantitative criteria to measure and reward performance. Certainly it is easier to measure the number of nutrition counseling sessions given, for example, than the quality of that nutrition counseling. What results is goal displacement. Second, the emphasis on highly visible behaviors lessens the importance of those behaviors that are not visible. For example, team building and creativity are frequently not rewarded, simply because they are hard to observe. Last, there has been an emphasis on equity rather than efficiency. Inherent in this view is that everyone should be treated the same. This approach has failed. People are all different and have diverse needs and aspirations. Treating everyone the same leads to a dissatisfying, ineffective, dehumanizing work environment, which lowers employee self-esteem.

These reasons, combined with some practical issues surrounding the bureaucratic reward systems, point to further problems. Most food and nutrition managers in large healthcare facilities have limitations on the use of rewards. These facilities have criteria for rewarding people, limitations on the amount of money that can be awarded, and rigid guidelines regarding when rewards can be given. The paperwork to recommend a reward often deters its use. Furthermore, the time lag between the behavior and the receipt of the reward lessens its positive impact.

From this review of reasons why reward systems are failing emerges important concepts to consider when designing a reward system. Most important is the fact that rewards have to be meaningful to the employee. Money is still an important incentive because it improves one's standard of living. It cannot, however, be the sole incentive in a reward system. Herzberg (1968) suggested a new direction in managing reward systems. He recommended that rewards be restructured from extrinsic motivators (eg, salaries) toward intrinsic ones (eg, the content of the work itself, hours of work, degree of control and responsibility, opportunities for achievement and recognition, and personal growth and learning).

When redesigning the reward system, the leader should consider two distinct aspects. First, the leader should understand the issues surrounding money as a reward. Then he or she needs to consider nonmonetary rewards.

Managing Monetary Rewards

Monetary reward systems, such as merit pay, cannot reward everyone equally. Most employees will tolerate differential benefits (ie, one person getting more than another). However, employees cannot accept a disproportionate use of the reinforcement process with only a few people receiving all the rewards (Lashbrook 1986, p 131). This leads to a feeling of favoritism and mistrust of the leader. It can also cause employees to compete rather than cooperate with one another.

These issues should be considered when redesigning a monetary reward system:

- Competent behavior that contributes to the organizational vision and goals should be rewarded.
- Rewards should reinforce high performance, not just improve low performance.
- Staff involvement in designing the reward system results in a greater commitment to it.
- Rewards should reflect a person's skills, educational background, and accomplishments. These can form the basis for determining starting salaries and promotions. If pay is attached both to quality of work and length of experience, the issue of salary compression can begin to be addressed.
- The leader should know how the reward system in the organization works. This ensures that the dietetics department gets its full and fair share of the limited financial resources of the healthcare institution.
- Ideally, each unit head should have access to some money that can be used to reward individual and group accomplishments. This money should be used to reward behaviors that are consistent with the vision and goals of the department and each unit.

Nonmonetary Rewards

In a service industry such as food and nutrition, tying pay to performance is much harder than in manufacturing or sales. Thus pay and individual performance become blurred. Pay is tied more to overall organizational performance than to individual performance. Thus people want to have more input into policies and decisions that increase overall organizational performance. Having one's idea listened to and implemented can be more satisfying and rewarding than money. Employees need to see that an increase in their productivity will cause an increase in the performance and productivity of the overall organization. They also need to know that they will personally benefit from organizational successes.

The issue of nonmonetary rewards has received little systematic attention and research. However, most scholars would agree that intrinsic elements need to be used to reward people. This is true for two reasons: (1) intrinsic rewards appeal to the values of people and a higher level of needs, and (2) because of scarce financial resources and the bureaucratic problems of administering a reward program, other forms of rewards need to be sought. Fortunately, most of these rewards can be used at the will and discretion of the dietetics leader (Schiller and Wolf 1994).

Employee-of-the-month or unit-of-the-month programs have been very successful in foodservice and other organizations. The leader may need a small budget to use for plaques, free meals, or some other small recognition. Free, desirable parking spaces provide a meaningful recognition and a highly visible one as well.

To be most successful, the decisions regarding who is rewarded need to be participatory, not autocratic. One way to achieve this is to permit anyone to submit a recommendation for deserving individuals. A small committee can review and make the decision for the monthly recipient.

The provision of positive verbal feedback is cited frequently as an underused method of rewarding people. Leaders can assess their use of positive feedback and determine a goal for its use. Successful leaders who use this technique have to "work at remembering it." A written note to oneself is one external way to remember.

Promoting people, delegating tasks with increased accountability and responsibility, seeking advice, and providing opportunities for further growth and development can all be used to reward behaviors. The leader needs to clearly state that the reason the person is being recognized in one of these ways is to reward his or her behavior.

Support

Support is a critical management function that has not received much attention in the available literature on management until recently. *Support* means to guide and coach others while allowing them to stay in power. Employees need to know that they can seek help from the leader and not be punished. The norms of the department, however, should encourage employees to support one another as well. Support cannot threaten the self-esteem of others. If employees seek support and are met with a managerial response (eg, telling the employee what to do, offering an "I used to do it this way" solution, or solving the problem for the employee instead of empowering the employee to solve it himself or herself), then employee self-esteem is destroyed.

In contrast, to protect employee self-esteem, the leader can question the employee about what has been tried and elicit the employee's reasoning around why something has not worked. By seeking ideas from the employee, helping the employee see the strengths and pitfalls of each idea, and encouraging the employee to explore alternatives, the leader not only protects the employee's self-esteem but enhances it. Rinke and Finn (1990) recommended that dietetics professionals take responsibility for themselves, take steps to enhance their self-esteem, and set personal goals for self-improvement.

Development

The development of people in the organization includes both formal teaching and informal guidance by helping people to learn from events and from mistakes. The importance of developing people, the greatest resource of service organizations, cannot be overemphasized. In healthcare, millions of dollars are devoted to having the latest equipment, but very little time and money are spent on developing people. In times of crisis, money for formal, personnel development is the first "perquisite" to be cut.

Development of staff through formal workshops is undervalued because, in general, people cannot bring back what they've learned or implement it because of the constraints of the work environment. Furthermore, the results of development are not concrete and are therefore difficult to evaluate (Schiller et al 1991, p 112–116).

Changing and creating organizational cultures requires that leaders replace existing ideologies, symbols, and customs with new ones (Trice and Beyer 1993, p 393). In most healthcare organizations today, dietetics leaders cannot simply maintain the current culture, which is often based on outmoded approaches to productivity and the work environment. Rather, they need to transform the organization to ensure that everyone in the department is aligned with the mission, vision, and goals of the unit. Such leaders must necessarily find and cultivate innovative leadership within the department to help bring about changes inherent in such a shift in social architecture. Leaders need to understand employee resistance to such change, and provide stability when many changes are introduced over time (Trice and Beyer 1993, p 404).

Flower (1992) suggested the use of a leadership grid to facilitate the understanding of change, motivation, and team building in the work environment. In addition to the usual "concern for production" and "concern for people," Flower's grid includes a third dimension: motivation. Motivation is shown on the grid as a bipolar dimension running from negative to positive. Negative motivation is driven by fear (fear of failure, fear of rejection) and positive motivation is fueled by desire (desire for control, desire to please). Successful leaders inspire positive motivation and have a balanced concern for workers and for productivity. These leaders can create dynamic work teams, engage in intergroup conflict resolution, and engineer revolutionary changes. When people understand the desired change, they are fully prepared to implement it (Flower 1992).

Implications for Dietetics

The tasks of the transformational leader are complex. By using the elements of the social architecture presented in this chapter, leaders can thoroughly assess their organizations and restructure those elements that require changes. The dietetics leader-manager needs to establish a vision, determine goals and objectives, select and assign personnel, provide individual and group feedback, design appraisal and reward systems, and support and develop staff. At times, these tasks may seem overwhelming.

As mentioned, the first step in managing these elements of the social architecture should be to develop a vision statement. From the vision, all other elements should flow to provide internal consistency.

The importance of internal consistency cannot be overstated. Internal consistency helps everyone in the organization to think in a similar way. For example, a few dietetics departments have a written philosophy that states that dietitians use Standards of Practice, which may include the nutrition care process of assessment, planning, implementation, and evaluation. The permanent goals of the dietetics department should then include some statement regarding Standards of Practice and use of the nutrition care process. Often this is not stated in the departmental goals. Rarely are staff dietitian applicants questioned about or selected based on their understanding of Standards of Practice and the nutrition care process.

Feedback to staff regarding their use of Standards of Practice and the nutrition care process may or may not occur, depending on the section chief. Many appraisal systems include an element for nutrition care documentation. Neatly written, completed medical record notes are relatively easy to observe and quantify. However, few appraisal systems truly emphasize the quality of nutrition assessment and evaluation, for example. The reward system, which is tied to the performance appraisal system, loosely reinforces Standards of Practice and the nutrition care process. Yet instances in which dietitians are rewarded for their expertise in applying the nutrition care process to attain positive outcomes for a patient or group of patients are virtually unknown. Support for assisting staff with the nutrition care process is negligible. In most dietetics departments, dietitians and dietetic technicians would not willingly ask for help in what is deemed to be basic knowledge and skill. Last, those few individuals who attend programs in nutrition assessment, diagnosis, and so on, seldom are able to implement what they have learned in their practice. New approaches are needed.

Application to Dietetics Practice: Case Study

The Setting

A one-thousand-bed medical center that is part of a for-profit corporation is in the process of installing an integrated hospital information system (HIS). All departments will be connected to the system. Clinical and management data will be stored, processed, and distributed.

An HIS coordinator, who will be in charge of the computer installation for the entire medical center, was recently hired. The chief executive officer, who interviewed and selected the HIS coordinator by himself, was interested in hiring someone with computer expertise. The selected HIS coordinator is fully competent with computers and computer installation, but is not familiar with hospital operations. The coordinator has been assigned the responsibility of ensuring interdepartmental communications and coordination. Each department is responsible for implementing its software packages and training all staff who will use the package. For instance, the foodservice, nutrition service, pharmacy, and laboratory will train nursing staff on the use of pertinent data.

In the dietetics department, the quality management coordinator has been delegated the responsibility of overseeing the installation of the computer system in dietetics, including working with other departments and the HIS coordinator. This person was selected because of her expressed willingness to learn about computers and her proven competence in working with large programs. A dietetics computer task force, chaired by the dietetics educator, has been convened to advise the quality management coordinator.

The dietetics department will use two software packages, one for medical nutrition therapy and the other for patient food services. The medical nutrition therapy component of the software application will include order entry for nutrition assessment, specialized nutrition support, supplements, special diets, diagnostic diets, diet counseling, nutrient intake, and tracking of patients receiving nothing by mouth or clear liquid diets. The food service component will include patient menus, diet orders, room transfers, special meals, and planned discharges. Other on-line data will include reports from the laboratory, radiology, and pharmacy. Nursing will not chart on-line; however, patient acuity will be computerized and information will be sent to the central nursing department once per shift. Budgeting, staffing, and electronic mail software packages within the hospital will be available. The dietetics office will be able to communicate via computer with administrative departments, including purchasing, personnel, central supply, and finance.

Current Situation

The first portion of the system is on-line. Patient files, admission data, and the bed control functions are operational with some minor difficulties. Diet order entry and patient meal management functions are now ready to go on-line. The HIS coordinator, however, has failed to keep the dietetics computer information coordinator aware of the progress in the nursing units. The foodservice manager is suddenly faced with the notice that, in three days, all patient information will be available only on computer. None of the foodservice personnel, diet clerks, or staff dietitians have been trained on how to access this information or how to request needed information. In addition, nurses need to be trained on use of the system—a responsibility of the dietetics department in this case. The department quality management coordinator has proposed several ways to train personnel, including reading the documentation, training those nurses, dietitians and clerks available in three days between 10 AM and 2 PM, and making these individuals responsible for training their counterparts over a three-day period. The clinical nutrition manager and the nursing supervisors want the responsible party (dietetics quality management coordinator) to train all dietetics and nursing personnel, as previously agreed upon, at convenient times throughout the day and night. It is impossible to guarantee that this can be accomplished in three days. The chief executive officer wants the computerized foodservice information up and running in three days, because he is being pressured by the corporate office.

Case Study Discussion

1. What might be included in the vision statements of the organization and the dietetics department regarding the installation of an HIS?

2. Write hospital, foodservice, and nutrition care unit permanent and temporary objectives for the installation of an HIS.

3. How might the selection of the HIS coordinator have been better handled?

4. What support and development should be provided for the HIS coordinator and the dietetics computer information coordinator?

5. What type of feedback should be provided to the HIS coordinator and the dietetics computer information coordinator about the current problem with implementation of the foodservice application?

References

Dubnicki C, Williams JB. The people side of TQM. *Healthcare Forum Journal.* 1992;35:55–61.

Fairbanks JA, Prue DM. Developing performance feedback systems. In: Williamson JN, ed. *The Leader-Manager.* New York, NY: John Wiley & Sons; 1986:331–354.

Flower J. Human change by design. *Healthcare Forum Journal.* 1992;35:85–89.

Herzberg FH. *Work and the Nature of Man.* Cleveland, Ohio: World Publishing Co; 1968.

Kerr S. On the folly of rewarding A, while hoping for B. In: Williamson JN, ed. *The Leader-Manager.* New York, NY: John Wiley & Sons; 1986:417–432.

Lashbrook WB. Management as a performance system. In: Williamson JN, ed. *The Leader-Manager.* New York, NY: John Wiley & Sons; 1986:125–136.

Parks SC. Challenging the future: dietetic leadership in the twenty-first century. *Courier.* 1994;33:5.

Pheysey DC. *Organizational Cultures: Types and Transformations.* New York, NY: Routledge; 1993.

Rinke W. *The Winning Foodservice Manager: Strategies for Doing More With Less.* Rockville, Md: Achievement Publishers; 1992.

Rinke W, Finn SC. Winning strategies to excel in dietetics. *J Am Diet Assoc.* 1990;90:935–938.

Schiller MR, Gilbride JA, Maillet JO. *Handbook for Clinical Nutrition Services Management.* Gaithersburg, Md: Aspen Publishers; 1991.

Schiller MR, Wolf KN. Motivating clinical staff: new variations of an old theme. *Clinical Nutrition Management Newsletter.* 1994;13:1–6.

Stevens BJ. *The Nurse as Executive.* 3rd ed. Gaithersburg, Md: Aspen Publishers; 1985.

Trice HM, Beyer JM. *The Cultures of Work Organizations.* Englewood Cliffs, NJ: Prentice-Hall Inc; 1993.

Yankelovich D, Immerwahr J. Why the work ethic isn't working. In: Williamson JN, ed. *The Leader-Manager.* New York, NY: John Wiley & Sons; 1986:407–416.

8

Organizational Trust

Chapter Objectives

1. Define trust from both a sociological and psychological perspective.
2. Describe three behaviors of trusting individuals that contribute to organizational effectiveness.
3. Describe eight sources of organizational trust.
4. List four stages of development of organizational trust.
5. List three assumptions that lead to organizational distrust.
6. Describe research findings that demonstrate the positive benefits of organizational trust.
7. Compare and contrast the effects of trust and distrust in a dietetics organization.
8. Describe behaviors that build and maintain organizational trust.

Introduction

Although trust is a complex concept, the beliefs and behaviors of leader-managers are the single most important determining factors of organizational trust. If the leader-manager is committed to trusting others and building a trusting environment, then trust will exist. If he or she does not trust others and believes that distrust is inevitable, there will be no organizational trust. For a leader-manager, trust is not an inherent part of his or her position. It must be earned and nurtured every day and in every situation. It takes time, patience, and unending attention.

Trust has long been associated with leadership. Sitting Bull used trust to instill heroism and teamwork in his people at the battle of Little Bighorn (Murphy and Snell 1993, p 24). Trust or credibility is built on the qualities of being honest, inspiring, and competent (Berlo et al 1969). These qualities are similar to the qualities of honesty, competence, and inspiration, which ranked in the top four in a "Characteristics of Admired Leaders" survey conducted nationwide (Kouzes and Posner 1993a, p 14). Kouzes and Posner (1993a, p 22) concluded that, above all else, people want leaders who are credible; thus credibility is the foundation of leadership. Similarly, trust is viewed by Block (1987, p 138) as pivotal in helping a leader achieve his or her vision. Bennis (1989, p 160) also believes that trust is the fundamental basis for leadership, because trust is the underlying issue in not only getting people on your side but having them stay there.

The work of dietetics involves a great deal of interdependence with others. Dietetics professionals need to rely on one another and on people in other disciplines to accomplish their goal of providing high-quality nutrition care. Credibility or trust is the foundation upon which individual and group relationships can flourish. Distrust, however, degenerates into conflict, wasted energy, paranoia, and hostility. In healthcare organizations designed as semiautonomous work units or teams, trust is essential for effective group functioning.

Meaning and Characteristics of Trust

Trust From a Sociological Perspective

The sociological perspective of trust is grounded in role theory. According to this theory, organizations are social systems and the members of the organization assume roles within this system. The concept of expectations is the basis for understanding trust. Two expectations are specific to leadership: the expectation of competent role performance and the expectation that people will fulfill their fiduciary responsibilities to others (Barber 1983).

The first expectation means that people presume others to be technically competent in their role, bringing expert knowledge and skills to the activities of their role in society. For example, in healthcare organizations the dietetics leader-manager expects dietetics personnel to be knowledgeable and skillful in their practice. Reversely, dietetics staff expect the leader-manager to demonstrate competencies in food and nutrition and management as he or she attempts to accomplish organizational goals.

Individuals fulfill their fiduciary responsibilities and obligations when they place the concerns of others above their own. This avoids misuse of power and makes honest use of knowledge and position in society. Fiduciary responsibilities are moral obligations that are placed more heavily on the individual with specialized knowledge, skill, and power. For individual dietetics professionals, this means that their concern for their patients' well-being overrides their concern for themselves. Similarly, leader-managers have more power and organizational resources for their use than do staff. Thus, in order to be trusted, they need to place the concerns of staff and patients above their own. In other words, for organizational success, dietetics leader-managers act in behalf of the interests of others, not in behalf of their own interests. This is not to say that dietetics leader-managers are disinterested in their own personal success. However, this success will be realized in the organizational context only when they do not take advantage of their position in the organization.

Trust From a Psychological Perspective

In contrast but not in conflict with the sociological perspective of trust is the psychological perspective, which considers the behaviors of trusting and distrusting individuals. When a person trusts another person, his or her vulnerability to the other person is increased. The consequences one suffers if the vulnerability is abused are greater than the benefits one gains if the vulnerability is not abused. Trust, then, is the conscious regulation of one's dependence on another. This dependence will vary with the task, the situation, and the persons involved (Deutsch 1962).

For example, the daily occurrence of delegation of tasks involves both trust and vulnerability. The delegator trusts another person to complete a task on time and correctly, while at the same time his or her vulnerability is increased. Consider, for example, budget preparation, which could often be delegated by the director of nutrition services to the clinical nutrition manager. If the clinical nutrition manager abuses the trust placed in him or her and does not prepare the budget on time or prepares it incorrectly, the director will be forced to delay submission of the departmental budget. This may cause the director to appear inept in the eyes of his or her boss and peers. However, if the clinical nutrition manager completes the delegated task, the benefit for the department director will be the routine submission of the budget. Although this will increase trust between the clinical nutrition manager and the department director, it will not attain any special privileges for the director or the nutrition services department. Thus, in this situation, the consequences the department director may suffer are greater if the trust is abused than the benefits gained if the trust is not abused.

A person's inner state of trust or distrust can be transformed into behaviors that are either trusting or distrusting. These behaviors are communications with others, exerting influence over others, and controlling others. Trusting behaviors beget trust and distrusting behaviors beget distrust. Relationships stabilize at either low or high levels of trust (Zand 1972).

Figure 8-1 displays a model, based on one by Zand (1972), in which trusting behaviors increase mutual trust. Because trusting leader-managers are more willing to be open and vulnerable, they will communicate more

Figure 8-1. A model of trusting behaviors.
Reprinted from Trust and managerial problem solving, by DE Zand, published in *Administrative Science Quarterly*, 17(2), by permission of *Administrative Science Quarterly.*

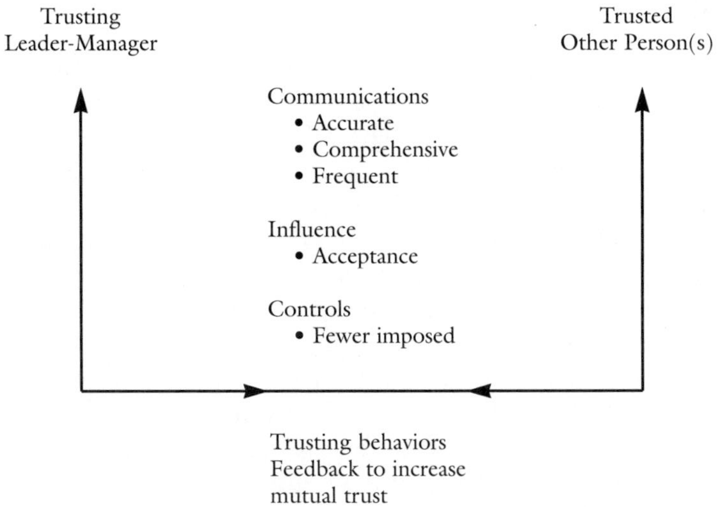

fully, more accurately, and in a more timely manner. This openness of information exchange feeds back to people, who then see the leader-manager as someone who can be trusted. Therefore, they will likewise disclose more accurate, comprehensive, and timely information about facts, thoughts, and feelings. This interchange strengthens feelings of mutual trust.

This model holds true for mutual influence and control as well. The leader-manager who trusts others will accept more influence from others in goal setting, selecting means to accomplish goals, and evaluating progress toward goals. This willingness to be influenced feeds back to others. It increases mutual trust and the willingness to be influenced by the leader-manager. Similarly, the trusting leader-manager accepts more interdependence with others and imposes less control over them. This shows confidence that they will do what was agreed upon.

Since the aim of the leader-manager is to provide a work environment in which people can contribute their talents and skills to the organization, it is clear that only if trust exists can people fully contribute. This is done through the openness of information exchange, the mutuality of goal setting, and empowering rather than controlling others.

The importance of trust to organizations becomes clear when viewing trust from this perspective. The true measure of success for dietetics leader-managers is the wisdom and effectiveness of their decisions. These decisions can be those made by leader-managers alone or those made by a group. If information is not shared and if people are unwilling to set and work toward mutually agreed-upon goals, organizational success will not occur. Trust is the ingredient that will ensure that information is shared appropriately and that will enable members of the group to influence and be influenced by one another.

Effects of Distrust

If leader-managers enter relationships distrusting other people, they will disclose less information, attempt to control other people, and refuse to be influenced by others. If other people also enter the relationship lacking trust in the leader-manager, they will perceive the behaviors of the leader-manager as untrustworthy. Other people will respond by withholding information, refusing to be influenced by the leader-manager, and attempting to control the situation. The leader-manager will now believe that his or her initial impression that people cannot be trusted is correct. Likewise, others will also confirm their initial impression that the leader-manager cannot be trusted. Relationships will then settle at a low level of trust, with everyone attempting to minimize their vulnerability and maximize their control.

Ryan and Oestreich (1991, p 88) describe this development of a lack of trust as the cycle of mistrust, which repeatedly traps both supervisors and employees (Table 8-1). Distrust is devastating to organizational relation-

Table 8-1. Cycle of Mistrust

Action	Explanation
Negative assumptions	Manager negatively stereotypes employee based on assumptions about employee's self-interest and ability to create organizational problems
Self-protective behavior	Manager behaves in self-protective ways to defend against employee's potential negative behavior
Observed aggressive behavior	Employee interprets manager's self- protective behavior as aggressive and closed
Reinforced negative assumptions	Employee believes manager's aggressive behavior signals mistrust and possible manipulation, reinforcing employee's own negative stereotypes about managers
Self-protective behavior	Employee acts self-protectively to defend against the manager's potential negative behavior
Observed aggressive behavior	Manager interprets employee's self-protective behavior as aggressive and closed
Reinforced negative assumptions	Manager believes employee's aggressive behavior signals mistrust and possible manipulation, reinforcing manager's own negative stereotypes about employees

Adapted from Ryan and Oestreich (1991).

ships and functioning and leads to feelings of anxiety and anger. These feelings prevent the effective use of people's talents and skills. Thus leader-managers are challenged to develop an atmosphere of trust throughout the dietetics department or their area of work.

Development of Trust in the Individual

As a first stage of ego development, the roots of trust or distrust can be found in infancy as a result of the mother/child relationship. A sense of trust results if the infant learns that the mother will feed and comfort. The mother becomes for the child both an inner certainty and an outer stability, providing consistency, continuity, and sameness of experience (Erikson 1950, p 247–251).

It is important to have an understanding of the development of trust in infancy. However, the leader-manager cannot stop his or her understanding at this point. More practically, the leader should understand the development of trust in adulthood, specifically in organizations. The dietetics leader-manager cannot simply dismiss the presence or absence of trust in an individual to his or her infancy and believe that nothing can be done to build trust. In organizations, leader-managers are constantly working with people and facing new situations. In each situation, people confront the issue of trust vs distrust, either consciously or unconsciously. Thus the leader-manager needs to understand the sources, development, management, and maintenance of organizational trust.

There is evidence that trust may be easier to adopt than distrust. Distrust absorbs one's energy to explore and adapt to the environment in an objective and unprejudicial way. Hence one has fewer options for learning and growing. Because of this phenomenon it is easier for the human being to trust than not to trust (Luhman 1980, p 71).

Sources of Trust in the Organization

In order for leader-managers to generate trust in organizations, it is necessary for them to understand the sources of organizational trust. These sources of trust are behaviors that determine whether to trust another person. Observing superior/subordinate relationships over a period of three years, Gabarro (1978, p 295–298) discovered eight sources of organizational trust. He categorized them into three groups: character-based, competence-based, and judgment-based. These aspects apply both to the trust of the leader by subordinates and the trust of subordinates by the leader. However, each group viewed the importance of individual categories differently. Table 8-2 summarizes the discussion that follows and suggests behaviors that enhance trust.

Character-Based Sources of Trust

These sources of trust are found in the character of the person. They include integrity, intentions and motives, openness and discreetness, and consistency and reliability. The first and most important determinant of trust for both managers and staff is trust in the basic honesty and moral character of individuals—that is, their integrity. Without trust in the integrity of another, all other sources of trust are meaningless.

The second source for determining trust in organizations is trust in the intentions and motives of others. Subordinates perceive this source of trust as more important than do superiors, because followers discern the manager to have control and dominance over their work lives. Thus subordinates want to believe the manager's intentions are favorable to them (ie, lacking a hidden agenda). Clearly, dietetics leader-managers whose intentions and motives are truly in the best interests of their followers will promote organizational trust.

Along with integrity and intentions, subordinates view openness and discreetness of communications as an important foundation for trust. This third source of trust includes being open and honest about organizational problems and employee performance. At the same time, the leader-manager cannot violate confidences or divulge harmful information.

The last character-based source of trust is consistent, reliable, and predictable behavior. Although both superiors and subordinates base decisions about whether to trust another on this characteristic, superiors viewed it to be one of the most important bases of trust. The dietetics leader-manager, whose task is to accomplish the goals of the organization through other people, must rely on staff to get their jobs done consistently and predictably.

Competence-Based Sources of Trust

These sources of trust refer to a person's competencies, skills, abilities, and knowledge. This category includes technical competence, interpersonal skills, and business sense. One of the most important sources of trust for superiors is the expectation that staff will be technically competent to perform their assigned task. Competency in interpersonal relationships–that is, the ability to work with others to accomplish the goals of the organization—is the second source of trust in this category. Since organizations rely on teams of people to work harmoniously, interpersonal relationships are important to organizational effectiveness and success. Trust in the general business sense of others—their common sense and wisdom about the procedures and workings of business—is the third source in this category.

Table 8-2. Sources of Organizational Trust

Sources of Trust	Important to Superior*	Subordinate*	Leader-Manager Behaviors
Character-Based			
Basic honesty and moral character	x		Is honest Never lies Does not withhold information Acts in the interests of others
Intentions and motives		x	Has no hidden agendas Has intentions that are in the interests of staff and organization Is an advocate for staff
Openness and discreetness of communications		x	Is open and honest about organizational problems and employee performance Does not violate confidences Does not divulge personal, harmful information
Consistent, reliable behavior	x		Acts in accord with the vision and objectives of the organization Considers "past practices," but does not rigidly adhere to them Considers future implications of a decision
Competence-Based			
Technical competence	x		Continues to learn and develop leadership, managerial, and professional skills Keeps abreast of clinical theory
Interpersonal skills			Nurtures relationships Shows concern for both personal and professional issues
Business sense			Develops business knowledge and skills Knows economic trends and health policy
Judgment-Based			
Ability to make good decisions			Is flexible but consistent Learns from experiences

From Gabarro (1978).

* x indicates the three most important sources of trust for each group.

Judgment-Based Sources of Trust

A person's ability to make good decisions regarding his or her work and behaviors more or less encompasses all the other sources of trust. For example, openness and discreetness are manifestations of both a person's character and his or her judgment.

In summary, four relationships for trust development emerge:

1. The leader-manager's trust of staff
2. The staff's trust of the leader-manager
3. The leader-manager's trust of his or her superior
4. The superior's trust of the leader-manager

These four relationships can actually be viewed as two. What the dietetics leader-manager looks for in his or her boss to determine whether to trust the boss are the same characteristics that the leader-manager's followers are looking for in the leader-manager. The most important of these characteristics are integrity, the intentions and motives of the superior, and openness and discreetness. The leader-manager's boss, however, is looking for the same behaviors in the leader-manager as the leader-manager looks for in his or her subordinates. These behaviors include integrity, consistency of behavior, and technical competence.

Development of Organizational Trust

Developing organizational trust starts with the leader-manager. In studies of organizational trust, the leader's behavior was more important than that of followers' in setting a trusting tone in the group (Boss 1978, Zand 1972). Common sense confirms this research. It is difficult to imagine a dietetics staff member being the pivotal developer of trust in a dietetics department. The responsibility starts with the top and filters down through all levels of dietetics management. Although the formula for building trust is somewhat simplified (trust begets trust), trusting and believing in the trustworthiness of others is not always easy.

Building and maintaining organizational trust occurs over time. The nature of the trust becomes more concrete and differentiated as people come to know one another better. Four stages of trust development have been described:

Stage 1. Early in the working relationship there is initial impression making and mutual orientation with a general clarification of expectations.

Stage 2. Stage 1 is followed by more intense exploration and learning with more specific, in-depth clarification of expectations, including the discovery of the other person's expectations and articulation of one's own.

Stage 3. During this stage of tacit testing of mutual expectations, the eight sources of trust are tested to determine in which specific areas a person can or cannot be trusted. For example, the leader-manager may learn that a particular subordinate is consistent and reliable in the technical aspects of nutrition care, but that the person does not enjoy good relationships with peers. Thus the individual cannot be trusted in this regard.

Stage 4. The relationship stabilizes unless some new or different information is presented to the parties in the relationship (Gabarro 1978, p 301–302).

Trust can be enhanced by building an interpersonal relationship between manager and employee that supports the success and performance of both. Such a relationship often includes these behaviors:

1. Giving credit for good work that is done instead of blaming each other
2. Taking responsibility rather than making excuses
3. Sharing rather than restricting information
4. Collaborating on important issues
5. Talking in terms of "we" instead of "us and them"
6. Focusing on the big-picture issues and not becoming sidetracked by differences in the details
7. Respecting organization structures and roles and not using them as weapons
8. Valuing each other's backgrounds and experiences rather than discrediting each other's competence
9. Openly voicing concerns, criticisms, and conflicts
10. Speaking positively about their work, organization, and future, rather than expressing cynicism (Ryan and Oestreich 1991, p 104–110)

Similarly, Kouzes and Posner (1993b) describe six disciplines that build a leader's credibility or trust. Kouzes and Posner explain that to be credible as a leader you must first clarify your own values, or "discover yourself." Since leadership is a relationship, and strong relationships are built on mutual understanding, you must then go on to develop a deep understanding of the collective values and desires of others, or "appreciate constituents." The next discipline, "affirming shared values," means finding a common ground for agreement on which everyone can stand and where individuals will come together to support a cause. In the discipline of "developing capacity" the leader helps individuals learn what to do and how to do it. Thus the leader continuously develops the capacity of others to keep their commitments. Kouzes and Posner also believe leadership is service, where the leader "serves a purpose" for the people who have made it possible for him or her to lead. In this way, the leader is not self-serving, but other-serving. Finally, a credible leader keeps hope alive. In "sustaining hope" he or she has an upbeat attitude, which is essential during troubling times of transition.

Managing Organizational Trust

Three Assumptions That Create Mistrust

Barnes (1986) described three assumptions that, acting together, can lead to pervasive mistrust in an organization. The first assumption, "either/or" thinking, limits decisions to two options and stifles creativity. People therefore view an issue in only one of two ways and do not consider alternatives. A popular illustration of this is exemplified in the decision whether to centralize or decentralize a foodservice operation. When there is a focus on centralizing vs decentralizing, other alternatives may be overlooked, such as the modification of either design or choosing a matrix design.

An even more serious effect of either/or thinking is that it places people on two sides of an issue with emotional overtones attached to each option. The two sides become marked as "good" and "bad," leading to an "us-vs-them" relationship. If leader-managers then label their choices as "good" and attack and criticize those who do not agree with their view, they set up adversarial relationships. This leads to a climate of distrust.

Unfortunately, this climate can frequently be a part of food and nutrition service departments: labor vs management, dietetics staff vs dietetics administration, and foodservice administration vs clinical nutrition services. However, in order for a dietetics department to be powerful and strong and to compete successfully for organizational resources, the us-vs-them environment cannot exist. Dietetics leaders are only as strong and successful as the support, trust, and respect they receive from the rest of the department.

The second assumption described by Barnes is the principle that "hard" facts and data are better than "soft" feelings and abstract possibilities. To defend an either/or choice, leaders may look for facts, figures, and short-term tangible results. In today's climate of cost containment, this tendency is particularly strong. For instance, bottom-line financial figures may guide many decisions. Again, as a result of this assumption, people within the organization take sides—facts vs feelings. Consequently, leaders might adopt a nonproductive behavior style, taking a wheeler-dealer or hard-nose, shoot-from-the-hip, buccaneer approach to defend an either/or choice. These behaviors, combined with ignoring feelings and soft data, further contribute to organizational distrust.

The third assumption, that the world is a dangerous place, entrenches feelings of organizational distrust. People approach relationships with one of two views: to trust people until they prove they cannot be trusted or to distrust people until they prove they can be trusted. If the second view is adopted, as has been demonstrated, relationships settle at a low level of trust.

To develop organizational trust, the leader should first be aware of these three assumptions and how they operate within the organization. If present, these assumptions should be replaced with alternative assumptions. The new assumptions should not be the exact opposites of the three that lead to organizational distrust. In fact, the three exact alternatives, ambiguity in decision making, soft feelings, and pervasive trust, are likewise not consistent with organizational success.

"And/Also" Thinking and Paradoxical Actions

By adopting a view that "things are not always what they seem" and by choosing an and/also style of thought and behavior (such as listening, exploring, and confronting), the leader will discover options and alternatives. At the same time the leader will demonstrate his concern about the organization and about other people.

Barnes prescribed the use of paradoxical actions as a way of becoming an and/also thinker. A paradox is "any conclusion which at first sounds absurd but that has an argument to sustain it"—although the arguments are often buried, ignored, or brushed over quickly (Quince 1976, p 1). Paradoxical actions involve adopting a viewpoint in which the elements in a particular situation are kept separate but are not necessarily assumed to be in conflict. These actions also help the leader-manager cope with new information, confront important discrepancies, and care for individual people and issues.

In dietetics management the leader-manager is often confronted with two concerns: the goals of the organization and those of dietetics. The dietetics leader-manager can view an issue solely from the dietetics perspective or solely from the organizational perspective. This then becomes an either/or situation in which the leader-manager risks losing the trust of either the dietetics staff or his or her superior. To be an and/also thinker, the dietetics leader-manager can seek solutions that are best for dietetics and also for the organization.

For example, what the dietetics staff believes is a desirable new technology (eg, hand-held, programmable computers) to provide good patient care and what the organization can afford may be totally different. To some dietitians, the idea of systematically rationing this technology may at first seem absurd, because only a few years ago healthcare organizations routinely upgraded to new technology, often without question. When sound criteria are developed for applying the technology, the solution becomes more acceptable and appealing. If managed appropriately, the needs of both the organization and the dietetics staff can be satisfied.

Neither pervasive distrust nor pervasive trust is healthy for an organization; both lead to inflexibility. Organizations with too much distrust lack unity, and the people in them succumb to either/or thinking and prefer hard data over soft. However, organizations with blind trust become overly integrated and people lapse into prolonged ambiguity and "soft is better than hard" behavior. Both extremes rely on emotions rather than on data and self-awareness. Barnes recommended adopting tentative trust by performing these paradoxical actions:

- Viewing the elements in the organization as both certain and uncertain
- Dividing and blending these elements
- Seeing questions in answers
- Viewing a situation from both inside and outside
- Learning while teaching
- Finding unity in opposites and opposites in unity

For example, in deciding about the use of the aforementioned hand-held, programmable computers, the leader-manager should ask the following questions about the organization and about the dietetics staff. What are the financial limitations on the use of the computers? Is this a real estimate of the resources or are additional funds available? Has the dietetics staff accurately predicted the need for the computers? Is there a danger the computers could be a substitute for basic routine clinical care, such as nutrition assessments? Are the computers as effective as the manufacturer states? If the dietetics staff is correct in its estimate, what are the financial implications? Is there a way to meet the estimated needs through means other than the capital budget?

This line of questioning can continue until the dietetics leader-manager has a firm grasp on all the elements in the situation. Through this thorough examination, the leader-manager can glean those elements that are certain and those that are not; blend the elements or pull them apart; continue to question and learn in the process; and find a unifying solution.

Research on Trust and Organizational Effectiveness

It is evident from the following review of research findings that without trust, organizations cannot excel. Trust affects many aspects of an organization, including the individuals, the leader's effectiveness, staff motivation and satisfaction, performance, decision making, and communications.

Individuals

Trustful individuals are more innovative and creative, more emotionally stable, and have more self-control than distrustful individuals. They are less likely to feel the need to psychologically defend themselves against real or perceived threats (Rogers 1961). A trusted person is highly influential (Savery and Waters 1989). At the same time this individual has a low need to control others and is open to influence by others. A trusting person has high self-esteem, the single most important characteristic of successful leaders (Frost et al 1978, p 107). In addition, trustful people are more dependable, more likable, and better adjusted psychologically than persons who do not trust (Rotter 1980, p 35).

Leadership Effectiveness

A leader-manager cannot be a transformational leader unless he or she is trusted by followers. The leader-manager's ability to appeal to the values of followers is directly related to whether they trust him or her. For example, one's ability to define a vision and commit people to it cannot occur unless the leader-manager is credible and demonstrates the eight sources of trust (Table 8-2). When trust is lost, leader-managers may resort to coercive means or reward power and therefore practice transactional leadership (Frost and Moussavi 1992).

Motivation and Satisfaction

Organizational trust is the best predictor of satisfaction with participation in decision making and the best predictor of overall job satisfaction. The environmental climate of the organization is more important in determining satisfaction than a person's background or the individual's participation in decisions (Driscoll 1978, p 50). When distrust exists in an organization, people need outside pressure to motivate them. When trust exists, people are motivated from the inside out by being self-directed (Tannenbaum and Davis 1969, p 76).

Performance

Trust has a positive effect on both individual and group performance in organizations. High trust stimulates high performance. In turn, high performance reinforces trust. Generally, subordinates will respond positively with high performance in response to a superior's genuine confidence in them. This high performance will beget a higher level of trust by the superior (Haney 1967, p 12). Further, trust enhances the performance of groups. Groups in which members have a high degree of trust in one another are more effective than groups composed of distrustful individuals (Friedlander 1970, p 397).

Problem Solving and Decision Making

Zand (1972) designed an experimental research project with two groups: one having low levels of trust and one having high levels of trust. He found that in groups with a high level of trust, problem solving was more effective. Specifically, the high-trust group exchanged relevant ideas, searched extensively for alternative courses of action, exerted influence on solutions, were satisfied with the problem-solving efforts, were motivated to implement decisions, saw themselves as a team, and had little desire to leave the group.

Communication

Both the frequency and accuracy of communications are functions of trust. Good communication leads to more consensus of opinion and to more accurate perceptions about one another's views. In the absence of trust, communications tend to exaggerate differences and to diminish consensus of opinion. Distortion of communication occurs if the transmitter of information is distrusted (Mellinger 1956). The credible or trusted leader-manager learns how to discover and communicate the shared values and visions that will form a common ground, finding unity among diverse interests, points of view, and beliefs. Upon this strong, unified foundation, leader-managers and employees can act consistently with spirit and drive to build viable organizations (Kouzes and Posner 1993a, p 48).

Implications for Dietetics

In this chapter, the important issue of organizational trust has been reviewed from a variety of perspectives. Trust is essential for organizational success. It is a vital ingredient for dietetics departments to thrive. The task of developing and maintaining trust falls heavily on the shoulders of the dietetics leader-manager. There are some practical leadership behaviors that will build, enhance, and maintain trusting relationships in dietetics departments. However, there are no set formulas that automatically guarantee trust.

Trust is built every day and in every situation. It is developed through formal mechanisms, such as meetings with groups or individuals, and through activities, such as budget preparations, determining goals, or preparing reports and strategic plans. More often it is developed during the day-to-day, routine interactions and decision making. In this setting, expectations are often made explicit and immediate feedback occurs.

Building trust starts with an awareness of its importance to organizational success and of the devastation caused by distrust. Trusting others is not trite, superfluous behavior. It involves deep soul searching about one's beliefs about others in the organization. The leader-manager can reflect on the question, "Do I trust others?" If the answer is no, the leader should explore why not.

Trust, like other human behaviors, is enhanced by expectations. If leader-managers believe others are lazy and not trustworthy, others will respond accordingly. However, if leader-managers behave in a way that shows they expect trust from others, they will receive it.

Steps in Building Trust

The *first* step in building trust is to assess the strength of its presence in the organization. Figure 8-2 is an assessment questionnaire that can be used to do this. It is not only a useful tool for leader-managers to use for their own purposes, but it can also be used to assess the level of trust in a group. Ironically, however, a leader-manager's comfort in using the tool to assess group trust may be a function of how trusting the group is initially.

The *second* step in building trust is to treat people with respect, courtesy, care, and concern. This well-worn advice often goes unheeded. Again, the leader-manager has to examine his or her personal value system and beliefs about people. Trust begets trust. The leader-manager is thus the first to trust and to adopt appropriate trusting behaviors.

Trusting behaviors are those that support followers, peers, and superiors. Support means giving people both help and freedom so they can achieve. At the same time, the leader-manager should be cognizant of people's need to maintain a sense of personal worth and self-esteem.

By supporting both cooperation among group members and the independence of the individual, the leader-manager further builds trust. To do this the leader-manager can use several techniques. He or she can support the individual and the group by giving them information and resources to accomplish goals. Although in some cases follow-up may be necessary to ensure that people do not get distracted from working on mutually agreed-upon goals, the leader-manager balances this by stepping back and observing. Interfering inappropriately squashes initiative. Encouraging people to work together not only for the benefit of the organization but for themselves will also build trust.

Figure 8-2. Questionnaire to assess organizational trust.
From PR Britton and JW Stalling, *Leadership Is Empowering People* (Lanbam, Md: University Press of America; 1986). Reprinted by permission.

How much trust is there in the organization? To get an idea, circle your responses to these questions. "1" indicates low and "5" indicates high.

	Low High
1. How willingly is information shared among the group?	1 2 3 4 5
2. How much do you trust others to use information that you share for the good of yourself as well as for themselves or the department?	1 2 3 4 5
3. How free do people feel to be themselves, even in competitive struggles?	1 2 3 4 5
4. How much mutual support do you give one another?	1 2 3 4 5
5. How much mutual respect does the group have?	1 2 3 4 5
6. How much empathetic understanding of others' positions is there?	1 2 3 4 5
7. To what extent do people reserve judgment while respecting complexity and subtlety?	1 2 3 4 5
8. To what extent is there an openness to look at motives?	1 2 3 4 5
9. How much are helpful (nonmanipulative) motives prized?	1 2 3 4 5
10. How much of an attempt is there to flatten the traditional hierarchical line and staff structure?	1 2 3 4 5
11. Are people and the mission of the dietetics department seen as compatible?	1 2 3 4 5
12. To what extent is stability of jobs a goal of the dietetics department?	1 2 3 4 5
13. How much bureaucratic inflexibility is there?	1 2 3 4 5

Delegating also demonstrates trust in a very concrete, measurable way. It is, in fact, an act of trust. By giving people power, authority, and responsibility, the leader-manager enhances the other's self-esteem and places his or her trust in them.

The leader-manager's subtle reactions to others speak loudly. Negating others' viewpoints, criticizing others' work or behaviors, and nonverbal reactions of disapproval all send messages to others in the organization. If a particular employee is deemed to be out of favor, he or she will have difficulty securing the cooperation and trust of others. Being sensitive to one's own subtle messages about others and sending only positive ones is another technique for building trust within the group.

Successful transformational leaders rarely use punishment and disapproval as techniques of control. These should be used only sparingly and thoughtfully. If a person makes a mistake, look for something the person did right and compliment him or her on that. Showing someone how to avoid the mistake in the future builds both trust in the leader and self-esteem in the other person.

A *third* step is to communicate openly and honestly. The leader-manager needs to communicate not only facts but also feelings of both encouragement and disappointment. In other words, the leader-manager should show his or her humanness. The leader-manager should share all information except that which is confidential or harmful to divulge. Deciding what is harmful to divulge is not easy, because every situation is different.

Within the group, people need to feel comfortable about exploring and expressing differences of opinion. Thus the group norm should not be to criticize others who express unpopular ideas or bring out negative information. In fact, even poor ideas should not be penalized.

Fourth, one of the expectations of people in leadership roles is that they will fulfill their fiduciary responsibilities. This means that one cannot take advantage of a managerial position. There should be a sense of fairness for all.

A *fifth* step in building trust is to be consistent. This can be achieved by keeping the vision of the department always in mind and using it in decision making and when taking actions. By clarifying expectations and giving people a clear sense of goals, the leader-manager ensures consistency and competency.

Sixth, by always being genuine with people, the leader-manager maintains personal integrity and honesty and gains the trust of his or her followers. Some popular ways of not being genuine that should be avoided are to test people by withholding information or setting up an event to see their reactions. Another action to avoid is spying on people rather than getting information directly from the source.

These six steps for building organizational trust in dietetics departments are neither new nor inspirational. Leader-managers, however, need to apply these techniques consistently. To do this, they need to take the time to think before acting and to consider how their words and behaviors will affect others' level of trust.

Application to Dietetics Practice: Case Study

The Setting

The setting is a five-hundred-bed medical center in the Northeast that offers medical, surgical, and psychiatric services on an inpatient and outpatient basis. The medical center is a public facility, serving patients from a lower socioeconomic background within a one-hundred-mile radius of the medical center. The medical center is affiliated with a nearby prestigious medical school.

The dietetics department includes foodservice, clinical nutrition, and outpatient nutrition management. The major problems facing the department are low morale, staff vacancies, and an employee turnover rate of 35 percent. The dietetics department is run by a contract food and nutrition services company. The current organizational chart is displayed in Fig 8-3.

The regional contract food and nutrition services director is new to her position, having assumed the role six months ago. This is her first position as a regional contract director. The previous regional contract director was rigid and believed in a centralized structure. She seemed to have little influence within the department; the outpatient nutrition services dietitian and clinical nutrition specialists had the most influence.

The regional contract director believes in a decentralized structure, a belief she has expressed since beginning her new position. She is concerned about the large turnover of staff and the 25 percent vacancy rate, and the low visibility and perceived value of the department within the hospital. She thinks these situations are due to poor leadership in the past.

Current Situation

After six months, the regional contract director has determined that it is time to flatten the hierarchical chart. She proposes the organizational chart

Figure 8-3. Current organizational chart.

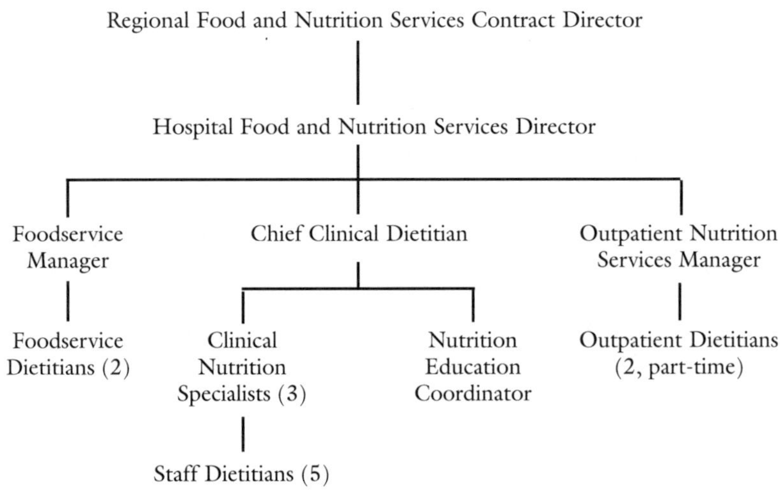

in Fig 8-4. She has hired one person to fill the current position of chief clinical dietitian with the intention of promoting her to the position of director of clinical nutrition services in the new structure. This new chief clinical dietitian and the regional contract director worked together in a previous hospital account. They are seen by the clinical nutrition specialists and outpatient nutrition services manager as having a close friendship as well.

At a meeting of the dietetics management staff, the regional contract director proposes the new organization chart. Positions for all displaced current managers and the director had been previously discussed with the people affected. In the meeting the outpatient nutrition services manager and clinical nutrition specialists are very vocal about decentralization. They voice many concerns about the staff dietitians and feel that they are not capable of assuming additional, more sophisticated responsibilities such as nutrition education program development, specialty disease management, and discharge planning and outpatient services. They cite many problems, especially poor clinical care and patient outcomes.

The regional contract director counters these concerns by stating that the new structure would improve communications, strengthen staff dietitians, and ultimately improve satisfaction. Citing the large turnover and vacancy rate, the regional contract director states firmly, "Something has got to change." She suggests that the outpatient nutrition services manager and clinical nutrition specialists would have to take charge of helping develop the staff dietitians. The meeting ends with two clashing sides evident: the new guard striving for decentralization and the old guard striving to maintain the status quo.

After the meeting, the regional contract manager talks to the new chief clinical dietitian about what has occurred. The regional contract manager says she does not trust the outpatient nutrition services manager and clinical nutrition specialists and believes they would attempt to undermine any changes.

Figure 8-4. Proposed organizational chart.

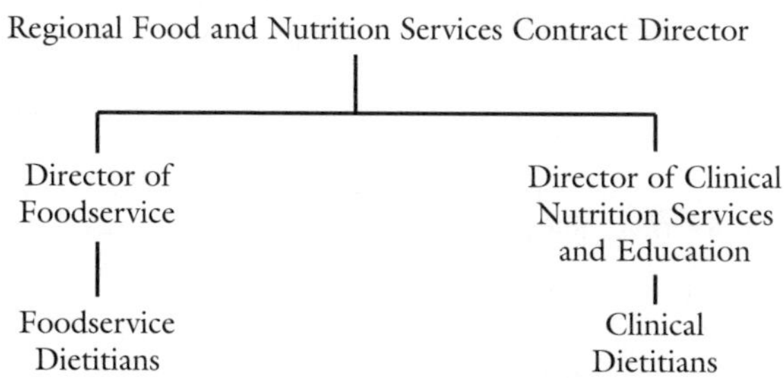

Case Study Discussion

1. How would you assess the level of trust in this situation?

2. Using the assessment tool in Fig 8-2, answer questions 1, 3, 5, 6, 8, 10, 12, and 13 for this situation.

3. Assume you are one of the clinical nutrition specialists. How would you rate the regional contract director in each of the eight sources of trust: integrity, intentions and motives, openness and discreetness, consistency and reliability, technical competence, interpersonal skills, business sense, and judgment?

4. What "hard" facts or figures did the regional contract director use to support her argument? In contrast, what "soft" information did the clinical nutrition specialists use?

5. How could the regional contract director have avoided the us-vs-them confrontation?

6. What can the regional contract director do to repair the damage?

References

Barber B. *The Logic and Limits of Trust.* New Brunswick, NJ: Rutgers University Press; 1983.

Barnes LB. Managing the paradox of organizational trust. In: Williamson JN, ed. *The Leader-Manager.* New York, NY: John Wiley & Sons; 1986:465–478.

Bennis W. *On Becoming a Leader.* New York, NY: Addison-Wesley Publishing Co; 1989.

Berlo DK, Lemert JB, Mertz RJ. Dimensions for evaluating the acceptability of message sources. *Public Opinion Quarterly.* 1969;33:563–576.

Block P. *The Empowering Manager: Positive Political Skills at Work.* San Francisco, Calif: Jossey-Bass Publishers; 1987.

Boss RW. Trust and managerial problem solving revisited. *Group and Organizational Studies.* 1978;3:331–332.

Britton PR, Stalling JW. *Leadership Is Empowering People.* Lanham, Md: University Press of America; 1986.

Deutsch M. Cooperation and trust: some theoretical notes. In: Jones MR, ed. *Nebraska Symposium on Motivation.* Lincoln, Neb: University of Nebraska Press; 1962:275–320.

Driscoll JD. Trust and participation in organizational decision making as predictors of satisfaction. *Academy of Management Journal.* 1978;21:44–56.

Erikson EH. *Childhood and Society.* New York, NY: WW Norton & Co; 1950.

Friedlander F. The primacy of trust as a facilitator of further group accomplishment. *Journal of Applied Behavior Science.* 1970;6:387–407.

Frost TF, Moussavi F. The relationship between leader power base and influence: the moderating role of trust. *Journal of Applied Business Research.* 1992;8:9–14.

Frost T, Stimpson DV, Maughan MR. Some correlates of trust. *Journal of Psychology.* 1978;99:103–108.

Gabarro JJ. The development of trust, influence, and expectations. In: Athos AG, Gabarro JJ, eds. *Interpersonal Behavior: Communications and Understanding in Relationships.* Englewood Cliffs, NJ: Prentice-Hall Inc; 1978:290–303.

Haney WV. *Communication and Organizational Behavior: Text and Cases.* Homewood Ill: Richard J. Irwin Inc; 1967.

Kouzes JM, Posner BZ. *Credibility: How Leaders Gain and Lose It, Why People Demand It.* San Francisco, Calif: Jossey-Bass Publishers; 1993a.

Kouzes JM, Posner BZ. The credibility factor. *Healthcare Forum Journal.* 1993b;36:16–24.

Luhman N. *Trust and Power.* New York, NY: John Wiley & Sons; 1980.

Mellinger GD. Interpersonal trust as a factor in communications. *Journal of Abnormal Psychology* 1956;52:304–309.

Murphy EC, Snell M. *The Genius of Sitting Bull.* Englewood Cliffs, NJ: Prentice-Hall Inc; 1993.

Quince WV. *The Ways of Paradox.* Cambridge, Mass: Harvard University Press; 1976.

Rogers C. *On Becoming a Person: A Therapist's View of Psychotherapy.* Boston, Mass: Houghton Mifflin Co; 1961.

Rotter JB. Trust and gullibility. *Psychology Today.* 1980:14:35–40,104.

Ryan KD, Oestreich DK. *Driving Fear Out of the Workplace: How to Overcome the Invisible Barriers to Quality, Productivity, and Innovation.* San Francisco, Calif: Jossey-Bass Publishers; 1991.

Savery LK, Waters HF. Influence and trust in a multinational company. *Journal of Managerial Psychology.* 1989:4:23–26.

Tannenbaum R, Davis SA. Values, man, and organizations. *Industrial Management Review.* 1969:10:67–86.

Zand DE. Trust and managerial problem solving. *Administrative Science Quarterly.* 1972:17:229–239.

9

Leadership and Self-Esteem

Chapter Objectives

1. Define self-esteem.
2. Discuss how self-esteem is developed.
3. Use visualization and affirmations to enhance one's self-esteem.
4. Discuss ways that self-esteem is damaged.
5. Discuss how to develop the self-esteem of others.
6. Cite an example of a self-fulfilling prophecy.

Introduction

The next three chapters discuss the most important resource leader-managers have available for transformational leadership—themselves. Although leader-managers seldom think of themselves as resources, they are. Like any other resource, the more people know about it, the more effective they will be in achieving results. Thus a vital element of leadership is self-awareness and self-development.

Definition of Self-Esteem

The most essential personal trait of successful leaders is having a positive self-regard (Bennis and Nanus 1985, p 57). Defining this is difficult. Maslow's (1970, p 45–46) classic definition of esteem needs is a useful way to look at positive self-regard. Self-esteem is a stable, firmly based, usually high evaluation of self, sometimes called self-respect. It includes the need for achievement, mastery, competence, confidence, independence, and freedom to act. When people's self-esteem needs are met they feel self-confidence, worthy, strong, capable, adequate, useful, and needed.

Maslow warned that it is dangerous to base self-esteem on the opinions of others. Rather, it must generate from real capacity, competence, and adequacy of task performance. These competencies and achievements must come from one's inner self. They do not occur out of sheer will power or determination to satisfy someone else's demands. A simpler definition of self-esteem proposed by Waitley (1978, p 17), an expert in the area of self-esteem and the psychology of success, is "a deep-down, inside-the-self feeling of your own worth." Douglas (1994, 53) defined self-esteem as "the reputation we have with ourselves."

There are two methods for quickly diagnosing one's level of self-esteem. First, the leader-manager can recall his or her internal response to making mistakes. If the most common response to a mistake is to berate oneself and tell oneself, "I'm stupid" or "I can never do anything right," then one's self-esteem may not be at its optimum. A person with high self-esteem might respond, "I goofed this one time, but I learned from it." A second technique to assess one's level of self-esteem is to think about interactions with other people. If a person continually kids others about their weaknesses, his or her own self-esteem is usually low. A person with high self-esteem looks for the strengths in others and compliments and "strokes" them (Rinke 1988).

Self-esteem is not ego self-centeredness, cockiness, or self-worship. It is a common misconception that "great leaders produce big results, and to produce big results you must have a big ego." Ego, in that context, means an overemphasis on self and personal self-aggrandizement. People with this type of ego development use the organization and the people in it for personal gain, whether financial or emotional (Ritscher 1986, p 68).

A leader who has a positive self-regard greatly benefits the organization for which he or she works. Leaders with positive self-regard create an atmosphere of excellence and greatness; the most significant result, though, of positive self-esteem in a leader is a positive regard for others. This is a pivotal factor in the ability of the leader to lead. A positive regard for others creates in them a sense of confidence and higher expectations. Confident employees can better use their talents and skills for organizational success.

Development of Self-Esteem

How people think about themselves has its foundation in the repeated thematic messages they receive from significant authorities. This is true particularly in the first twelve years of life. These authorities may be parents, other family members, teachers, ministers, other religious leaders, friends, and so forth. Some of the messages received are positive and some are negative, but they all provide the premise for how one feels about oneself. In one study of children who were tape recorded for several days, the psychologist investigators found that more than 90 percent of what children were told was negative—they were told what they could not do or that what they were doing was wrong (Fritz 1986, p 163). Self-esteem is also affected by three principles governing many children and teens: intelligence, beauty, and money. Teachers and parents favor the smartest students; children other than the most beautiful girl or handsome boy are often considered ugly; and children with the most money are considered superior (Douglas 1994, p 30–31).

These negative messages are unwittingly programmed into children's minds. To counterbalance these negative messages accumulated over time, leader-managers can tell themselves positive ones to enhance their self-esteem. In other words, leader-managers (and, in fact, anyone) can act or think as if a different premise about themselves is true.

Affirmations, Visualization, and Harnessing Mental Power

The subconscious mind records everything one experiences and has been told. It cannot distinguish between images, perceptions, or actual experiences. It also cannot distinguish between right and wrong. In other words, if people tell their subconscious that they are good at some particular task, the mind cannot distinguish whether it is true or not. However, if people assume that they are unable to do something, they will most likely be unable to do it.

To counteract negative ideas and thoughts, leader-managers can reprogram their subconscious using affirmations and visualization. Exactly how these techniques work is not known. People's actions, however, are often subconsciously motivated. Stated another way, people's behavior is a result of their thinking. Therefore, what people affirm or visualize becomes a part of their consciousness. This helps them bring about what they think about.

Affirmations. Affirmations are positive messages about oneself which, when repeated over and over again, the subconscious mind believes are true. Positive affirmations can become reality and govern behaviors in positive ways. One leader-manager used this technique to remember names. Over and over again, she told herself, "I can remember people's names." In a relatively short period of time, she was able to overcome her bad habit of forgetting people's names. Positive affirmations can be one of the most powerful ways to increase self-esteem (Rinke and Finn 1990).

Visualization. This is the natural power of the brain to create an idea or mental picture. Unlike recalling verbal images, the human mind can recall visual images with great accuracy. To maximize this human potential, images can also be used to reprogram the brain. It is often culturally unacceptable to fantasize and dream, especially in the workplace. However, the use and importance of visualization is becoming widely recognized. The technique is being used for many purposes, such as the treatment of disease, weight loss, and developing athletic skills. In management, visualization can be used for increasing one's self-esteem, making decisions, and managing time.

Real visualization is not daydreaming; instead, it is picturing and imagining a future event. When visualizing, the use of all five senses is recommended. First, leader-managers picture an event that they desire. The desired end should be a realistic, credible goal, but one that may seem slightly out of reach, something to strive for.

For example, dietetics leader-managers may wish to be the driving force behind a new program to include medical nutrition therapy as a benefit in a managed care organization. They can use visualization to "rehearse" their proposal to the managed care benefits director and medical director. While visualizing the scene, they would use all five senses: picturing the setting, hearing their voice, smelling the air, feeling the upholstery of the chair, and even tasting the coffee. They should further visualize the successful acceptance of their proposal by others.

Harnessing Mental Power. The use of affirmations and visualizations to develop self-esteem allows the leader-manager to harness his or her mental powers. The leader-manager knows that "the only thing in this world you may totally control is your own mind" (Douglas 1994, p 53). Harnessing mental power can be achieved by:

- Observing and recording existing beliefs and assumptions, self-talk, and mental imagery
- Analyzing these observations and determining whether they are accurate and constructive
- Identifying and developing more constructive beliefs, assumptions, self-talk, and mental imagery
- Substituting these more constructive beliefs and thoughts
- Monitoring and maintaining the constructive beliefs and thoughts over time (Manz and Neck 1991)

Other Ways to Develop Self-Esteem

Three further ways to develop a high self-regard are as follows:

- Recognize one's strengths and weaknesses and learn ways to compensate for weaknesses.
- Nurture one's talents and skill with discipline, and set high goals and objectives for oneself.
- Recognize the fit between one's perceived talents and what the organization requires (Bennis and Nanus 1985, p 58).

Having positive self-expectations is another key factor in the development of high self-esteem. A phenomenon called the Wallenda Factor illustrates this. Carl Wallenda was a successful tightrope artist for many years because of his positive self-expectations. However, according to his wife, he fell to his death during a performance in San Juan as a result of focusing too much of his attention on the upcoming feat and worrying about possible failure. The Wallenda Factor is the capacity to embrace positive goals, to expect success, and to pour one's energy into the task. It discounts the value of looking back at past failures or believing one will fail (Bennis and Nanus 1985, p 69–71).

Damage to Self-Esteem

One of the biggest detriments to one's self-esteem is the perceived need to be perfect and the avoidance of making mistakes. Since no one is or can be perfect, this is an unrealistic standard against which to measure oneself. The perfectionist never lives up to his or her own expectations, and so often feels a sense of failure, which then lowers self-esteem.

People with high self-esteem do not want to fail. However, when they do fail, they recognize that failure is sometimes inevitable. In fact, people who never experience failure are probably not trying hard enough and are not taking enough risks. People with high self-esteem are able to capture the energy from failure to reach higher goals.

In dietetics, our heritage and socialization often demand perfection. Yet, by striving for perfection in every situation, dietetics professionals run the risk of becoming paralyzed and missing opportunities to help others (McNutt 1986). Because nutrition is often not recognized as a routine part of medical care, some dietitians are hesitant to act or make recommendations to the physician until they "have all the facts." Dietetics professionals may not eagerly seek opportunities outside the realm of traditional dietetics practice because they were not trained in and thus do not have belief in their ability to develop skills in the new area. Ironically, other healthcare professionals seem to have confidence and interest in providing nutrition care and counseling, even though they may have very limited training in nutrition. To strengthen professional visibility and viability, dietetics professionals can use visualization and affirmation techniques to give themselves positive messages about themselves and the profession.

Developing Self-Esteem in Others

Leader-managers have an awesome responsibility. One definition of leadership is an ability to enhance the self-esteem of followers (Curtin 1988). Thus, as leaders of others, they have the task of enhancing the self-esteem of the people they supervise. Obviously, since self-esteem begins early in life, the leader-manager is not totally responsible for others' levels of self-esteem. The leader can, however, play an important role in either diminishing or enhancing others' self-esteem, particularly in the area of their work competency and mastery. For organizational success, the leader-manager can create in others a sense of confidence and high expectations.

There are two positive outcomes of enhancing the self-esteem of followers: increased productivity of people and enhancement of the leader's self-esteem. People with high self-esteem who feel good about their work will be more productive. Second, when leader-managers treat others with respect and expect success, their self-esteem will increase. As previously discussed, people with high self-esteem have a high regard for others. If the followers' self-esteem is increased, this will result in their having a higher regard for the leader. This feeds back to the leader and increases his or her self-esteem (Rinke 1988, p 14).

One technique used to enhance the self-esteem of others is to use coaching. While coaching may traditionally be viewed as a method used in sports to improve skill performance, it also includes the component of enhancing the trainees' psychological development. To build self-efficacy, the leader-manager can coach followers by:

- Defining clear parameters for success
- Building and structuring situations that have the potential for success
- Identifying factors that lead to success
- Identifying inner sources of success (Popper and Lipshitz 1992)

Another technique used to enhance the self-esteem of others is to look for people who are performing well and to publicly recognize them for accomplishments (Rinke 1988, p 14). This technique is the opposite of traditional management practices, which focus on negative performance and discipline rather than on positive performance and rewards.

Self-Fulfilling Prophecies

The Pygmalion effect, or self-fulfilling prophecy, was named after a king of Cyprus who carved a beautiful ivory statue named Galatea. Pygmalion fell in love with her, and she was brought to life for him by Aphrodite.

George Bernard Shaw's play, Pygmalion, was made into a Broadway show and movie, My Fair Lady. In one scene, Eliza Doolittle best explains the Pygmalion phenomenon:

> You see, really and truly, apart from the things anyone can pick up (the dressing and the proper way of speaking, and so on), the difference between a lady and a flower girl is not how she behaves, but how she's treated. I shall always be a flower girl to Professor Higgins, because he always treats me as a flower girl, and always will; but I know I can be a lady to you, because you always treat me as a lady and always will (Shaw 1948, p 270).

The essence of the Pygmalion effect is that a person, by his or her will and effort, can transform another person through expectations. People live up to the subtle, at times unconscious, expectations of others. This is called a self-fulfilling prophecy because one person's expectations of another's behavior, quite unwittingly, becomes a more accurate prediction of behavior, simply by having been made (Rosenthal and Jacobson 1968, p vii).

Stated another way and applied to management, if the leader-manager sets high, realistic, and achievable expectations for productivity and performance, people will live up to them. Yet when the leader-manager has low or negative expectations of others, they will have great difficulty in maintaining their self-esteem. Thus, to avoid further damage to their self-esteem, people will avoid situations in which they might fail. This becomes the self-fulfilling prophecy—low expectations and damaged self-esteem lead people to behave in a manner that fulfills the expectation or prophecy.

In his classic work, Livingston (1969) suggested there is scientific evidence to support the existence of this phenomenon in business organizations. In his research, he found that:

- The expectations that a manager has of subordinates directly affect their organizational performance and career progress.
- Superior managers have a unique ability to create high-performance expectations for subordinates. This characteristic seems to spring from the manager's confidence in his or her own skills to develop others.
- Conversely, less effective managers fail to expect the same level of high performance. Consequently, people do not perform as well. These managers have less confidence in their own abilities to set high expectations.
- Subordinates, most often, will behave in the way they think they are expected to behave.

It is the behavior, not the verbal communication, of the leader-manager that transmits positive or negative expectations. Merely hiding negative feelings will not successfully avoid the transferring of negative expectations.

Implications for Dietetics

The promotion of one's self-esteem and the self-esteem of others is important to organizational success. In dietetics, many dietitians possess thinking and behavioral styles that demonstrate confidence and energy. However, a number of dietitians also possess attributes associated with self-defeating, dependent behaviors (Schiller et al 1993). Thus specific techniques to enhance self-esteem—affirmations, visualization, and harnessing mental power—should be practiced. The techniques, though not time-consuming, need to become a part of one's daily routine. The more they are used, the easier and more effective they are.

Self-esteem is a key element in the theoretical framework of transformational leadership and in the design of the leadership strategies previously discussed. Some techniques may not directly develop self-esteem in others; however, they do not damage self-esteem. Such techniques include listening to people, giving people credit for their ideas and accomplishments, and using rewards appropriately.

Most important, the leader-manager must make a conscious effort to focus on the positive, the innovative, and the creative. Practicing this approach is important. The leader-manager needs to focus not only on positive individual performance but also on the positive aspects of the entire department and the dietetics profession. Furthermore, giving people sincere, warm compliments is important. Telling people that they did a good job will make them feel good, but telling them that they are fun to work with will make them feel even better.

Seemingly simple decisions might send subtle, unconscious, negative messages to people. This possibility presents a real dilemma for the dietetics leader-manager. Often only a few people can be given responsibility for a particular desirable task or inclusion in a prestigious event. Sharing the prerequisites and including everyone in a manner that is equitable and not damaging to anyone's self-esteem takes thoughtful consideration. When making decisions about these issues, the leader-manager should have a clear understanding of what is and what is not viewed as desirable and prestigious by the staff.

To further develop staff self-esteem and empowerment, the dietetics transformational leader can emphasize employee self-leadership. This concept involves working with the employee to develop more natural, intrinsic rewards that are built into the task rather than just giving the employee externally administered rewards. The employee then learns how to redesign his or her work and world to bring out his or her best qualities and maximum potential (Manz 1992a, 1992b).

Application to Dietetics Practice: Case Study

The Setting

Rita Jackson was recently awarded the contract to provide consultant dietetic services for a 150-bed nursing home in the Northeast. When she was interviewed for the position, she became concerned about the center's limited clinical nutrition and foodservice policies and procedures and subsequent state survey citations. Prior to starting with the new account, Rita wrote the dietary manager, asking her for information about documentation and for copies of existing policies and procedures.

Current Situation

On the day Rita began consulting with the nursing home, she received a resignation from the dietary manager, who left two weeks later. The consultant dietitian immediately began recruiting for the position. Two internal applicants who held part-time foodservice positions applied for and were interviewed by Rita for the job. Both candidates were excellent in their role and were looking for advancement and full-time employment.

After interviewing the two candidates, Rita discussed each applicant with the director of nursing and the dietetic technician. Although the dietetic technician supported one individual for the position, Rita chose the other person who currently held certification as a dietary manager. The decision came as a surprise to the dietetic technician and director of nursing. At that time, these individuals expressed their concern that the person chosen to be the dietary manager was not organized and could not handle the new responsibilities appropriately.

Case Study Discussion

1. How could the consultant dietitian perhaps have prevented the resignation of the first dietary manager?

2. How can she explain her choice to the person not selected without damaging this person's self-esteem?

3. What might be a self-fulfilling prophecy in this situation?

References

Bennis W, Nanus B. *Leaders: Strategies for Taking Charge.* New York, NY: Harper & Row; 1985.

Curtin JL. Putting self-esteem first. *Training and Development Journal.* 1988;42:41–44.

Douglas MR. *How to Win With High Self-Esteem.* Gretna, La: Pelican Publishing Co; 1994.

Fritz R. The leader as creator. In: Adams JD, ed. *Transforming Leadership: From Vision to Results.* Alexandria, Va: Miles River Press; 1986:159–182.

Livingston JS. Pygmalion in management. *Harvard Business Review.* 1969;47:81–89.

Manz CC. Self-leadership: the heart of empowerment. *Journal for Quality and Participation.* 1992a;15:80–85.

Manz CC. Self-leading work teams: moving beyond self-management myths. *Human Relations.* 1992b;45:1119–1140.

Manz CC, Neck CP. Harness your mental powers. *Executive Excellence.* 1991;8:15.

Maslow A. *Motivation and Personality.* 2nd ed. New York, NY: Harper & Row; 1970.

McNutt KW. Avoiding the pitfalls of perfectionism: resources allocation for the public good. *J Am Diet Assoc.* 1986;86:186–1990.

Popper M, Lipshitz R. Coaching on leadership. *Leadership and Organization Development.* 1992;13:15–18.

Rinke WJ. Maximizing management potential by building self-esteem. *Management Solutions.* 1988;33:11–17.

Rinke WJ, Finn SC. Winning strategies to excel in dietetics. *J Am Diet Assoc.* 1990;90:935–938.

Ritscher J. Spiritual leadership. In: Adams JD, ed. *Transforming Leadership: From Vision to Results.* Alexandria, Va: Miles River Press; 1986:61–80.

Rosenthal R, Jacobson L. *Pygmalion in the Classroom.* New York, NY: Rinehart & Winston; 1968.

Schiller MR, Foltz MB, Campbell S. Dietitians' self-perceptions: implications for leadership. *J Am Diet Assoc.* 1993;93:868–874.

Shaw GB. Pygmalion. In: *The Selected Plays of Bernard Shaw.* New York, NY: Dodd Mead & Co; 1948.

Waitley D. *The Psychology of Winning* [audiotape]. Chicago, Ill: Nightingale-Conant Corp; 1978.

10

Thinking and Decision Making

Chapter Objectives

1. Differentiate between the functions of the left and right sides of the brain.
2. Describe three mental abilities involved in decision making.
3. Discuss methods to improve one's analytical, synthesizing, and intuitive skills.
4. List five steps in the decision-making process.
5. Explain the pitfalls of each step.
6. Discuss the relationship of thinking and decision making to actions.

Introduction

Effective decision making is a key leadership skill for transformational leaders to be successful and to achieve excellence. Thinking and decision making are paired processes that lead to action:

Thinking → Decision Making → Action

Thus effective decision making entails both effective thinking and effective action, which is measured by the contribution of the action to the achievement of organizational success. In this chapter, all three components of this model—thinking, decision making, and acting—will be discussed.

Thinking

The ability to think, not years of experience, should be the most sought after attribute for today's leaders (Levitt 1990). According to Levitt, most leader-managers manage for yesterday's conditions because yesterday is where they obtained their experience, developed their skills, and had their success. But today's environment is extremely different, requiring leaders to:

> think seriously and deeply for themselves about the purposes of the organizations they head or functions they perform, and about the strategies, tactics, technologies, systems and people necessary to attain these purposes, about important questions that need always to be asked (Levitt 1990).

The brain has many powers, including logical thinking, sensing, judging, creativity, and intuition. The abilities of the brain that are specifically related to decision making (ie, analyzing, synthesizing, and valuing) are examined in this section.

Understanding Brain Functioning

Current research on the "split brain" provides insight into how people think. The two sides of the brain, the right and left hemispheres, perform different types of mental activities. The right hemisphere functions in the recognition of visual patterns, remembering faces, rhythm, control of large motor movements, music, and imagination. The left hemisphere is involved in analytical processes such as logic, reasoning, mathematics, and the use of language. Physically, the two sides of the brain are connected by a four-inch-long, pencil-shaped bundle of complex nerve fibers called the corpus callosum, which integrates information from the two sides of the brain. How people use each side of the brain, how the two sides interconnect, and how people can develop both sides of the brain are the subjects of ongoing research.

People differ in the predominance of one side of the brain over the other. For example, when confronted with similar problems, some managers use an intuitive process and some a more analytical approach to problem solving (Dokter and Hamilton 1978). However, people can intentionally focus on developing the functioning of the right and left sides of the brain. Research indicates that all areas of mental performance are enhanced by this focused development (Buzan 1983, p 14–15). For example, a person who wishes to develop the right side's capacity for visualization may also find increased capacity for recalling events.

Personnel can be selected for certain tasks based on their style of thinking. Veehoff (1992) noted that certain patients may need counseling from a dietitian who exhibits the right-brain characteristics of deep understanding and attentive listening. Such a health professional values highly the relationship of interacting and communicating, attributes cherished by some patients. Other patients may prefer working with health professionals who are more methodical, logical, and linear in their explanations and approaches to problem solving. Pairing dietetics professionals' natural skills with patients' preferences may improve adherence to difficult dietary regimens. Sensitivity to hemispheric functioning and preferences can facilitate communication and problem solving in other circles, too, such as conflict resolution among dietetics personnel, building alliances with other health professionals, and selling ideas to administrators.

The work of cognitive scientists and the use of artificial intelligence have contributed to the understanding of thinking and problem solving. Cognitive science involves the use of a "psychological laboratory" to observe human behaviors. Cognitive scientists propose that the memory holds information in patterns or sets, called chunks. Furthermore, the memory stores these chunks of information in relationship to other stored chunks of information. The work done with artificial intelligence confirms this research. Digital computers are used to model human thought patterns and to perform problem-solving/decision-making functions at expert levels. Artificial intelligence has been used successfully in the areas of medical diagnosis, chemistry, and electronics. Artificial intelligence uses an analytical process that works in "if-then" pairs. The "if" is a set of conditions or patterns to be recognized by the computer. The "then" is a body of information associated with the "if." For example, in medical diagnoses, if the patient exhibits symptoms a, b, and c, then the diagnosis is x. The if-then sequence of reasoning appears to be a universal scheme of thought and can be readily applied to management sciences (Simon 1987, p 59–61).

McKenzie (1992) suggested that the study of logic is one way to develop strong critical thinking skills. Logic may be approached from many different viewpoints. Logic can be deductive or inductive depending on whether one begins the thought process by thinking in generalities or specifics. Logic may be dialectical, as the evolution of a single conclusion drawn from truthful claims that conflict with each other. Finally, logic may by understood as symbolic logic. That is, symbols and signs may be used to draw inferences about reality. Critical thinking involves the generation and formulation of ideas and the systematic arrangement of these ideas into a line of correct reasoning. The use of logic can facilitate accurate data analysis, foster mental adroitness, and promote systems thinking in complex organizations.

Mental Abilities for Decision Making

As stated previously, the abilities of the brain that are used in decision making are analyzing, synthesizing, and valuing. All these abilities occur in the conscious mind. The work of Adair (1985) forms the basis for the following discussion of these abilities.

Analyzing. This mental ability enables a person to break the "total picture" into its parts. The following activities require analytical skills:

- Establishing the relationship of the parts (specifics) to one another and to the whole (general)
- Determining the causes of problems
- Identifying issues upon which a decision rests
- Discovering laws in nature
- Searching for the principles behind experiences

Analytical skills are developed in school through academic work and are the skills most often taken for granted. Because one's analytical skills can decline, however, the transformational leader is encouraged to continue to develop these skills in order to make sound decisions. To develop analytical skills, leaders need to question themselves and others about the elements of particular decision-making situations in which they find themselves. First, they can ask the basic questions of who, where, when, why, how, which, and why not. These questions will lead to others that will help the leader get to the heart of the problem.

Writing down the pros and cons of alternative courses of action is a visual way to organize facts and facilitate analytical thinking. By having information in writing, one can rearrange and restructure the facts to realize the full scope of each option. McKenzie suggested reading and writing as ways to improve critical thinking. Broad and comprehensive knowledge of the problem area facilitates problem analysis and enhances elucidation of multiple facets of the problem under consideration.

A knowledge of logic and logistical methods can also help leaders develop analytical skills. The science of logic is a prescribed method of drawing proper conclusions from information or premises. One of the major problems in managerial thought is basing logic and analysis on a false premise. Therefore, understanding the logical method can help the leader understand the importance of underlying premises.

There are two types of logical processes: inductive and deductive. Inductive logic is the process of deriving generalizations from specific data; this type of logic would be applied in nutrition or operations research. Deductive logic, the opposite, is the process of drawing particular inferences from general information. The following is an example of deductive logic:

All coins are round. (*major premise*)
You have a coin in your pocket. (*minor premise*)
Your coin is round. (*conclusion*)

In this example, the major premise is wrong; that is, all coins are not round. Yet the logic used could mislead one to believe that the conclusion is correct. Understanding the basic premises upon which analytic processes are built will strengthen the leader's analytical skills and the quality of any decisions. For example, if dietetics leaders base their actions on the following premise, they will not realize success in accomplishing goals:

Dietitians are powerless. (*major premise*)
I am a dietitian. (*minor premise*)
I am powerless. (*conclusion*)

Synthesizing. The mental skill of synthesizing is the opposite of analyzing. It is the ability to see things as a whole by combining parts. Behind this mode of thought is the belief that the whole is greater than the sum of its parts. It may also be called *holistic thinking.* This type of thinking is not well understood. Holistic thinking involves conceptual thinking, imagination, and intuition. Intuition is the only mental skill discussed in this chapter that occurs in the subconscious part of one's mind.

Holistic thinking, balanced with analytical thinking, is important for the transformational leader (Senge 1990, p 68). Systems or holistic thinking focuses on the interaction of the parts and allows leaders to create new futures rather than just developing strategies for coping with the present. One type of holistic thinking is *conceptual thinking.* A concept is something conceived in the mind to which the person attaches attributes. Conceptualization involves taking something concrete and making it more general. A person develops concepts by making them whole through life experiences. Dietetics literature shows that conceptual thinking is valued (American Dietetic Association 1975). The in-basket technique was recommended as one method of developing these skills among students (Sifferman and Hoover 1981). Rinke et al. found, however, that most entry-level dietitians had poorly developed conceptual skills (Rinke et al. 1982), perhaps because competency-based education is widespread in dietetics education (Rinke 1980). Consequently, conceptual thinking should be included in continuing education programs for dietetics professionals.

Another form of holistic thinking or synthesizing is *imaginative thinking.* This is a vital mental ability for innovation and creativity in management. Imagination has five components:

1. *Recall.* This is the ability to bring back to mind an idea of something not actually present to the senses, such as remembering one's twenty-first birthday.
2. *Visualization.* As discussed in the previous chapter, this is the ability to see or form a mental image of something that does not presently exist in its entirety.
3. *Creating.* This is the ability to form a mental image of something that has never existed, such as a new way to deliver dietetics services.
4. *Foreseeing.* This is the ability to mentally see an event or result before it happens.

5. *Fantasy.* This is the ability to create a fanciful design or invention. It is done by altering or combining the elements of reality in a particularly unrestrained and extravagant way.

To develop the skills of holistic thinking, leaders first develop an awareness of its importance. They then deliberately think about a situation holistically—that is, they purposefully view the situation, the dietetics department, the profession, and the organization as a whole. At the same time, they may also use some analytical skills to review the specifics of the situation. It is this holistic thinking that Senge (1990) refers to as the fifth discipline, a conceptual framework for clarifying the full range of complex, interrelated actions observed in organizations and helping people see how to change them.

All the leaders within a food and nutrition department should have similar beliefs about dietetics, quality, the nutrition care process, assessment, patient education, and so on. To achieve consensus on these concepts, it is important for leaders at all departmental levels to discuss their views of the organization and the department and their individual missions, strengths, and weaknesses. If they have similar concepts about the organization and the department, decision making will be easier to accomplish as a team. Developing a vision statement as a group would be one excellent way to stimulate discussion at the conceptual level.

To develop imagination, one must use it purposefully. For any problem situation, the dietetics leader can imagine ways of solving it. When using imagination purposefully, leaders should refrain from using solutions that they can recall or those read in a textbook. The technique of visualization can be used to develop imagination and strengthen thinking and decision making.

Valuing. This is a dimension of all thinking rather than a discrete entity. Valuing involves having a perception of the value, worth, or significance of something. It includes mental abilities such as judging, criticizing, and evaluating. Valuing helps to ensure the quality of thinking. It establishes the truth or reality of the situation and ensures consistency of values within the organization. As stated previously, thinking precedes action. For the action to be effective, the value of the thinking must be correct.

The Subconscious Mind

Until recently, the significance of the subconscious mind had not been intellectually respected. This was due to society's reliance on science and the highly rational scientific method. This attitude is now changing. Today's complex organizations demand new ways of thinking to achieve visioning, team learning, and personal mastery (Senge 1990, p 12). Very few mental activities take place at the conscious level. Most of these activities (eg, reflexes, habitual behaviors, and psychological defense mechanisms) occur at a subconscious level. Unconscious beliefs and values about oneself and one's environment affect behaviors and the social architecture of the workplace. These beliefs can limit or strengthen capacities for success in every aspect of one's life, including leadership abilities, relationships with others, the ability to heal from illness, and effectiveness of communication.

Intuition

Intuition is the constant, "behind-the-scenes" processing of information and imagination. It is the power or faculty of the mind to immediately grasp that something is the case, without the intervention of any reasoning process. It manifests itself consciously as a hunch or gut feeling. People also experience intuitive moments when something forgotten suddenly pops into their consciousness. Unfortunately, people seldom tap into their intuition and use it wisely.

How this inner mind works is not known. What is known, however, is that the more a person uses it and trusts it, the better it seems to perform (Harmon 1986, p 107). Transformational leader-managers can appeal to their intuition when developing their vision, establishing relationships with people, dealing with the complexities of designing the social architecture, and making decisions. Listening to and using one's intuitive mind should be balanced with rationality and logic. Checking an intuitive thought with common sense before acting is one technique to avoid misusing one's intuition. Intuition can be negatively affected by strong emotions and mental or physical stress. Thus if dietetics leader-managers wish to follow their intuition, they need to be feeling well and not under any undue stress.

Leaders can access their intuition and subconscious through a variety of recommended techniques (Buckley and Steffy 1986, p 235–240):

1. If the leader's skills are rational thinking and logical thought processes, he or she can take up a creative venture such as music or poetry. If the rational side of the brain needs developing, the leader might try learning to use a computer or taking a logic course, both of which will strengthen left-brain abilities.
2. *Nondesk thinking* is a term used to describe a break from left-brain activities. This can be achieved by pursuing a relaxing activity, such as exercise, in a relaxing environment. Following this interlude, leaders have reported more precise thinking, clearer vision, and even a more acute sense of smell.
3. Consciously making a request of one's intuitive, subconscious mind is another way to access one's intuition. The technique can be used when the problem to be solved is clear and reduced to its most basic level. For example, the leader can ask his or her subconscious who to

select for a particular job once the options have been limited to two or three candidates. After making such a request, it is best to engage in nondesk thinking. Sometimes the answer will just come into one's mind. At other times, the answer might be found unexpectedly somewhere in the environment. For example, something someone says or an article in a magazine might trigger an idea that leads to the solution.

4. A similar technique is to ask the subconscious to work on a problem while sleeping. Sometimes the answer may come in a dream or upon waking. As soon as the answer comes into consciousness, the leader should write it down so the thought won't be lost.
5. Experimenting with inner listening is a technique that decreases activity in the left brain and increases activity in the right one. This five-step framework facilitates inner listening:

   - Let go of answers that you "think" are right.
   - Empty the mind, quieting internal noise.
   - Ask yourself a simple, specific question.
   - Listen, do not pass judgment. (These first four steps can be repeated several times.)
   - Examine the information rationally and act.

6. Self-talk or affirmation, reviewed in the previous chapter, is "reprogramming" a belief about yourself that is held in your subconscious.
7. Self-suggestion is a similar technique that can be used to repeatedly remind oneself to refer all choices to the subconscious mind.

Reflective Thinking

One reason organizations are plagued with bad decisions may be that managers do not take time out for reflective thinking. Ritscher (1986, p 65) proposed the following:

> The power of quiet and solidity cannot be overemphasized. The single largest problem in organizations is a kind of anxiety and low-grade confusion. Leaders often make decisions based on anxiety, ego, insufficient experience, and the slightly crazy atmosphere that frequently accompanies group decision making. Such decisions are no match for ones made by going to a quiet place, steeping oneself in the nature of the problem, and using clarity of mind to uncover the right solution.

The value of reflection is that it slows down action and thus makes subsequent actions more thoughtful (Weick 1983). The dietetics leader-manager needs to take time to reflect on the foodservice or nutrition care department, the organization, and the profession. These moments of reflection can influence decisions and improve their quality. The daily work of the typical dietetics leader-manager seldom allows for this time. Furthermore, often one wishes to leave the work behind when at home with family and friends. Yet a time for reflection can be invaluable and should be part of the transformational leader's schedule.

Decision Making

Levy and Loomba (1973, p 169) defined decision making as

> the conclusion of a process by which one chooses among available alternatives for the purpose of achieving a set of desired objectives. Decision making involves all the thinking and activities that are required to produce a choice among alternative courses of action; it is the central activity of all human beings.

Decision-Making Models

Although a variety of decision-making models have been presented in the management literature, they all have common elements (which form the model proposed below). Some are presented as five- or six-step models; they differ according to how each activity is categorized. The following is a typical decision-making model:

1. *Identify the problem.* Be aware that a problem exists in the organization that requires some action; that is, recognize the need for a decision. This process involves the collection and assessment of data; an examination of facts and the opinions of others; identification of possible causes of the problem; and recognition of time and other resource constraints.
2. *Define objectives.* Define a goal and develop standards to assess the options.
3. *Develop alternative courses of action.* At this stage ideas for possible options are generated; the pros and cons of each alternative are listed; the consequences of each are examined and measured against the objective.
4. *Make a decision and implement it.* Select the best course of action and follow it through with action.
5. *Evaluate results.* Monitor the results based on predetermined criteria and the objective; revise the decision, if necessary, by repeating step 1.

The model presented above is simplistic; decision making does not necessarily proceed from step 1 to step 5. In real situations there is often overlap, and some steps are eliminated completely. Moreover, the model is seldom consciously used by managers in today's complex situations. However, effective decision making is the hallmark of good management and leadership. Therefore, even if the realities of the situation dictate not following a textbook prescription, the leader needs to understand the pitfalls of decision making that lead to poor decisions.

There is no such thing as a perfect decision. An effective decision, or best decision, is one in which the leader uses the resources available to best achieve the desired goals of the organization. The leader is cognizant of this especially when searching for solutions and evaluating outcomes. Lynch (1992) developed a unique decision-making model suited to sensing-thinking personality types who prefer structured methods to solve problems. The use of personality-specific decision models may improve both the decision-making process and the results of decisions.

Problem Identification. The first step, sensing a problem and giving it form, involves a great deal of skill and time. How the problem is eventually defined is the foundation upon which the entire process lies. If the problem definition is not correct, the solution will not be either. For example, if a foodservice manager sees rivalry and fighting between two members of the department, he might label this an interpersonal relations problem and attribute the cause to the different cultural backgrounds of the two. By defining the problem in this manner, his solution may be to call in a third party to mediate. The real problem, however, may be that one of the involved parties does not trust either the other person or the foodservice manager. He or she may, in fact, be jealous of their relationship. This situation requires a different type of intervention. In this case, the solution needs to involve the direct intervention of the foodservice manager.

Stevens (1985, p 173) used Dewey's approach to problem solving, viewing problem definition as the key to effective decision making. The following hypothetical situation illustrates the process of accurate problem definition.

On one patient care unit, patient satisfaction with attentiveness and the response time of dietetics personnel are exceptionally low. The associate director for patient foodservice has explored the environment to get a sense of the problem. Is the poor service related to the initial selection of people for the unit? Are the patient nutrition care demands too strenuous? Are members of the work group resentful because they are viewed as responsible for the department's poor quality ratings? Is the problem the dietitian leadership, the patient mix, or nursing and medical staff perceptions of nutrition services?

The first statement of the problem could be that the workload is too heavy and the time schedule too demanding in relation to other similarly staffed units. Based on this, the associate director resurveys the environment to see if these are truly the causes of the problem. This process of tentatively defining the problem, surveying the environment, and redefining the problem is repeated, often with the help and input of a quality team, until the true cause of the low morale is determined.

In the example, it may be that the workload and time schedules are definite problems. (However, they may be symptoms of the problem rather than the problem itself.) The associate director, with the aid of a quality committee, at this point may propose one or more solutions to the problem: shift personnel from other units to handle the excessive workload or realign job assignments to improve equity among units. Solutions are continuously suggested as the problem is defined and refined and as various solutions are implemented into the environment. A tentative solution may be tried and it may fail to correct the problem; this indicates that either the solution is wrong or the problem needs redefinition.

Defining Objectives. If there is a vision and goals to guide the process, defining objectives is one of the easier steps in decision making. In the above example, the objective of the decision may be to improve patient satisfaction as measured by staff attentiveness and response time to patient requests.

Developing Alternative Courses of Action. Generating ideas, developing alternative courses of action, listing pros and cons, and examining the consequences of each course of action form the core of the decision-making process. However, the process is fraught with difficulties. It is not possible or necessary to develop every possible course of action to a problem. It is more appropriate to develop feasible alternatives—that is, those actions that are possible and realistic in view of available resources. Eliminating unfeasible alternatives helps the leader to scan realistic options and evaluate them quickly (Adair 1985, p 109).

The decision maker, though, needs to search widely for *feasible* alternatives. By narrowing possibilities too soon, the leader may inadvertently eliminate better, more creative options. Rather than limiting themselves to one obvious tried-and-true alternative, dietetics leader-managers should make a determined effort to come up with more than one alternative to any problem situation. Using one's imagination to construct assumptions is a good way to generate options. For example, the leader could imagine that there were more financial resources available or that the administrator would agree to an unusual scheme.

Brainstorming. Limiting options to feasible ones does not mean that brainstorming should not be used, but it should be used thoughtfully and in more complex situations. Brainstorming usually involves a group of people who suggest many different options and scenarios for a solution (Schiller et al 1994, p 70–72). In brainstorming, everyone involved in the decision-making process is able to contribute both extreme and moderate options. The essence of brainstorming is that judgments on each proffered option are suspended until there are sufficient options available. Each person should have the opportunity to explore and understand all the options. Consequently, elements of one idea may be combined with those of another to produce a third, even more creative solution. This is a good technique for solving complex problems, such as methods for improving patient satisfaction with nutrition services or for defining the future roles of dietitians and dietetic technicians in nutrition services. Brainstorming's usefulness for more routine decisions, such as the problem of inadequate medical record documentation, may result in delaying a vital decision that needs to be made quickly.

Functional fixedness. The decision maker also needs to avoid functional fixedness, which is the tendency to see things in association with a given function (Adair 1985, p 112). Use of the imagination can overcome this tendency by letting one's mind roam freely. In hospitals, inpatient foodservices require seven-days-a-week, three-meals-a-day operations. One creative foodservice director came up with the cost-saving idea of a cook-chill system that requires the use of food production personnel for only one eight-hour shift five days a week. In presenting this alternative work week, he was not fixed on the traditional assumption that all food production services need to be operational seven days per week or for each meal served.

In generating ideas, the decision maker(s) should avoid negative talk (Umiker 1993). The danger in this is that good alternatives will be dismissed before they can be fully explored. Frequently heard statements, such as "We tried that before and it didn't work" or "Theoretically, it's a good idea, but in practice it is impractical" or "That option will cost too much" can shut down exploration or worthwhile alternatives.

One problem in considering options is that a desirable alternative may not be available. When this happens, decision making is delayed, which may cause more problems than if an undesirable decision is acted on. If this is the case, it is best to make a decision and take action as quickly as possible.

One option that might be considered is not to make any decision at all. On rare occasions this may be a viable alternative. Its use, however, should be limited. Deciding not to decide may cause inertia. Often it is better to be wrong than to make no decision at all (Dawson 1993, p 16–17).

Consequences. The consequences of each option cannot be determined or predicted precisely. However, the more familiar leaders are with the situation, the better they can judge the consequences. In situations that are not familiar to the leader and/or the decision-making group, the use of someone else's expertise is important. Another danger in predicting consequences is that in unraveling so many and such extreme possible outcomes, the group or individual becomes immobilized.

Evaluation and Implementation. Once a decision is reached, it should be evaluated before it is implemented. Questions to help this evaluation follow:

- Does the decision meet the objective?
- Will the decision move the organization toward its vision and mission?
- Has someone been overlooked in the decision-making process?
- Are there resources available to implement the decision?
- Does the decision feel right?

Action and decision making mean taking risks, but taking risks does not mean being reckless. Good risks are those taken only after careful consideration. To assist in assessing risks, both imagination and quantitative methods may be helpful. In management literature, there are mathematical formulas and methods to diagrammatically calculate risks. Although the practical use of such tools is doubtful, there may be times when they could be valuable. In implementing a decision, planning and foresight can help minimize the risk. Questions to ask include: What is the worst possible outcome? Are we willing to accept this outcome, if necessary?

The next step is implementation of the decision. Implementation can range from simple to complex, depending on the scope and breadth of the decision. The more people who are involved in and affected by the decision, the more complex the implementation will be. For decisions that affect the entire foodservice or nutrition department, such as a new foodservice system or the shift of all nutrition counseling to outpatient services, the implementation might progress on a step-by-step basis over many months. Oftentimes demonstration projects are used to implement a decision and evaluate it before implementation on a wide-scale basis occurs.

Evaluating the Results. Once a decision has been implemented, the leader needs to evaluate it. This is done by evaluating the results against the objectives and standards determined in the second step of the process. If the implementation does not achieve the intended objectives, the entire decision-making process is again initiated.

The Myth of Rational Decision Making

Nicholas Nicholaidis (cited in Adair 1985, p 6) found that emotions, organizational politics and power, and the values of people play a large role in decision making. Transformational leaders seldom consciously use the steps of the decision-making process that were previously discussed.

Furthermore, they do not choose prescribed textbook solutions when reaching a decision and taking action. Instead, the following factors influence decisions:

- The individuals' values, interests, and needs
- The standards of their superiors and the vision of the organization
- The acceptance of those people affected by the action and those who have to implement it
- The reasonableness of the decision
- Whether the decision contained a built-in protection that could provide an excuse if the actual results differed from the expected ones

Experienced leader-managers also use intuition to make decisions, because they have a large amount of knowledge gathered from their experience, training, and education. They organize this information in their minds into recognized chunks and patterns. In this case, intuition is seen as making thoughtful leaps from one chunk of information to another. Experienced leaders are able to do this because these patterns and chunks of information are contained in their memory (Simon 1987, p 60).

Bhaska (cited in Simon 1987, p 61) researched a "thinking-aloud" protocol with business school students and experienced businesspeople. Both groups reached similar decisions. The experts, however, using intuition, arrived at solutions more quickly. The novices used a more conscious analysis to arrive at the solution. Thus knowing and learning the steps of the decision-making process are also valuable for developing decision-making abilities.

In complex decision-making situations it seems that solutions are obtained by combining conscious deliberation and intuition. Decision-making styles can be seen to exist on a continuum with the nature of the problem to be solved and the predominant decision-making style of the decision maker deciding which process will be used (Simon 1987, p 61).

Acting

Weick (1983, p 223–236) argues that when managers act, they also think. Thinking is not a separate and distinct activity, occurring in isolation. Acting is continuous, and thinking is woven into it. Thoughtful acts are characterized by attention, intention, and control. When a manager acts thinkingly, attention is paid to what is happening, order is imposed, and action is corrected when it strays from a predetermined set of standards. Thus managerial actions are significant and have important consequences.

In contrast, actions taken unthinkingly are acts of impulse, mindlessness, or rigidity, done without sensitivity to the environment or others.

The following example illustrates thinking and unthinking actions in decision making.

The Situation: A staff clinical dietitian is requesting two months off during the summer to take a European honeymoon. The departmental policy limits vacations at this time of year to two weeks so that everyone can have a vacation during this time. Because the dietitian has been with the department for five years and is considered to be outstanding, the clinical nutrition manager has petitioned the department head to waive this policy in this case.

Response 1: To act thinkingly, the department head would pay attention to the facts, such as the seniority of the dietitian, the likelihood of his or her resigning if the request is denied, and the feelings of the clinical nutrition manager and dietetics staff. The department head would then look at the available options and outcomes—losing the dietitian forever vs not having his or her services for two months—and the effect of each on the other staff's morale. With careful consideration, the department head decides to approve the request only if the other dietitians and dietetic technicians agree to it and if they understand the implications on their vacation time, if any.

Response 2: In contrast, to act unthinkingly, the department head would simply state, "The policy says only two weeks. I will not approve this request."

Acting with thought is important for another reason. There is, in reality, a sparsity of discreet decision making in managerial actions. Decisions seldom occur by people meeting at the same time and using a model similar to the one presented. Rather, decisions occur through small, gradual actions that tend to limit alternative courses of action and possibilities. In other words, decisions are made without anyone realizing it. Therefore, the leader needs to act thinkingly in small actions (memo writing, correcting policy drafts, in meetings, etc), because these small actions help mold decisions (Weiss 1980).

Implications for Dietetics

Three general types of conscious mental abilities are involved in decision making: analyzing, synthesizing, and valuing. There is also a large realm of unconscious mental activities that has been labeled intuition. The effective thinker needs to know which of these skills or combination of skills to use in any given situation. The leader-manager should balance intuition with rationality, analysis with synthesis, conceptualization with imagination, and valuing with all these processes. For example, in developing alternative courses of action, analytic skills are used to view the whole situation and break it into its parts. However, when deciding on the course of action to take, synthesizing skills are used to perceive how the action fits with the overall organization (Rinke 1992, p 63–86). Furthermore, an effective thinker is sensitive to his or her intuition and unconscious mind and knows when to listen to them.

The best way to become an expert decision maker is to make many decisions; the best way to become a leader is to lead (Ford and Ford 1993). After reaching a decision, the leader can study the differences and similarities between this decision and various decisions made in the past.

Application to Dietetics Practice: Case Study

The Setting

The hospital is a six-hundred-bed, not-for-profit facility offering tertiary care services in a large city on the West Coast. Because of changing demographics and a shift of population to the outskirts of the city, the hospital is experiencing a daily census of approximately 330. Changes in hospital reimbursement have resulted in decreased length of stay and a shift toward outpatient services. The hospital has expressed interest in opening an ambulatory health center and there are rumors that home care services may be developed; no one, however, has initiated specific plans for either enterprise.

Current Situation

Because of downsizing and cost-containment initiatives, the hospital nutrition support team was discontinued and the nutrition support dietitian was offered a vacant clinical position. There are two other clinical dietitians; each will provide nutritional care on his or her unit for patients who require specialized nutrition support. There is no "chief clinical" dietitian; all report directly to the department head, a foodservice director who is not a dietitian.

The foodservice director lets each clinical dietetics team function as an autonomous work unit. As a result, each dietitian provides leadership of nutrition care services for defined nursing units. The clinical dietitians are aware that the hospital has discussed expanding ambulatory services, but they have not taken steps to promote the development of outpatient nutrition services or home care. Although the clinical dietitians have a great deal of autonomy, any expansion of dietetics services must be approved by the department head.

The nutrition support dietitian recognizes the potential for expanding outpatient nutrition services; the idea of providing specialized nutrition support to patients at home is especially attractive. During informal discussions with the hospital planning department and the director of nursing, the nutrition support dietitian learns that a business plan for home care would be well received and could create a new, more desirable position for herself. The major constraint for the dietitian is lack of direct Medicare reimbursement; the plan will need to delineate the benefits of including a dietitian on the home care team sufficient to offset the lack of direct reimbursement.

The nutrition support dietitian has a good working relationship with the other dietitians and decides to meet with them to discuss the opportunities and generate a strategy for expanding their services and strengthening their positions in the healthcare organization. They agree to develop and submit plans to the foodservice director that ensure a leadership role for each clinical dietitian in expanded nutrition services.

Case Study Discussion

1. How can the dietitians use (a) analyzing, (b) synthesizing, and (c) valuing to think about this situation?

2. How should the dietitians use the steps of the decision-making process to reach a decision about the best design for their expanded services?

3. What would be one acceptable approach to expanded services that would provide a defined leadership role for each dietitian? Support your decision.

References

Adair J. *Management Decision Making.* Hants, England: Gower Publishing; 1985.

American Dietetic Association. Position paper on the administrative dietitian. *J Am Diet Assoc.* 1975;67:478–479.

Buckley KW, Steffy J. 1986. The invisible side of leadership. In: Adams JD, ed. *Transforming Leadership: From Vision to Results.* Alexandria, Va: Miles River Press; 1986:233–243.

Buzan T. *Use Both Sides of Your Brain.* New York, NY: EP Dutton Inc; 1983.

Dawson R. *The Confident Decision Maker.* New York, NY: William Morrow & Co; 1993.

Dokter RH, Hamilton WF. Cognitive science and the acceptance of management science recommendations. *Management Science.* 1978;19:884–894.

Ford JD, Ford LW. The challenge of leadership: models in nursing and dietetic leadership: what can we learn from each other? *Report of the Thirteenth Ross Roundtable on Medical Issues.* Columbus, Ohio: Ross Laboratories; 1993.

Harmon WW. Transformed leadership: two contrasting concepts. In: Adams JD, ed. *Transforming Leadership: From Vision to Results.* Alexandria, Va: Miles River Press; 1986:11–23.

Levitt T. The thinking manager. *Health Management Quarterly.* 1990;12:6–9.

Levy S, Loomba NP. *Health Care Administration: A Managerial Perspective.* Philadelphia, Pa: JB Lippincott; 1973.

Lynch JJ. An operational decision-making model for the cognitively sensing-thinking manager. *Topics in Health Information Management.* 1992;13:56–64.

McKenzie L. Critical thinking in health care supervision. *Health Care Supervisor.* 1992;10:1–11.

Rinke WJ. Competency-based education. *J Am Diet Assoc.* 1980;76:247–251.

Rinke WJ. *The Winning Foodservice Manager.* 2nd ed. Gaithersburg, Md: Aspen Publishers; 1992.

Rinke WJ, David BD, Bjoraker WT. The entry-level dietitian, II: Employers' perceptions of the adequacy of preparation for specific administrative competencies. *J Am Diet Assoc.* 1982;80:139–147.

Ritscher J. Spiritual leadership. In: Adams JD, ed. *Transforming Leadership: From Vision to Results.* Alexandria, Va: Miles River Press; 1986:61–80.

Schiller MR, Kovach KM, Miller MA. *Total Quality Management for Hospital Nutrition Services.* Gaithersburg, Md: Aspen Publishers; 1994.

Senge PM. *The Fifth Discipline.* New York, NY: Doubleday & Co; 1990.

Sifferman CK, Hoover LW. In-basket exercise to teach computer-assisted food systems management. *J Am Diet Assoc.* 1981;78:165–168.

Simon HA. Managing management decisions: the role of intuition and emotions. *Academy of Management Executives.* 1987;1:57–64.

Stevens BJ. *The Nurse as Executive.* 3rd ed. Rockville, Md: Aspen Publishers; 1985.

Umiker W. Optimism, self-image, and self-esteem. *Health Care Supervisor.* 1993;12:23–28.

Veehoff DC. Whole brain thinking and the nurse manager. *Nursing Management.* 1992;23:33–34.

Weick KE. Managerial thought in the context of action. In: Srivasta S, ed. *The Executive Mind: New Insights on Managerial Thought and Action.* San Francisco, Calif: Jossey-Bass Publishers; 1983:221–242.

Weiss CH. Knowledge creep and decision accretion. *Knowledge.* 1980;1:381–404.

11

Time Management

Chapter Objectives

1. Explain the importance of time management for effective leadership.
2. Assess one's time management skills.
3. Distinguish between boss-, system-, and self-imposed time.
4. List ten guidelines for setting goals.
5. Discuss the importance of planning and delegation as techniques for managing one's time.
6. List tasks that can and cannot be delegated.

Introduction

The most traditional view of time management, and an important one, is that time is a precious resource. As such, time needs to be managed so that one can effectively and efficiently achieve intended results. The importance of time management, however, transcends this conventional view. Transformational leaders who have control over their time can have clear, calm minds when confronted with multiple demands. Unfortunately, a clear vision and articulated objectives often get forgotten in the confusion and muddle of daily events and crises. If leaders are not composed and if they are struggling to accomplish daily tasks, their actions and decisions tend to become reactions to events; they will not have the time or peace of mind to act thoughtfully and proactively. The most important step in achieving clarity of mind is to gain control over one's time.

Time is also a reflection of personal energy and how it is consumed. A leader, no matter how spirited, has a limited amount of energy to use both for self and for the organization. There are many possible demands on the personal energy of the leader, including daily routine tasks and crises, vision and goal accomplishment, personal and professional activities, and home and family obligations. The goal of time management is to minimize the number of demands facing the leader at any one time. This management will ensure that there is adequate energy for the tasks that advance the vision of the organization and the leader's personal goals and purpose. Kofodimos (1993) suggests completing a "life spheres assessment" to evaluate one's time/energy imbalance. This exercise will help elucidate the factors that contribute to the pressure to overwork, such as new technology that encourages bringing work home, high-tech communication devices that demand constant interaction, and heightened competition in the workplace, including healthcare organizations.

Furthermore, how the leader spends time is important, because it sends messages to others. Ideally, dietetics leader-managers should be spending most of their time in activities that move the dietetics department toward its vision and objectives. If dietetics leaders become involved in all daily routine situations, they send the message that the vision and objectives are not really important.

For example, a vision statement may purport a "decentralized" management philosophy and structure in which every staff dietitian, unit manager, and foodservice supervisor is encouraged to assume full leadership for food and nutrition services for his or her area of responsibility. However, if the department head, administrative dietitians, or clinical nutrition managers do not delegate to others, allow others to participate in decision making, or permit others to act independently, they are signaling that they really prefer a centralized approach to management. Even though the vision statement avows "decentralization" and trust, the real message (the managers' behavior) is "centralization" and distrust.

Effective time management also contributes to feelings of well-being and happiness. Personal success is measured by the amount of time spent in endeavors the individual enjoys. This is true for both personal and work time. In other words, the way one spends time brings satisfaction and success to one's life. To illustrate, Smith et al (1994) surveyed a select group of dietitians nominated to receive Awards of Excellence. All these successful dietitians reported using some form of time management tool and planned for daily, weekly, and monthly time blocks.

From the opposite view, there are serious consequences of poor time management. Most important, managing one's time is managing oneself. If a leader is incapable of managing self, then it is doubtful that he or she can manage others. Furthermore, a leader's difficulty in managing time can result in project completion delays. Consequently, the entire organization is negatively affected and can be immobilized. Superiors, subordinates, coworkers, and collaborators rely on the leader-manager to complete reports, provide information, make decisions, and take actions in a timely fashion. The inability to be timely on a consistent basis does not help the organization progress toward excellence and success.

This chapter will explore techniques that can be used by leader-managers to organize and therefore make the best use of available organizational time and personal time; to maintain peace of mind, the leader-manager needs to realize a balance between the two. Both the amount of time available for an activity and how this time is spent are important considerations when searching for effective use of time.

Assessing Time Management

There are three ways to assess a person's skills in managing time. First is the appearance of one's work space or office. Despite the popular saying, "A cluttered desk is a sign of a genius," a clear desk and a neat office symbolize control over one's time and responsibilities (Mayer 1990, p 23–24). Developing a system to file papers and to present an uncluttered front to the world is important. Some other visible signs of not having control of time are rushing from meeting to meeting, being late for appointments, and not taking time to fully discuss and consider issues.

Second, many people seem to measure their success and importance by the number of hours they devote to their job. Frequently, people "complain" or even "brag" about the hours spent on their jobs. This may be the result of a need for increased self-esteem, a need to be needed, or a belief that one is indispensable. Consistently spending time in excess of the officially designated hours may signal both ineffective time management and an unfulfilled need.

Leaders and managers in the field of dietetics often give conflicting messages regarding the hours to be spent on work. Frequently, they will implore their personnel to determine priorities and to not stay past the end of their shift, yet the managers will take work home, stay late every night, and spend the weekends doing paperwork.

Similarly, in some organizations one's dedication and loyalty are measured by the number of extra hours devoted to the organization. If this is an organizational cultural belief, people will burn out. Transformational leaders are responsible for ensuring this is not the norm in their departments.

Time Logs

A third, more systematic way to assess one's skill in time management is to use a time log. Some experts believe that people, on the average, waste two to three hours per day as a result of ineffective use of time (Davenport 1982, p 52). A time log will help one become aware of this wasted time, determine the degree of effective time use, and assess other factors of time management (Douglass and Douglass 1993, p 37–45).

Generally, a log is kept for a typical week. However, leaders may decide to keep a log for a longer period if they have particular needs. Keeping a time log on a periodic basis will help leaders see their progress in managing time and identify new areas for further growth. If the leader changes positions, a time log can be kept to assess if there are new areas of concern after several months on the new job. Because the leader's primary reason for time management is to seek clarity of mind, it is helpful to keep the log for both organizational and personal time (Covey et al 1994, p 82–86).

Covey (1989, p 151) also recommended dividing one's time into four categories or quadrants to better analyze time utilization. The four categories are urgent/important, urgent/not important, not urgent/important, and not urgent/not important. Urgent activities, such as crises and pressing problems, require immediate attention. Activities in the important/not urgent quadrant should receive a good deal of attention. This quadrant holds activities that are results-oriented and lead to goal achievement. These activities include planning, problem prevention, reaching toward production capabilities, recognizing new opportunities, and recreation. Successful dietitians said they spent less than a third of their day on such activities, but they would like to increase this to 45 percent of their time (Smith et al 1994). This type of analysis can be used with a traditional time log.

A sample of a time log format is found in Table 11-1 and a partially completed log is found in Table 11-2. (Some people may prefer to keep an ongoing narrative diary instead of using this form.) In column 1 of the time log, the activity and the length of time spent on the activity are recorded; the purpose or objective of the activity is indicated in column 2. For example, the purpose of a phone call may be to get information, give information, make a decision, or to procrastinate.

The purpose of the third column is threefold: to identify time wasters, to categorize the time, and to assess one's energy level. Time wasters are activities that engage the person's time and are not important or vital to the accomplishment of organizational or personal goals (Ferner 1980). Time wasters can be both internally and externally generated. In a comprehensive, international survey of executives, LeBoeuf (1980, p 41) reported the major time wasters experienced by them:

> telephone interruptions; drop-in visitors, meetings (scheduled and unscheduled), crises; lack of objectives, priorities, and deadlines; cluttered desk and personal disorganization; ineffective delegation and involvement in routine and detail; attempting too much at once and estimating time unrealistically; lack of, or unclear communication or instruction; inadequate, inaccurate, or delayed information; indecision and procrastination; confused responsibility and authority; inability to say no; leaving tasks unfinished; and lack of self-discipline.

Table 11-1. Sample Time Log Format

Time and Activity	Purpose of Activity	Assessment	Effectiveness of Time Spent
Indicate activity and length of time spent on it	Before beginning the activity, write down its purpose or objective	Identify time wasters	Assess each task by asking:
			• Did the task contribute to goal accomplishment?
Make entries every 15 minutes unless some activities extend for a longer period of time		Categorize the time as boss-, system-, or self-imposed time	• Could the task have been done in a better way?
		Assess energy level	• Was the task performed at the right time?
			• Could the task be delegated?
			• What were the benefits of completing the task?
			• Was it enjoyable or unpleasant?
			• Were there many interruptions?

Also in the third column, for those hours spent in organizational activities, the leader categorizes the type of time. Oncken and Wass (1990) describe three categories of managers' time:

1. *Boss-imposed time* is time spent in activities required by one's superior. These may include attending organizational meetings, preparing reports, developing policies and procedures, participating in special task forces, attending ceremonial events, and communicating with the boss. Gaining control over this time may not be possible. There are some activities, however, such as preparation of reports, that may be delegated. Leaders need to know how much of their time fits into this category and they need to recognize that managing some of this time more effectively may not be possible. At the same time, they have the opportunity to assess what can be delegated to others or eliminated by negotiating with the superior.
2. *System-imposed time* is time spent in activities that support organiza-

Table 11-2. Sample Completed Time Log for a Dietetic Internship Director

Time and Activity	Purpose of Activity	Assessment	Effectiveness of Time Spent
7:30–8:00 Weekly preceptor meeting	Get information regarding weekly status of dietetic intern rotations and educational concerns	Interrupted twice by staffing problems on the units; much digression from the agenda; system-and boss-imposed time; energy level high	Meeting could be longer; must do this myself
8:00–8:30 Weekly meeting with department head	Give information and receive information from various units	Boss-imposed time; meeting seems to be a gripe session and not useful; energy level still high	Cannot delegate; meeting not useful but have no control over this
8:30–8:45	Return to office	Stopped by 3 interns with problems (payroll, library references, scheduling VCR); subordinate-imposed time	I volunteered to take care of problems; could have redirected them to others
8:45–9:15 Reading; answer phone calls	Get and give informal information	This is discretionary time that could be better spent; procrastination	Enjoyed! Some of the information is useful in understanding the social networks
9:15–10:00 "In" box	Time set aside for routine correspondence	5 phone calls interrupted time; only 2 were important; energy level high	Resented 3 phone interruptions; task does not demand energy; thus move this to a late afternoon function and use this time in personal meetings
10:00–11:00 Nutrition Services Committee	Get and give information regarding new quality improvement program	Discretionary time	Goal accomplished; enjoyed task completion
11:00–11:30 Solved interns' problems	Resolve problems for the 3 interns	Subordinate-imposed time; time waster	Could have delegated this task and taught interns to solve problems independently

tional peers. This includes activities similar to those mentioned above, but the purpose of the activity is different. For example, time spent receiving information about new institution policies and passing it on to subordinates is system-imposed time. As with boss-imposed time, the leader can assess this time and determine ways to decrease time spent in these activities.

3. *Self-imposed time* is time spent doing things the leader initiates or agrees to do. It has two components. Subordinate-imposed time is spent in activities requested by subordinates; discretionary time is time for doing what a leader initiates and wishes to do. The true purpose of time management is to increase discretionary time (Covey 1994), and this "new" time should be devoted to important/not urgent activities. An increase in discretionary time can be achieved by improving control over subordinate-imposed time.

For example, in Table 11-2, the dietetic internship director agreed to follow up on three interns' questions regarding a payroll problem, the availability of a library reference, and scheduling a videocassette recorder for class. These questions could have been handled by the interns. The internship director could have referred the interns directly to payroll, the library, and the media center, respectively, while offering support if the problem was not resolved at that level. Instead, the internship director spent a half hour communicating with the appropriate personnel and getting back to the interns.

The third column can be used to analyze one's emotional status and energy levels. Leaders sometimes slip into the practice of spending their most productive time in doing the least important, least demanding tasks. Consequently, they end up doing their most important work when their energy levels are lowest. By rearranging the schedule, leader-managers are able to give the most energy to the most important tasks, such as solving problems, making decisions, starting projects, attending important meetings, developing new ideas, or writing important reports or meaningful correspondence (Ulrich 1985).

In the fourth column, the effectiveness of the time spent can be analyzed. This should be done as soon as possible after completing a task, but must be done at least at the end of each day. This analysis has both an emotional and objective component.

At the end of the week, the entire log can be analyzed for time wasters, time spent in unimportant activities, and ways to more effectively use time. Questions to consider when analyzing the time log include:

- What were the most significant accomplishments of the week?
- How many activities were enjoyable or detestable?

- If you continue spending time the way you did the past week, where will you be in five years?
- Are the most important tasks being accomplished during periods of high or low energy?
- How much time is spent in each category: boss-imposed, system-imposed, and self-imposed?
- How much time is spent on activities in each quadrant: important/urgent, important/not urgent, not important/urgent, and not important/not urgent?
- How can discretionary time be increased?
- How much time was spent in moving forward the vision and goals of the organization and dietetics department?
- How does wasted time affect the overall foodservice and nutrition department?
- How does subordinate-imposed time affect time management?

Goals and Goal Setting

Goals give people purpose in life—reasons to pursue daily routines and tasks with energy and enthusiasm. Furthermore, goals help leaders avoid wasted efforts and to use their time most effectively. Most important, goals provide focus in one's life, which contributes to clarity of mind.

Goals work because they set up a discrepancy between what a person desires and current reality. This generates creative tension and personal energy, which help motivate a person toward the goal (Harmon 1986, p 107). There are a number of guidelines for goal setting:

1. Determine holistic goals that include all aspects of one's life: professional, organizational, family, social, financial, spiritual, physical, and psychological or self-improvement.
2. Choose goals that open doors of opportunity, such as meeting new people who can assist and support the attainment of the goal. Determine goals that force one to leave one's comfort zone.
3. Determine goals that are measurable, concrete, achievable, and challenging.
4. Consider organizational constraints, resources, and personal strengths and aptitudes to determine realistic goals.
5. Develop goals that fit one's life purpose. This means that the goal will assist the individual toward self-actualization. Thus well-designed goals not only benefit the self but also are in the service of others.

6. Set time frames for completion of goals. By having realistic time frames, tasks and activities seem less overwhelming. Appropriate time frames do not allow for procrastination, but should be realistic. It is not always easy to achieve such a balance. When a goal is not reached by a specific deadline, the date can be changed. The leader should not feel personal failure if a goal is not achieved by the desired date.
7. Periodically, reassess movement toward goals and set new deadlines if appropriate.
8. Reward self upon completion of goals.
9. Spend time each day, even if it is only five minutes, on tasks that move toward goal accomplishment. Decide each morning what is the most important thing to be accomplished that day toward achieving a goal.
10. Enjoy working toward goals. In many cases, the pursuit of the goal is more fun than its actual achievement.
11. Visualize goals.
12. Pursue a goal with enthusiasm, even if the enthusiasm is a pretense.
13. Periodically, evaluate progress toward goal achievement. In this process, some goals may be dropped and new ones added.

Time Management Techniques

There are many practical time management techniques. Some of the most common techniques include managing the time spent in meetings, controlling and minimizing interruptions, mastering one's use of phone conversations, and eliminating nonessentials such as reading junk mail. The focus of this section is on two of the most important techniques: planning and delegating.

Planning

The foundations of planning are based on goals, both organizational and personal. Writing down goals, carrying them around, and referring to them daily places the goals firmly in the leader's subconscious mind. This creates sensitivity to opportunities that can lead to goal attainment. Without this subconscious awareness, a person might miss opportunities to reach a goal.

In chapter 7 the use of positive reinforcement as one technique for rewarding people was suggested. This is a commonly recommended yet frequently forgotten behavior. The leader can write a goal to give one person positive reinforcement every day. If this goal is referred to daily, the leader will be less likely to miss an opportunity to give positive reinforcement to others.

Leaders determine both organizational and personal goals. If time management is a problem, the leader can choose time management goals as well. Table 11-3 illustrates the goals of a hypothetical transformational dietetics leader-manager. These goals are concrete, measurable, and include time frames for completion. It is recommended that these goals be carried in a commercially designed calendar and appointment system. Either at the end of the day or the beginning of the day, refer to these goals. Plan activities for the day based on them, determining daily priorities. Next, write down three to five activities to be accomplished. These tasks are to be done before anything else.

Work seems to expand to fill the amount of time allotted for it. Thus setting realistic time frames for daily tasks, without allowing for procrastination, is an important skill. It can be frustrating to set too many goals for the day and then leave some unfinished. From a time management perspective, however, it is better to err by having too many daily goals than to have too few. Setting unrealistic goals every day can increase frustration and stress levels. Thus, the leader should learn how long it realistically takes to accomplish tasks.

In planning time, the leader-manager should ensure that the day will include adequate discretionary time. One of the most helpful techniques is to set aside a block of time for completion of routine, nonpriority, "must-do" paperwork. How much time and when the time is set aside are determined by other organizational demands and by one's energy level. However, at least two hours at any one time is recommended for discretionary time. An entire day per week can be set aside, or a morning or afternoon once or twice per week. This block of time can also be used for activities that move the vision, leader-initiated meetings, concentrated writing, or nonroutine activities.

Delegating

Knowing how to delegate effectively is essential for organizational and personal success. Delegation is both a science and an art. The science involves first assessing what can be delegated. To do this, decide what activities will provide the greatest return on the time investment. Delegate those with low returns. In general, the leader's time is best spent on activities that advance the vision, mission, goals, and objectives of the department or work group and on those that build trusting relationships within and outside the department.

Jenks and Kelly (1985, p 56–63) categorized tasks that should and should not be delegated. Tasks that can be delegated include:

1. *Routine tasks.* These tasks are done repeatedly and can be delegated

Table 11-3. Sample Goals for a Transformational Dietetics Leader-Manager

Personal Goals Goals	Work Goals	Time Management
1. Walk 30 minutes daily (ongoing).	1. Consciously work on building trust every day (ongoing).	1. Spend 10 minutes every morning planning the day. Write down 3 to 5 things to accomplish, and do these first.
2. Buy a new car by March 1.	2. Develop a vision statement by July.	2. Negotiate with department head to decrease the length of the morning meeting by defining exactly what information is needed. Complete in 1 month.
3. Entertain friends at least monthly.	3. Follow up on restructuring task force; meet weekly with dietitians during implementation phase.	3. Rearrange schedule so that the taxing tasks are completed in the morning. Complete in 2 months.
4. Develop a system by January 1 for remembering birthdays, etc. Buy all the cards for one year by January 15.	4. Initiate a formal dietitian and technician development program by September.	
5. Practice visualization and affirmations twice daily to remember people's names. Reevaluate in 1 month.	5. Start reimbursement system on one unit by January.	

without difficulty. The organizational chart is, in reality, a preplanned system of delegation. Responsibility and authority are delegated to people based on this system of hierarchy. Periodic evaluation occurs when dissatisfactions are expressed or people change positions. An example of delegation can be seen in the handling of the mail in the dietetics department. This can be a cumbersome and time-consuming task. Secretaries can be taught to screen mail by:

- Identifying junk that can be immediately discarded
- Separating correspondence that provides information from correspondence that requires action
- Taking routine actions
- Signing some paperwork for the dietetics leader
- Sending some mail directly to other people
- Attaching routing slips to information that needs to be distributed to several people.

2. *Boss or system-imposed tasks.* Even tasks that are deemed absolutely necessary and may involve decision making can be delegated. Usually, the leader retains responsibility for those tasks that involve a high degree of evaluation and judgment. For example, approval of over-

time can be delegated to supervisors, yet decisions about how to trim payroll costs may still reside with associate directors or the department head.

3. *Trivial activities.* These tasks have little impact on the results that one is trying to achieve. They may include presiding over a meeting about the facility picnic, dealing with equipment repair, or giving information to someone about a minor matter. These activities take a great deal of time and usually do not require the skills of professionals.
4. *Tasks involving special expertise and skills.* These tasks can easily be delegated. For example, the chairperson of the quality improvement committee would be the most qualified to prepare a quarterly quality improvement report.
5. *Chores.* Chores may be categorized under any of the above categories, but they are tasks that one does not enjoy doing. A chore for the boss may be seen as a reward for the "delegate." At the foodservice or patient care unit level, time scheduling can be delegated easily and efficiently. Managerial leaders who are freed of this responsibility gain a significant amount of time to fulfill other responsibilities. For the staff, there are added benefits as well. When a peer is responsible for time schedules, people may be more willing to cooperate and negotiate. At the same time, there may be more chance for input from everybody on the staff. Furthermore, it is possible that the staff might do the job better. Since the schedule involves their own time, they have a greater vested interest in its timely completion and equity.
6. *Pet projects.* Although it may seem paradoxical, the tasks enjoyed by the leader might better be delegated to someone else. For example, although a dietitian might thoroughly enjoy working with figures and managing the inventory, this may not be the best use of professional time.

Just as some tasks or activities can be delegated, others cannot. Some leaders err by delegating too much or by delegating inappropriate activities. As with everything a leader does, a sense of balance is important. Jenks and Kelly suggested that the following tasks *should not* be delegated:

1. *Ritual activities.* Tasks that would be ineffective without the influence of the position, prestige, and title of the dietetics leader should not be delegated. They may include both internal and external events. For example, dietitians and technicians should be involved in National Nutrition Month activities and the department head should preside over annual award ceremonies.
2. *Decisions affecting dietetics department policy.* These include both informal and formal policy. For example, an administrative dietitian

may choose to use a search committee for selecting a foodservice supervisor. The search committee can help screen and interview applicants, yet the administrative dietitian retains ultimate authority for hiring. Prior to the work of the search committee, guidelines for the selection or rejection of a candidate are determined by the administrative dietitian.

The dietetics leader accepts final authority and accountability for formal policies. Staff can and should have input into the policy, and several people may actually write it. Even if the policy is designed in a truly participatory manner, final authority and accountability for the policy rests with the dietetics leader.

3. *Personnel matters.* The dietetics leader needs to assume responsibility for the evaluation of direct subordinates. In addition, the leader must adhere to the disciplinary routines and practices of the organization and play a defined role in order to avoid costly technical mistakes for the organization. Any delegation that involves divulging confidential information is inappropriate.

   The knowledgeable leader will not delegate conflict resolution or the handling of crises that call for direct involvement. Judging what does and does not call for direct involvement is not always easy. Once the leader decides that intervention is needed, however, the task cannot be delegated to someone else.

   Praise and positive reinforcement is strongest when given directly by the leader. Secondhand praise loses its meaning. It signals that the task and the person are not important enough to be given direct feedback.

4. *Delegation itself.* The delegate needs to have direct contact with the leader to understand the parameters and standards of the task. The direct contact builds trust and mutual respect as well.

The Delegation Process

The leader decides to whom specific tasks should be delegated. Jenks and Kelly (1985, p 63–68) provided guidelines for making this decision. In a sense, this is an intuitive decision that involves fitting the best person with the right job. Most important, the leader-manager should know the expertise, strengths, knowledge, interests, aptitudes, and attitudes of the followers. These factors should be matched with the job to be delegated. The attitudes of individual followers are also important considerations. For example, if the delegated task is an innovative, nonroutine, boss-imposed task, then an enthusiastic, eager delegate could be chosen. If the matter is routine and trivial, another person might be more appropriate.

Second, the leader should assess the current workload of the delegate.

Can the person handle the delegated duties along with his or her current responsibilities? In delegating to an individual with a high workload, the leader might wish to help the person delegate other activities. Workload and deadlines can be reassessed and the person relieved of certain tasks.

Another consideration in choosing the right person for the job is the reason for delegating. Most often the reason for delegation is the completion of a task. However, a leader may choose to delegate to assist someone's development or to evaluate someone's performance. Once the person is chosen, the process of delegation becomes the focus. First, the person needs to be aware of the relative importance of completing the task. The leader then secures the commitment of the person for completion of the activity, outlines the requirements of the task, and provides the necessary information and resources. At this time, standards should be set; however, expectations of perfection are as inappropriate for others as they are for oneself. The assignment needs to be explained in terms of the organizational vision and should appeal to the values of the individual. Compare the following two approaches:

> *Leader A:* "The Joint Commission requires that this quality improvement report be completed. I really don't agree with it, but it has to be done. Do you think you can pull something together by Friday?"
>
> *Leader B:* "High-quality care is important to our patients, and I want to be able to assure them that we are delivering the best care possible. We therefore need to complete a survey of client satisfaction with our nutrition counseling program. Medical nutrition therapy is getting a lot of attention from dietitians, administrators, legislators, and the public right now. In today's healthcare environment it is really important to have a reputation for comprehensive, cost-effective, high-quality care."

In the first response, the leader minimizes the importance of the task by stating her disagreement with it. Since Joint Commission accreditation is important to an institution's long-term survival, the task is an important one to the mission of both the organization and the dietetics department. In the second approach, the leader emphasizes the societal value of the survey in ensuring high-quality healthcare. This approach will have more success than the first, because it appeals to the value of medical nutrition therapy as an integral part of high-quality care.

Results should be the emphasis of the assignment, not the means. The person to whom the task is delegated is given the flexibility to decide on the means as long as those means are consistent with the department's vision. The delegate is free to ask for advice, support, and guidance from the leader. Firm deadlines and points of evaluation, if determined, help ensure that the task is completed on time.

For effective delegation, the leader should give rewards once the task is completed. Rewards will vary, depending on the scope and breadth of the delegated task. However, it is vital to give the person recognition and credit for the task (Schiller and Wolf 1994).

Many leaders are aware of these scientific principles of successful delegation outlined above, but they still fail to delegate because of an inability or unwillingness to apply them. The art of delegation depends on the leader-manager's personal attitudes toward delegation, including:

- Receptiveness to other people's ideas and ways of doing things. This includes supporting others, praising their efforts and accomplishments, and accepting differences in approaches.
- Willingness to let go of tasks and not to be "in control."
- Willingness to let others make mistakes. Usually these mistakes are minor. Serious, repeated mistakes can be avoided through counseling, support, being available for questions, asking discerning questions, and providing thorough explanations of expectations.
- Willingness to trust.
- Willingness to establish and use broad controls rather than rigid, inflexible standards (Koontz and O'Donnell 1976, p 382–384).

Implications for Dietetics

Many demands are made on the time of transformational leaders. In order to have clarity of mind in dealing with these demands, leaders must manage their time. Managerial time is characterized by variety, fragmentation, and brevity. This means that the leader can easily get caught up in superficiality and be all action and no thought (Mintzberg 1973). Therefore, it is important that leader-managers assess their own time management skills. This can be done by asking a number of questions:

- Am I spending many hours over and above my regularly scheduled hours to complete my work?
- Am I delegating appropriately?
- Do I allow too many interruptions?
- Do I take time out every day for planning and thinking?
- Do I set daily goals and accomplish them?
- Have I determined my long-term professional and personal goals? Do I work on them each day?
- Am I able to say no when appropriate?

Application to Dietetics Practice: Case Study

The Setting

The hospital has a cafeteria for staff and visitors. The cafeteria is open eighteen hours a day and serves an average of five thousand meals per day with an average ticket of $2.25. There is a grill, deli bar, soup and salad bar, breads and dessert station, and a hot entree counter. The hospital is in a residential area and there are few other eating establishments in the neighborhood.

Current Situation

The foodservice director recognizes that more staff members are bringing bagged meals from home or from brand-name restaurants. Cafeteria revenue has dropped 12 percent and the average ticket has decreased from $2.45 to $2.25 over the past six months. After brainstorming with foodservice management leaders, the foodservice manager decided to explore the feasibility of offering brand-name foods in the cafeteria with the goal of increasing the number of patrons purchasing meals by 10 percent and increasing the average meal receipt to $2.50 within the first year.

The cafeteria manager was charged with the overall responsibility of coming up with a proposal for brand use. He was given freedom to create a project task force and to include whomever he wished as task force members. A preliminary proposal would be due in three months.

The next day the cafeteria manager asked to meet with the foodservice director to discuss potential task force members, brand options, and the possible use of kiosks, carts, or designated cafeteria counter space. At the meeting the foodservice director shared his views and presented some desirable options. The meeting lasted forty-five minutes.

Later that afternoon the cafeteria manager named four foodservice associates to the task force. Meetings were scheduled for 2:30 on alternate Wednesdays.

Meetings were held as scheduled, but task force members were often late or absent if they were on their scheduled day off. After two months the foodservice director asked for a progress report and was told that the group was still considering the variety of brand options to be offered, including soda brands, coffee brands, baked brands, pizza brands, yogurt brands, and dry snack brands. Two more meetings were held, but the group failed to reach consensus.

At the sixth meeting of the task force, the day of the three-month deadline, the cafeteria manager presented to the group a completed plan similar to the one laid out earlier by the foodservice director. When three of the four task force members objected to the plan, the cafeteria manager announced that this was the plan desired by the foodservice director and he intended to submit it.

Case Study Discussion

1. For the cafeteria manager, is the initial request for a proposal boss-, system-, or self-imposed time?

2. Was the decision appropriately delegated?

3. What category of activities for delegation does this decision fit?

4. Was the task delegated to the appropriate person? Were the right people involved in decision making?

5. Could the task have been delegated to someone else? If yes, who else could have handled the project?

6. Did the cafeteria manager have appropriate guidance in making the decision?

7. What time management problems are apparent in this case situation?

References

Covey SR. Effective leadership begins with seven habits [interview]. *J Am Diet Assoc.* 1994;94:382–385.

Covey SR. *The Seven Habits of Highly Effective People: Powerful Lessons in Personal Change.* New York, NY: Simon & Schuster/Fireside; 1989.

Covey SR, Merrill AR, Merrill RR. *First Things First.* New York, NY: Simon & Schuster; 1994.

Davenport R. *Making Time, Making Money: A Step-by-Step Program for Setting Your Goals and Achieving Success.* New York, NY: St Martin's Press; 1982.

Douglass ME, Douglass DN. *Manage Your Time, Your Work, Yourself.* New York, NY: American Management Association; 1993.

Ferner J. *Successful Time Management.* New York, NY: John Wiley & Sons; 1980.

Harmon WW. Transformed leadership: two contrasting concepts. In: Adams JD, ed. *Transforming Leadership: From Vision to Results.* Alexandria, Va: Miles River Press; 1986:105–110.

Jenks JM, Kelly JM. *Don't Do. Delegate!* New York, NY: Franklin Watts; 1985.

Kofodimos J. *Balancing Act.* San Francisco, Calif: Jossey-Bass Publishers; 1993.

Koontz H, O'Donnell C. *Management: A Systems and Contingency Analysis of Managerial Functions.* New York, NY: McGraw-Hill; 1976.

LeBoeuf M. Managing time means managing yourself. *Business Horizons.* 1980;23:41–46.

Mayer JJ. *If You Haven't Got the Time to Do It Right, When Will You Find the Time to Do It Over?* New York, NY: Simon & Schuster; 1990.

Mintzberg H. *The Nature of Managerial Work.* New York, NY: Harper & Row; 1973.

Oncken WO, Wass DL. Management time: who's got the monkey? *Journal of Nursing Administration.* 1990;20:6–9.

Rinke WJ. *The Winning Foodservice Manager.* 2nd ed. Rockville, Md: Achievement Publishers; 1992.

Schiller MR, Wolf KN. Motivating clinical staff: new variations of an old theme. *Clinical Nutrition Management Newsletter.* 1994;13:1–6.

Smith DP, Rhoades PK, Gines DJ, Tolman NM. The seven personal habits of highly effective dietitians. *J Am Diet Assoc.* 1994;94:377–380.

Thompson BA, Huston JL. How to break down tasks so they don't break you: coping with overwhelming demands on your time. *Health Care Supervisor.* 1994;12:39–43.

Ulrich B. Time management for the nurse executive. *Nursing Economics.* 1985;3:318–323.

12

Leadership in Groups and Teams

Chapter Objectives

1. Define working groups.
2. List the advantages and disadvantages of working in groups.
3. Discuss a descriptive model of group theory.
4. Describe the five stages of group development.
5. Describe success strategies for formal and informal team leadership.
6. Discuss practical techniques for facilitating group work.

Introduction

Throughout this book it has been seen that dietetics leader-managers spend all of their organizational time in one of three ways. They are involved in tasks by themselves, with one other person, or with a group or team. This book has provided discussions of their role in each of these activities. Because group theory and team dynamics are more complex than working alone or with one other person, it is important for dietetics leader-managers to have additional information about groups and teams.

Although dietetics professionals are often engaged in activities in which they act on a one-to-one basis with patients, they also become involved in activities as members of various groups. In dietetics there is a great reliance on groups to reach organizational goals, but group activities have not always been valued. Some people have considered work groups a "waste of time" or another "useless committee." Groups have also been denigrated for being expensive or leading to "groupthink." This means that groups make bad decisions because of distortion in the group process (Janis 1972). On the other hand, many organizations today view teams as effective for problem solving, planning, decision making, and getting the job done.

There are valid reasons why groups should be used in dietetics and why they are necessary for the accomplishment of goals. Groups help to secure commitment, bring together a wide range of skills and expertise, give individuals a sense of belonging, and allow people a forum to express their views. It is also true that two minds are better than one. In fact, there is a phenomenon called a *third mind* or *master mind,* which is the "coordination of knowledge and effort, in a spirit of harmony, between two or more people, for the attainment of a definite purpose" (Hill 1960, p 168–169). In other words, energy springs from two or more people who think and work together toward a goal; this energy is not present when a person works in solitude.

The leader-manager needs to structure, value, and manage groups appropriately so that people recognize the usefulness of groups and teams. This chapter will consider group theory by focusing on what the leader-manager needs to know to assess a group or team. He or she may be a member of the group, the leader of the group, or the composer who forms the group and to whom the group is responsible.

Work Groups

The primary characteristic of work groups is that they are composed of three or more individuals who are working together for an expressed organizational purpose. The group may be formally constituted as committees, task forces, formal meetings, boards, councils, and so on. The task of a formal group may be to make a decision, develop policies and procedures, determine goals and objectives, or plan organizational change. Work groups may also be informally constituted, such as the gathering of people to solve daily problems. The focus of this chapter will be on both formal and informal groups and teams.

Group Assessment Model

The following descriptive model proposed by Ephross and Vassil (1988) defines and describes concepts that are useful for the leader-manager to assess dietetic work groups. This understanding can enhance a leader's skills for using groups to accomplish organizational tasks.

Temporary vs Permanent Groups

In dietetic organizations, both temporary and permanent groups are formed. Temporary groups, usually task forces, ad hoc groups, or project committees, are formed to complete a time-limited, discrete task. In these groups, people may behave differently and bring a different set of expectations than in permanent groups. Members of temporary groups may take more risks and be less tolerant than members of permanent groups. There are two reasons for this. First, the temporary group is motivated by a set deadline. This means that the work of the group may need to proceed quickly. Thus people will be more vocal and less tolerant. Second, in temporary groups, the members usually have a lower emotional commitment and investment in the group, knowing it is going to disband (Ephross and Vassil 1988, p 29–30).

Permanent groups typically have the opposite characteristics of temporary ones. They are formed for fulfilling some ongoing purpose. Permanent groups may be patient care teams, committees, quality circles, boards, advisory councils, and so on. Because group members must work together for an indefinite period, they are more likely to be tolerant of one another. Because they may not be motivated by deadlines, permanent groups are likely to progress slowly through the stages of group development. Because reputations may be determined by the outcomes of the group, people make more commitment and psychological investment in permanent groups than in temporary ones.

Structure and Process

Group structure can be defined as the stable characteristics of the group, including its roles, norms, subgroups, affection ties, and patterns of conflict management. In contrast, *group process* can be seen as ever-changing characteristics, such as giving opinions, suggesting ideas, seeking cooperation, making plans, responding to ideas, expressing feelings, and responding to them (Ephross and Vassil 1988, p 30–31).

Stages of Group Development

Groups go through *phases* or *stages* of group development. Various authors of group theory define between four and six phases. The phases adopted for this book contain four stages of group development with some stages having substages (Ephross and Vassil 1988, p 56–73).

Pregroup Stage. This stage, initially described by Hartford (1972), is a preparatory stage in which members are chosen, expectations are defined, and goals and objectives are determined. The better the planning and thinking in the preparatory phase the more likely the group will succeed and be productive.

In their role as either group leaders or group composers, leader-managers should consider the following list of questions. Although these questions can be used when forming a group, they can also be used when reevaluating an existing group:

- Who should be in the group?
- What is the purpose of the group?
- How long will the group exist?
- What are the expectations of each individual in the group? Of the group itself?
- What is the group's formal structure?
- How will the group relate to other groups, the dietetics department, and the organization?
- What are the deadlines for task completion?
- What are the expected outcomes? (Shulman 1984)

Members should be selected for the contributions they can make to the group. Likewise, the membership of the group should be representative of the people who will be affected by any decisions the group makes. At times the membership of groups may only be dietetics staff; increasingly, however, the membership includes other healthcare professionals.

When selecting members and asking them to serve on a group, the leader's expectations of them should be made clear. One universal expectation is that as a member of a group, the individual is expected to contribute to both the group process and the outcome. By knowing expectations, individuals can contribute to the group more fully and in a timely way.

Formation Stage. This stage includes the *exploration* and *involvement* subphases. Once the group has formed and members are working face-to-face, they begin to interact. They explore with one another their understanding of what the task is, their expectations of one another, and their commitment to each other. Once this exploration is completed, the group members begin to become involved with one another. To do this, they begin to take risks by expressing their ideas and feelings.

From Power and Control to Problem Solving. During these two subphases, the conflicts within the group become evident. As the struggles are played out, a sense of solidarity and group cohesion develops. Group cohesion is a sense of attachment to one another and sense of pride and investment in the group and its accomplishments. At this point, people are able to participate in the group and express their opinions.

Termination. When a group has completed its task, people may withdraw from the group or have ambivalent feelings about the group. In this phase, the group should be helped to recognize what they have learned. This will enable them to transfer the learning to another setting. The group should also be rewarded for its accomplishments.

Public vs Private Sentiments

Members of the group may express themselves publicly about an issue, but what is stated may not reflect everyone's feelings. An individual may have private thoughts, feelings, and beliefs that are not expressed publicly within the group (Ephross and Vassil 1988, p 31–32). The sensitivity to the private feelings of group members vs what is spoken publicly can assist the dietetics leader-manager in better understanding and managing the group.

Molecular and Molar Characteristics

The molecular and molar characteristics of a group are the parts of the group and the relationship of the parts to the whole, respectively (Ephross and Vassil 1988, p 33–34). Leader-managers can use both analytical and synthesizing thinking skills (see chapter 10) to assess how individuals relate to one another, to subgroups, and to the entire group; how subgroups relate to each other and to the group as a whole; and how the group as a whole functions. By doing this, they can detect the problems that can occur, such as competition for resources among different groups or within groups.

Leadership

As with leadership theory in general, there is no universally accepted theory about group leadership. However, the elements of transformational leadership can be applied to group leadership. Group leaders need to appeal to the values, motives, and aspirations of the members to define the group's collective purpose. In a formal group, the collective purpose is often defined during the formation of the group. The group leader needs to show how the purpose of the task relates to the broader perspective. To do this, he or she can define how the task fits the vision and mission of the organization. The group leader also needs to:

- *Understand the internal workings of the group.* This can be done by using information in this chapter to assess the group. By allowing the group to fully explore issues, by asking questions, and by expressing personal feelings and allowing others to express theirs, the leader-manager can better understand the dynamics within a group.
- *Plan the work of the group.* Planning enables group activity to flow well and ensures that deadlines are met. Efficient planning includes using agendas, recording minutes, assigning tasks, and so on.
- *Be a visionary.* By showing how the task of the group relates to dietetics, the organization, and even to society, the leader can achieve the

role of visionary. If the task is quality improvement, then the leader can discuss how the group tasks relate to dietetics, to the healthcare environment, and to societal trends such as consumerism.

- *Manage interpersonal relations.* When deciding who is assigned which tasks, the leader-manager is attempting to manage interpersonal relationships. Leaders also may have a role in mediating conflict and working toward group cohesiveness.
- *Be proactive.* The leader need not be controlling and talkative, but should provide guidance, resources, and support. The concepts of empowerment are as important to groups as they are to the individual in the organization.

Work

Task accomplishment and the satisfaction of members' needs comprise the work of groups. Despite conflicts and differences of opinion, ultimately a group is judged by its ability to become cohesive and accomplish the assigned tasks (Ephross and Vassil 1988, p 35–36).

Learning

Although the purpose of work groups is not to change a person's attitudes or behaviors, learning can and, it is hoped, does take place in groups. Through the exposure to other people and their ideas and through full discussion of issues, group members may experience a change in attitude brought about by new knowledge and understanding (Ephross and Vassil 1988, p 36–37).

Participation in a group may be a particularly valuable way for people to understand various organizational constraints. For example, when a staff dietitian, nutrition educator, or clinical nutrition specialist works in a group, he or she may become more familiar with constraints facing dietetics managers such as declining full-time-equivalent positions and limited financial resources. The opposite can occur when a manager works with a group concerning clinical or educational issues. Furthermore, by having the experience of working with a group, the members may gain skills that they can transfer to other settings.

Organizational Setting

The group's tasks, where the group reports within the organizational hierarchy, and to whom it reports all form the organizational setting for the group. Ephross and Vassil (1988, p 104) hypothesized that the higher a group is in the organizational structure, the broader the members' field of reference and the greater their concern for the entire organization. At the same time, those groups that report at lower levels in the organization may be more innovative and creative.

In dietetics departments there are two types of groups to consider. The first type is composed primarily of members with line responsibility and authority. The tasks of this group may be people promotion and selection, safety issues, or delivery issues (eg, developing an efficient tray line service). The other type of group includes groups that are assigned staff responsibilities, such as dietetics research, quality improvement, staff development, and strategic planning.

Democratic Microcosm

A democratic microcosm is the ideal to strive for when managing group activities. Although democracy as a concept may have varying meanings (from anarchy to total equality), there is one definition most suited to groups—the concept of democracy as shared participation. Democratic groups are more creative, more productive, and appeal to the human need to belong. Democratic groups have the following characteristics:

- Members should have some voice in who the leader of the group will be.
- Each person can express his or her ideas and participate in the decision-making process.
- Formal and informal procedures for participation exist.
- There is an agreed-upon and used method of making decisions.
- Members agree to support group decisions or dissent in a particular defined way.
- The individual accepts responsibility for his or her own actions, respects other group members, and accepts responsibility for the group (Ephross and Vassil 1988, p 4354).

Decision Making and Groups

Groups, like individuals, function according to the decision-making model presented in chapter 11. The difference between individual and group decision making lies in how the decision is reached. Schein (1969) stated that groups can reach decisions by any of the following six ways:

1. *Lack of response.* This can take several forms. The group may simply not be interested in a particular issue or the dynamics of the group may not allow for full participation. Another possibility is that the group is a "rubber-stamp" committee or the issue at hand dictates

that the committee rubber-stamp another person's or group's decision.

2. *Authority rule.* In this case, the leader makes the decision.
3. *Majority rule.* In reaching a decision, the sentiments of the majority serve to make the decision.
4. *Voting or polling.* This technique is often used in very formal groups and search committees. Although voting may be necessary and useful at times, voting tends to polarize people. Thus, in setting up a group, it may be useful to decide under what circumstance a vote can be called for. The purpose of this is to keep voting to a minimum.
5. *Consensus.* This is what every group should strive for. It is a sign of group strength. Consensus means that although some group members do not fully agree with the decision, they are willing to support the decision and give it a chance to succeed.
6. *Unanimous vote.*Decision making seldom happens with everyone in total agreement. In fact, if there is never disagreement, this may be a sign of too much group cohesion or groupthink.

Self-Esteem and Groups

As with decision making, the basic principles of self-esteem that were explored in chapter 9 can also be applied to self-esteem and groups. The leader-manager should understand that individuals can join groups to enhance their self-esteem. If they are allowed to contribute in a meaningful way and if the group affirms the principles of a democratic microcosm, members' self-esteem can be enhanced. However, if the group does not allow for the respect and contributions of each member, self-esteem can be damaged.

Furthermore, the self-esteem of the group as a whole needs to be considered. The group needs to have a sense of accomplishment. This will lead to confidence in the group and its processes. Simply acting on the decisions and recommendations of the group promotes group self-esteem.

Leading the Team

Just as the popularity of work groups has increased as a method to generate energy, ideas, and enthusiasm, so too has the use of teams in the organization. Although teams are often equated with groups, the two are not synonymous. The unique feature of a team is shared commitment. Without shared commitment, groups simply perform as individuals. When shared commitment exists, groups become a powerful unit of collective performance. The best teams invest time in shaping their own purpose and translating it into specific goals (Katzenbach and Smith 1993).

Another fundamental distinction between teams and other groups is performance. Group performance is simply the sum of individual contributions. Teams, however, strive for performance greater than individual accomplishments; thus they achieve more (Katzenbach and Smith 1993).

Formal Teams

In an organization teams can exist as formal or informal groups. Many of the principles of group leadership can be applied to both formal and informal team leadership as well. Certain structural characteristics of the formal team and personality characteristics of the leader are important for success. The structural elements can include the following:

- Purpose, supported by structures and systems that provide empowerment and authority
- Skilled and diverse membership who support purpose and share a common set of principles and values
- A leader who can link members with the organization and its systems
- Measures of individual and team performance and effectiveness (Reynolds 1994, p 129)

For the leader of a formal team, personal characteristics that are beneficial include charisma, empathy, and trust, with trust being the most important. Trust is crucial to getting people on your side and keeping them there (Bennis 1989, p 155–160).

Informal Teams

Trust is also an underlying factor for informal teams with which the leader-manager interacts. Members of the leader-manager's informal team could include customers, bosses, subordinates, bystanders, or others. The informal team may never even meet as a "group," but it is linked by a common purpose, often the goal or vision of the leader-manager. Critical skills for working effectively with an informal team include negotiating agreement and negotiating trust. These dimensions also serve as the basis for developing strategies to categorize and influence members of the informal team (Fig 12-1). Categories of informal team members can include:

- *Allies (high agreement/high trust)* who share the leader's vision and goals and want the leader to succeed.
- *Opponents (high trust/low agreement)* who do not share the leader's

Figure 12-1. Informal team member categories.

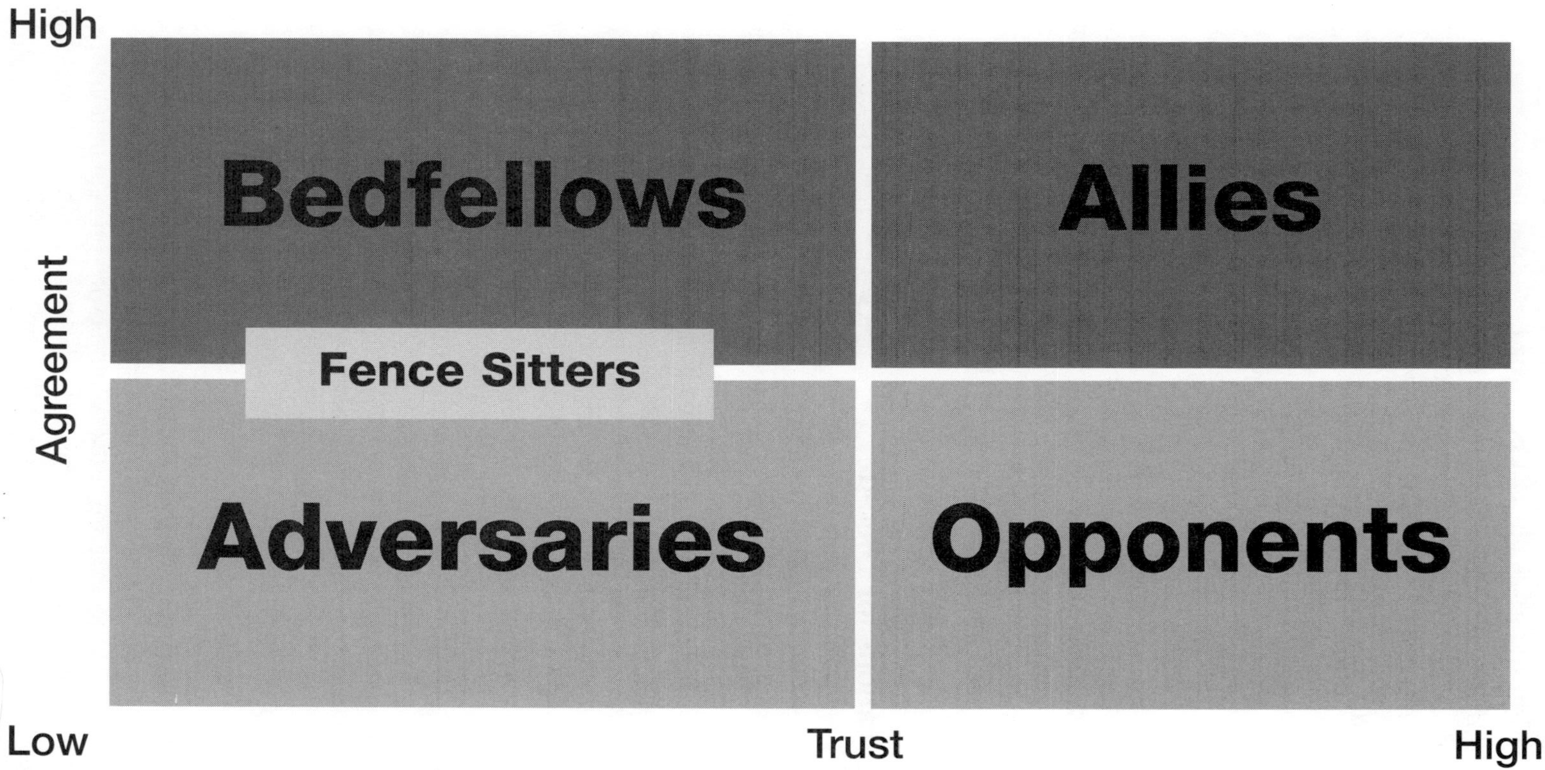

From Peter Block, *The Empowered Manager: Positive Political Skills at Work* (San Francisco: Jossey-Bass, Inc); p. 139. Copyright 1987 by Peter Block and Jossey-Bass Inc, Publishers.

vision and goals but can be trusted.

- *Bedfellows (high agreement/low trust)* who share the leader's vision and goals but cannot be trusted and may not be willing to "share the whole story."
- *Fence sitters (low trust/unknown agreement)* who will not take a stand for or against a vision or goals and even if a decision is reached may not uphold it. Therefore, they cannot be trusted.
- *Adversaries (low agreement/low trust)* who do not share the leader's vision and cannot be trusted. They can be very difficult to deal with because there is lack of trust (Block 1987, p 138–152).

Common steps to use with all members of the informal team are to exchange vision, purpose, or goals; affirm or negotiate agreement; and affirm or negotiate trust (Block 1987, p 139). Further strategies for influencing and working with informal team members are described in Table 12-1.

Implications for Dietetics

Whether the transformation leader is a member, a leader, or composer of a formal or informal group, he or she has an obligation to ensure that dietetics work groups and teams are supported and effective. There are some relatively simple, well-known techniques for facilitating the work of groups and teams. Often these mechanisms are forgotten and put aside. Yet the effective leader-manager should expect that groups and teams will use them to accomplish their tasks.

Agendas for meetings should be prepared ahead of time and distributed to members in advance of meetings. Having a specific format for agendas will ensure that items are not forgotten and will not fall through the cracks. One suggested format includes (1) announcements, (2) old business, (3) new business, and (4) additions. Under "old business," the person preparing the agenda can review previous minutes and list those items needing further discussion or follow-up. If this is done faithfully, the person preparing the agenda will only need to review the minutes of the previous meeting.

All group meetings should have *minutes*. The minutes can follow the same format as the agenda. One of the most useful ways to keep minutes is to have a routine format to label recommendations and further actions separately. If recommendations and actions become part of a narrative discussion, they often get lost and forgotten. There are two approaches to keeping minutes. One is to use three columns with one column listing the topic, the next the discussion, and the third the recommendations or follow-up action. Another format is to have the topic and discussion in one narrative

Table 12-1. Strategies for Influencing and Working With Informal Team Members

Classification	Definition	Strategy
Allies	High Agreement/ High Trust	Affirm agreement on vision Reaffirm quality of relationship Acknowledge doubts/vulnerability Ask for advice/support
Opponents	High Trust/ Low Agreement	Reaffirm quality of relationship, one based on trust State your position State in a neutral way what you think their position is Engage in problem solving
Bedfellows	High Agreement/ Low Trust	Reaffirm agreement Acknowledge lack of trust that exists Be clear about what you want in working together Ask bedfellows to do same Try to reach agreement on how to work together
Fence Sitters	Low Trust/ Unknown Agreement	State your position on project—your goals, vision, purpose Ask where fence sitter stands Apply gentle pressure Encourage thought on issue, and letting you know what it would take for their support
Adversaries	Low Agreement/ Low Trust	Eliminate contact or reduce threat State vision State your understanding of adversary's position in a neutral way Identify your contribution to problem End meeting with your plan and no demand

Adapted from Block (1987).

paragraph followed by a second paragraph marked "Recommendation/ Action." This will make agenda preparation easier as well.

To whom recommendations are sent, either an individual or another group, should be clearly defined. If the group has the authority to act independently on its recommendations, this should also be known. Most important, the leader-manager should ensure that the recommendations made by the group are heeded and acted on or implemented.

Attendance at meetings in dietetics departments can be a major problem. When the group is formed, expectations about attendance should be clearly defined. Guidelines should be developed for how many meetings can be missed before a person is removed from a group. Attendance should be listed at the beginning of each minutes. There should also be a system of excused and unexcused absences, and this should be noted in the minutes as well.

Application to Dietetics Practice: Case Study

The Setting

The Regional Medical Center recently made the decision to implement critical pathways, beginning with four primary diagnoses that traditionally had been money losers for the institution. Chris Jones, a chief clinical dietitian, was selected to attend a training program on critical pathway development and has been appointed chairperson of the critical pathways advisory panel. The advisory panel reviews the recommendations of each individual critical pathway committee and from this review recommends pathways that should be taken before the medical staff for approval. The membership of the group is as follows:

- The chief clinical dietitian, chairperson
- Four utilization review nurses who serve as chairs of each of four individual committees for which pathways are initially being developed
- Three head nurses
- One staff physician
- One nursing instructor, who chairs the nursing staff development committee
- The quality improvement nurse who chairs the quality committee
- One staff nurse who chairs the staff nurse advisory council
- One senior clinical nutrition specialist

An agenda is prepared and distributed about one week prior to the meeting. Each critical pathway committee chairperson is asked to report on his or her committee during the monthly advisory panel meetings. At the first meeting, the chief clinical dietitian asked each person to introduce himself or herself. Each member was asked to explain his or her perceived role in the group, current position, and responsibilities in the hospital. Committee chairpersons were asked to discuss the goals and current activity of their respective committee. Following this, the purpose and objectives of the advisory panel were discussed. The chief clinical dietitian advised the membership that the advisory panel was not to be pro forma and merely ratify recommendations of the committees. However, the advisory panel was cautioned not to usurp the authority and responsibility of the other committees.

At the second meeting of the advisory panel, two critical pathways committee chairpersons expressed their concern that the advisory panel would become a rubber-stamp committee. They felt the advisory panel was possibly a waste of time and would prove to be cumbersome.

After about three months it became clear that one head nurse, Nina, was frequently asking for the opinion of another head nurse, Jan. Nina had been in her position one year and Jan had been in hers for fifteen years. When Jan would express her opinion, Nina would defer to her.

Current Situation

The current issue before the group is a recommendation from the hip-fracture critical pathway committee that their pathway be implemented throughout the hospital following medical staff approval. The three head nurses are in favor of this because of the need to reduce the wide variability in care protocols currently being used to treat patients with hip fractures. The quality improvement nurse feels that the hip-fracture critical pathway should be tried out on a unit on a trial basis before being implemented hospital-wide. The nursing instructor is opposed because of the immediate training that will have to be developed and coordinated with an already overloaded training schedule. The senior clinical nutrition specialist states that she is opposed because the pathway does not include provisions for medical nutrition therapy. After heated discussion, a vote is called for with the results being nine agreeing to accept the recommendation and four opposed.

Case Study Discussion

1. Is this a temporary or permanent group? Is it formal or informal? What are the implications of this for the chief clinical dietitian?

2. Do biases exist in the composition of the membership of the advisory panel?

3. What was the purpose of the chief clinical dietitian's introduction of members at the first meeting?

4. Were the concerns expressed by the two critical pathway committee chairpersons at the second meeting healthy?

5. How could the advisory panel's work be better facilitated?

6. Is the interaction between Nina and Jan an example of structure or process?

7. Which subgroups are evident in the case, and how do they relate to the whole?

8. How was the decision to implement the hip-fracture critical pathway reached? Could a better approach have been taken?

References

Bennis W. *On Becoming a Leader.* New York. NY: Addison-Wesley Publishing Co; 1989.

Block P. *The Empowered Manager: Positive Political Skills at Work.* San Francisco, Calif: Jossey-Bass Publishers; 1987.

Ephross PH, Vassil TV. *Groups That Work: Structure and Process.* New York, NY: Columbia University Press; 1988.

Hartford ME. *Groups in Social Work.* New York, NY: Columbia University Press; 1972.

Hill N. *Think and Grow Rich.* New York, NY: Fawcett Crest; 1960.

Janis I. *Victims of Groupthink.* Boston, Mass: Houghton Mifflin Co; 1972.

Katzenbach JR, Smith DK. The discipline of teams. *Harvard Business Review.* 1993;71:111–120.

Reynolds J. *Out-front Leadership: Discovering, Developing, and Delivering Your Potential.* Austin, Tex: Bard Productions; 1994.

Schein E. *Process Consultation: Its Role in Organization Development.* Reading, Mass: Addison-Wesley Publishing Co; 1969.

Shulman L. *Skills of Helping Individuals and Groups.* 2nd ed. Itasca, Ill: FE Peacock; 1984.

6. *Does the letter reflect the dietetics leader's skill in dealing with dietetics professionals' dissatisfactions with their practice? Why or why not?*

Not directly. This may be because the writer of the letter is not in the dietetics profession. To truly measure the effectiveness of this dietetics director, it would be important to know how she addresses these issues. One statement, "You have made a difference," implies that she has made changes.

7. *Does this letter reflect the dietetics leader's ability to use different leadership styles in different situations?*

No.

8. *Which of Maria's specific traits would you like to develop further in yourself?*

Spend a few minutes reflecting on your own leadership behaviors. List one or two of Maria's leadership attributes you would like to emulate. Write personal goals for growth in this area.

Chapter 2

1. *Describe one positive and one negative outcome of computerization in dietetics.*

Computerization of many routine dietetics tasks is on the horizon. One such example is the development of detailed nutrition screening and assessment software that can identify patients at nutritional risk and evaluate and help plan for their nutrition needs. Such software also has the potential to be integrated into the patient chart to provide any member of the healthcare team access to and an ongoing record of the patient's nutritional status.

One negative aspect of the development of elaborate nutrition screening and assessment software is that it may limit the need for dietetics professionals if it is widely used by other healthcare practitioners. Dietetics professionals need to be proactive and help other healthcare professionals realize that nutrition screening and assessment are but one part of the role of the dietitian. Translating nutrition screening and assessment information into an action plan for nutrition intervention that can successfully maintain or improve the patient's nutritional status is a skill that the dietitian alone is trained to perform.

2. *What are the possible benefits to the dietetics profession of improved global communications?*

With interactive communications and satellite communications, it may be possible for dietetics professionals to communicate with nutrition experts and other dietetics professionals throughout the world. Or there may be an "electronic dietetics library" in which a dietitian, confronted with a patient care problem, can from the bedside ask for and receive appropriate guidance from the literature.

3. *What opportunities do cost containment and the growing elderly population open to dietetics?*

The elderly are a group at high risk for poor nutrition. Nutrition care for this group is most cost-effective when nutrition problems are identified and treated early. Dietetics professionals have a significant opportunity to create and implement effective nutrition screening and intervention programs with the elderly, such as that developed by the Nutrition Screening Initiative. These programs can lead to more cost-effective care by preventing the complications and prolonged recoveries resulting from poor nutrition care.

4. *Are semiautonomous work units in healthcare a credible future reality?*

These units do seem to be somewhat of a pipe dream. However, with a movement toward models like patient-focused care, decentralized services do appear to be becoming more commonplace. In addition, the changing values of people and the need to be competitive may force bureaucratic healthcare facilities to search for alternative organizational structures in the future. Semiautonomous units can be one answer.

5. *What will be the characteristics of future dietetics leaders?*

Most important, the future leader's primary concern will be matching and maximizing the talents and skills of the dietetics staff with the organization's goals. This will mean that the leader will need to be flexible, creative, innovative, and caring. He or she will have to balance people and tasks.

Chapter 3

1. *What is the value conflict in this situation?*

There is value in increasing revenue from cafeteria sales; this may enhance the foodservice director's bargaining power with administration. Reimbursement for clinical nutrition services and attaining professional roles for staff members are factors that affect professional image and the desire to engage in meaningful work. Conflicting values in this situation are concentration on task (obtaining increased resources) vs the personal needs of dietetics professionals. In addition, there is conflict between the dietitians' desire to employ dietetic technicians and their personal insecurity about upgrading their professional roles. In transformational organizations, managers and employees work together toward a common vision that helps satisfy both institutional and personal needs. The clinical nutrition manager has the challenge of helping to build the self-esteem and self-efficacy of the clinical dietitians so they are comfortable in meeting new demands of medical nutrition therapy.

2. *Would you describe this clinical nutrition manager as a transformational leader? Why or why not? Is the department head a transformational leader? Why or why not?*

Although there is not sufficient information from which to draw a conclusion, the clinical nutrition manager has demonstrated one important transformational leadership strategy. She has proposed a strategy and worked with the staff to obtain a collective goal—creating dietetic technician positions. This is the first step toward improving the work environment of clinical dietitians in this hospital.

The department head is transformational in that he recognizes the need for change. He would do well to work with personnel in the department to develop a futuristic vision, one that would incorporate new trends in medical nutrition therapy.

3. *What should the clinical nutrition manager do?*

The role of the leader manager in this situation is to identify the values apparent in the situation. She then would make staff consciously aware of these values and how they conflict. To do this, the leader first identifies her own values. In this case, the clinical nutrition manager's value is to have clinical dietitians take on a more professional role, and assume leadership for medical nutrition therapy in their assigned units. This is based on her belief that this will enhance image and personal satisfaction, and will increase staff morale and decrease turnover. This is a desirable purpose that espouses the aspirations and goals of both the leader and the followers. The leader then assesses the followers' values in this conflict and discusses them openly with staff. The leader uses a variety of skills in this situation: (1) she expresses the conflict in the values; (2) she assesses the character and intensity of the followers' willingness and ability to act; (3) she clarifies and shapes the values by identifying the sources of dissatisfaction; (4) she sees and articulates the contradictions in values; (5) she arouses dissatisfaction; and (6) ultimately, she forces a choice between expanding roles or continuing with the current structure and work processes. Throughout this process, the leader will have to negotiate between individual staff members, and between the department head and the clinical dietitians.

Chapter 4

1. *Did the department head, associate director, and clinical nutrition manager recognize the need for change? On what evidence do you base your conclusions?*

The department head desired less change; she wanted everyone to maintain normal work hours without overtime and she wanted clinical dietitians to continue supervising patient foodservices. Yet she had developed ambitious goals and had achieved most of them, including improvement of self-esteem, work autonomy, and flexible scheduling. Achievement of these goals required change in the department.

The clinical nutrition manager used overtime data as her quantitative indication of the need for change. She also used the department head's dissatisfaction with declining supervision of patient foodservices as the focus of a staff retreat to involve staff members in planning and problem solving.

2. *Why was the clinical nutrition manager unsuccessful in obtaining approval for dietetic technician positions the first time? What contributed to subsequent goal achievement?*

At first, the fiscal officer saw no benefit in allowing creation of a new personnel category. Later, when the clinical nutrition manager demonstrated the opportunity for increased reimbursement and upgrading of professional roles, the fiscal officer saw some benefit. The personnel department thus agreed to work with the department director to create the new personnel category.

3. *What high-control, high-speed tool of change did the clinical nutrition manager employ?*

The retreat served as a high-control, high-speed tool.

4. *What "mundane" tools of change were used?*

At the retreat, the clinical nutrition manager was present and she included all the clinical dietitians and foodservice managers. This is an example of the mundane tools listed as settings for interaction. Following the retreat the clinical nutrition manager used meetings, agenda, and memos as mundane tools of change. The fact that the clinical nutrition manager spent so much of her time on this issue signaled its importance.

5. *How would you classify the department head's response to the lack of time clinical dietitians spent supervising patient foodservices? Why?*

The department head responded with resilience. She also helped others to do so by supporting the retreat and by encouraging people to cope with job stress constructively.

Chapter 5

1. *How will the nutrition services unit ensure excellence and success?*

As stated in paragraph 2, the nutrition services unit fosters excellence by encouraging individual contributions to patient care and by maximizing job satisfaction.

2. *How will the dietitians provide nutrition education and other nutrition services?*

As stated in paragraph 3, nutrition services proposes to use a resource-driven model of care and evaluates outcomes in light of established standards.

3. *What is the overall purpose of this nutrition services department?*

As shown in paragraph l, the purpose of the department is to provide nutrition education, preventive care, and medical nutrition therapy that assists patients and other clients in making appropriate food choices for optimal health, preventing disease, maintaining nutritional status, or regaining health.

4. *How does the department ensure self-direction and fairness?*

In paragraph 6, it is stated that the nutrition service fosters individual growth and development and places people in positions appropriate to their knowledge.

5. *What is the management system of this department?*

In paragraphs 10 and 11, decentralization, involvement of others, and promotion of job satisfaction are mentioned.

6. *How does the department involve employees?*

In paragraph 5, it is stated that the nutrition services unit views dietetics as life work and acknowledges the commitment of professionals to their own growth.

7. *Is the system relatively flexible?*

Yes. As stated in paragraph 9, registered dietitians, not formal authority, set the tone and standards of patient care.

8. *What does the vision statement state about creativity and innovation?*

In paragraphs 7 and 8, it is stated that flexibility and creativity are needed in a resource-driven model of care. Because the nutrition services unit is on the leading edge of technology, innovation is needed.

Chapter 6

1. *How would you describe the organizational structure of the dietetics department? What is the social architecture?*

This is a decentralized organizational structure with only one managerial layer between the dietitians and the department head. It is an example of a formalistic social architecture.

2. *What are the elements of participatory management found in the dietetics department?*

The committee structure with the three advisory boards is an example of parallel organizations. The membership of each committee is a representation of people who are affected by decisions made by the committee. The extensive use of committees and the use of a coordinating council is another form of participatory management.

3. *How could participatory management be further enhanced?*

Wide representation of dietetics professionals and other staff on committees and task forces would enhance the committee functioning. Committee decisions should be carefully considered by the coordinating council, and these decisions should be implemented whenever possible.

4. *What are the benefits of the three advisory boards?*

The advisory boards provide staff who do not have managerial power a means of communicating directly to the department head about issues and concerns. Furthermore, since the advisory board chairpersons report to and sit on the coordinating council, the coordinating council can act on recommendations of the advisory boards.

5. *What norm guides the decision about who chairs committees?*

Dietetics professionals who are considered "the best and the brightest" are selected to chair committees.

6. *Would you describe the committee structure as informal or formal networks?*

The committee structure is an example of formal networks or prescribed networks, which are groups of people who relate to one another as defined by the organizational design.

Chapter 7

1. *What might be included in the vision statements of the organization and the dietetics department regarding the installation of an HIS?*

The vision statement of the hospital would include the use of advanced technology to enhance both the clinical and administrative functions of the organization. It should also mention that this technology can better utilize valuable human resources. For the dietetics department, the visionary statement would be consistent with that of the hospital. In addition, it could mention the use of technology to enhance the role of dietetics personnel by allowing them more time to interact with and help patients.

2. *Write hospital, foodservice, and nutrition care unit permanent and temporary objectives for the installation of an HIS.*

Example of objectives might be:

- To make use of advances in technology to provide high-quality, cost-effective patient care (hospital permanent objective)
- To implement the hospital information system for pharmacy and laboratory within the next twelve months (hospital temporary objective)
- To use technological advances to provide high-quality, cost-effective nutritional care (dietetics permanent objective)
- To develop the computer skills of dietetics personnel (dietetics temporary objective)

3. *How might the selection of the HIS coordinator have been better handled?*

The selection of this individual could have been accomplished easily by a search committee. The chief executive officer could have appointed a committee that was composed of staff for those services that would be implementing the largest software applications, both clinical and administrative. The chief executive officer would advise the committee that his major concern was to find someone with experience in computer installation. The committee might have been better able to also screen applicants and find someone with a knowledge of hospitals as well.

4. *What support and development should be provided for the HIS coordinator and the dietetics computer information coordinator?*

The HIS coordinator should spend time learning about each department and observing work activities. Particular emphasis should be placed on intradepartmental communications and cooperation. He should learn how to coordinate the implementation of applications with each department so that needs can be anticipated in advance.

In contrast, the dietetics computer information coordinator should be trained in computer literacy and in hospital information systems. She should spend time at the computer company and in a hospital currently implementing a system and one with a computer system fully operating.

5. *What type of feedback should be provided to the HIS coordinator and the dietetics computer information coordinator about the current problem with implementation of the foodservice application?*

Feedback should be provided to the HIS coordinator, appropriate dietetics personnel, and the dietetics computer information coordinator to prevent the recurrence of the problem. The information provided should review how the current situation occurred and show how the lack of coordination is not consistent with organizational goals. Both the process and the outcome should be discussed. This is feedback that should occur now to correct the current situation. Later, once the foodservice program is operational, further feedback and review can be provided.

Chapter 8

1. *How would you assess the level of trust in this situation?*

The level of trust is very low. It is affecting the ability of the group to make decisions regarding organizational structure, the ability of the regional contract director to lead, and communications.

2. *Using the assessment tool in Fig 8-2, answer questions 1, 3, 5, 6, 8, 10, 12, and 13 for this situation.*

The assessment should rate the dietetics department below 3 on every question except 10 and 12. The regional contract director is attempting to flatten the organizational structure while ensuring positions for those displaced by the reorganization.

3. *Assume you are one of the clinical nutrition specialists. How would you rate the regional contract director in each of the eight sources of trust: integrity, intentions and motives, openness and discreetness, consistency and reliability, technical competence, interpersonal skills, business sense, and judgment?*

Integrity—There is no evidence that the regional contract director's integrity is questionable.

Intentions and motives—As a clinical nutrition specialist, I would be concerned that decentralization might change my role. Thus I would have less say in decisions regarding the department. Therefore, the regional contract director's intentions may not be in my best interest.

Openness and discreetness—Before discussing the new organizational structure in an open forum, the regional contract director discussed it with those individuals who were displaced.

Consistency and reliability—Although I may not agree with her goal, the regional contract director has been clear about the move toward decentralization for her entire tenure with the facility.

Technical competence—There is no evidence in the case study regarding this source of organizational trust.

Business sense—There is no evidence in the case study to evaluate the regional contract director's business sense.

Interpersonal skills—The regional contract director is having difficulty in establishing good relationships with the clinical nutrition specialists and outpatient nutrition managers.

Judgment—The regional contract director did not prepare adequately for the arguments presented in the meeting. She seemed to be caught unprepared.

4. *What "hard" facts or figures did the dietetics leader use to support her argument? In contrast, what "soft" information did the clinical nutrition specialists use?*

The regional contract director used information about turnover and vacancy rates to support her arguments. The clinical nutrition specialists expressed concern about quality of care and the leadership effectiveness of the staff dietitians. This is an example of hard-fact-vs-soft-fact polarization.

5. *How could the regional contract director have avoided the "us-vs-them" confrontation?*

The regional contract director should have trusted the clinical nutrition specialists and outpatient nutrition manager, considered their feelings, and addressed their concerns. The regional contract director also could have acknowledged their input and their skills.

6. *What can the regional contract director do to repair the damage?*

This situation may never be characterized by complete trust. The regional contract director is desiring change that will take power from this group of dietetics managers. However, by trusting them and delegating appropriate tasks some trust can be established.

Chapter 9

1. *How could the consultant dietitian perhaps have prevented the resignation of the first dietary manager?*

The consultant dietitian should not have written the dietary manager the letter. Since survey citations were a major concern, there were evidently some problems with policies and procedures. The consultant dietitian should have talked with and explored the problems with the dietary manager rather than writing an impersonal letter. The consultant dietitian could also have assessed the situation firsthand before jumping.

2. *How can the consultant dietitian explain her choice to the person not selected without damaging this person's self-esteem?*

This is a very difficult situation. The most important thing is that the consultant dietitian should meet personally with the candidate who was not selected. This displays her concern for him or her as an individual. Since the consultant dietitian's decision was made because of the selected individual's current certification as a dietary manager, this should be emphasized. When telling someone he or she did not get a job, the consultant dietitian could explore future plans for the department and discuss goals with the individual.

3. *What might be a self-fulfilling prophecy in this situation?*

The new dietary manager is not expected to be able to handle the responsibilities of the job. If this is expressed in these terms or if the consultant dietitian accepts this "weakness" without attempting to explore it further, the person may live up to this expectation.

Chapter 10

1. *How can the dietitians use (a) analyzing, (b) synthesizing, and (c) valuing to think about this situation?*

(a) To analyze the situation the dietitian can start simply by asking, Who? What? When? How? Why? Which? Why not? This can lead to further questions such as, What will be the reaction of the foodservice director, the director of nursing, and the hospital planning department to a concrete proposal for expanding nutrition services? What other issues are involved, such as the reactions of the physicians, opportunities for reimbursement, changes in case mix, and the impact on income for the hospital? Are any overriding principles involved, such as maintaining the loyalty of staff to their unit; beliefs about job satisfaction; and feelings about downsizing the hospital?

(b) To synthesize, the dietitian should think about the entire department and the impact of expanding nutrition services on the whole department.

The dietitian should consider concepts such as job satisfaction, unit leadership, retention of staff, and high-quality nutrition care.

(c) Last, the dietitian should think about the value of her thinking and consider feelings that have been brought to light in the first two steps. The value of thinking about the skills and abilities of the other clinical dietitians is important. She should also consider the value of having a well-functioning home care team.

2. *How should the dietitians use the steps of the decision-making process to reach a decision about the best design for their expanded services?*

The dietitians should first ensure that the problem has been identified correctly. In this case, trends in hospital demographics, community healthcare needs, and expanding opportunities in nutritional services should be fully considered. Why has no one developed a concrete plan for development of outpatient services or home care?

Second, an objective should be defined. In this case, the objective should include identifying community needs for nutritional services, fully utilizing the dietitians' expertise, and contributing to the achievement of hospital goals. They might brainstorm possible opportunities for achieving these objectives. Insights may be gained by meeting with the hospital planning department and other supportive personnel.

Next, the dietitians would develop alternative courses of action and list the pros and cons of each. They should also consider other feasible alternatives for innovative approaches to the nutrition care of patients.

Once an alternative is chosen, a business plan should be developed, and the plan implemented and evaluated. In the case of this decision, however, it would be unlikely to reverse the decision and try another alternative in the foreseeable future.

3. *What would be one acceptable approach to expanded services that would provide a defined leadership role for each dietitian? Support your decision.*

The nutrition support dietitian can garner needed support from other key players and take the lead role in developing a plan for home care. Of course, this plan will include herself. In addition to providing nutrition support services, she may serve in a coordinating or managerial role. Another dietitian may develop a plan for initiating a nutrition clinic in the outpatient department with shared staffing by the clinical dietitians. Each dietitian would provide nutrition assessment and counseling services for the disease groupings for which they provide inpatient care. The third dietitian may opt to provide leadership for increasing the visibility and expansion of nutrition within the hospital by taking the initiative to serve on cross-functional teams and by starting a program for preadmission nutrition assessment and treatment of surgical patients at nutritional risk.

Chapter 11

1. *For the cafeteria manager, is the initial request for a proposal boss-, system-, or self-imposed time?*

This was self-imposed time. It is an example of volunteering to take responsibility for a task that is in line with one's area of responsibility. For the foodservice director, the meeting was subordinate-imposed time, which is one of two types of self-imposed time; the other is discretionary time.

2. *Was the decision appropriately delegated?*

Yes.

3. *What category of activities for delegation does this decision fit?*

This fits the category of either trivial or chore activities.

4. *Was the task delegated to the appropriate person? Were the right people involved in decision making?*

Yes. The cafeteria manager had the most interest in expanded offerings. Only a neutral third party might have been a better choice, although this type of person may not exist.

5. *Could the task have been delegated to someone else?*

Yes. Any of the foodservice managers or one of the dietitians or dietetic technicians would also be an appropriate person.

6. *Did the cafeteria manager have appropriate guidance in making the decision?*

No. The foodservice director could have given more guidance as to which brands were preferred, the range of options to be considered, and available space. If the cafeteria manager had known this information from the beginning, greater confidence might have been displayed and the decision may have been developed in a much shorter time period.

7. *What time management problems are apparent in this case situation?*

The main problem is time wasted at meetings. The meetings were scheduled at inconvenient times and participants were not committed to attendance. Since decisions were not reached, time was poorly spent. Poor meeting management lead to lack of consensus and a final decision to which a majority of the task force objected. The lack of consensus will probably lead to more lost time as the task force members vent their negative feelings about what happened.

Chapter 12

1. *Is this a temporary or permanent group? Is it formal or informal? What are the implications of this for the chief clinical dietitian?*

This is a permanent, formal group. As such, the chief clinical dietitian will need to permit the group to slowly proceed through the first two phases of group development—the formation stage, through the power subphase, to the problem-solving phase.

2. *Do biases exist in the composition of the membership of the advisory panel?*

Most definitely. The board is heavily composed of administrators and nursing managers. There is only one staff nurse, one physician, and one dietitian who have clinical patient care responsibilities and will be using the critical pathways.

3. *What was the purpose of the chief clinical dietitian's introduction of members at the first meeting?*

The purpose was to clarify expectations and group purpose during the formation phase of group development.

4. *Were the concerns expressed by the two critical pathway committee chairpersons at the second meeting healthy?*

Yes. This was indicative of the need for groups to explore each other's commitment to the purpose of the group.

5. *How could the advisory panel's work be better facilitated?*

Prior to meetings that have an agenda, the members should be given a copy of the minutes of all committees. If these minutes are in a standard format, recommendations could be easily read and acted upon.

6. *Is the interaction between Nina and Jan an example of structure or process?*

At first the interaction might be seen as process. However, once it becomes routine, it is structure.

7. *Which subgroups are evident in the case, and how do they relate to the whole?*

Subgroups of people hold similar positions in the nursing department. The utilization review and head nurses make up the two largest of such groups. In the decision about the hip-fracture critical pathway implementation, the two groups formed a large coalition of votes.

8. *How was the decision to implement the hip-fracture critical pathway*

reached? Could a better approach have been taken?

The decision was reached by vote. If the group had been allowed to discuss the issue further and even defer the decision for a month, the group might have been able to reach consensus. During the month, the quality assurance nurse could be asked to lead a pilot test of the pathway on a unit. The clinical nutrition specialist could work to implement appropriate medical nutrition therapy in the pathway. The nursing instructor could plan a training program into the education schedule.

INDEX